Teaching to Inspire Vocation

Teaching to Inspire Vocation

Restoring a Critical Element of Professional and Technical Education

Timothy C. Hohn

ROWMAN & LITTLEFIELD
Lanham • Boulder • New York • London

Published by Rowman & Littlefield
An imprint of The Rowman & Littlefield Publishing Group, Inc.
4501 Forbes Boulevard, Suite 200, Lanham, Maryland 20706
www.rowman.com

86-90 Paul Street, London EC2A 4NE, United Kingdom

Copyright © 2024 by Timothy C. Hohn

All rights reserved. No part of this book may be reproduced in any form or by any electronic or mechanical means, including information storage and retrieval systems, without written permission from the publisher, except by a reviewer who may quote passages in a review.

British Library Cataloguing in Publication Information Available

Library of Congress Cataloging-in-Publication Data

Names: Hohn, Timothy C., 1951– author.
Title: Teaching to inspire vocation : restoring a critical element of professional and technical education / Timothy C. Hohn.
Description: Lanham, Maryland : Rowman & Littlefield Publishers, 2023. | Includes bibliographical references. | Summary: "The book's theme is helping students find meaning, purpose, and vocation in their education. Its focus is on enhancing and amplifying the pedagogy and curricula of collegiate professional and technical education programs to meet the goals of this theme"—Provided by publisher.
Identifiers: LCCN 2023022083 (print) | LCCN 2023022084 (ebook) | ISBN 9781475864182 (hardcover) | ISBN 9781475864199 (paperback) | ISBN 9781475864205 (epub)
Subjects: LCSH: Career education—United States. | Vocational education—United States.
Classification: LCC LC1037.5 .H63 2023 (print) | LCC LC1037.5 (ebook) | DDC 370.1130973—dc23/eng/20230519
LC record available at https://lccn.loc.gov/2023022083
LC ebook record available at https://lccn.loc.gov/2023022084

Contents

Acknowledgments	vii
Preface	ix
1: Answering Mary Oliver's Question	1
2: Vocation in the History of Education	9
3: Vocation in Context	21
4: Authenticity, Mentoring, and Learning Community Elements	45
5: Contemplative Practice Element	59
6: Vocational Narrative Element	103
7: Experiential Learning Element	129
8: Teaching to Inspire Vocation	155
9: Conclusion	203
Bibliography	205
About the Author	215

Acknowledgments

I am most indebted to the many wonderful students at Edmonds College with which I shared a love of horticulture for twenty-two years. Most of these students had spent years pursuing professions that they soon realized were not for them. They came to Edmonds College with a vague but growing notion that horticulture was their calling. Through them, I realized how important it is to include explorations of meaning, purpose, and vocation in our curriculum and in my pedagogy.

I wish to acknowledge several author/editor/educators whose works were both an inspiration and a foundation for this project: Daniel Barbezat, Mirabai Bush, Arthur Chickering, David S. Cunningham, Timothy Clydesdale, William Damon, Barbara Jacoby, David Levy, Iain McGilchrist, Pamela Mutascio, Parker Palmer, Sharon Daloz Parks, Robert Pirsig, Neil Postman, William Sullivan, and Arthur Zajonc. Their work was an essential resource in the writing of this book, and I am very grateful. In addition, a special thanks to Timothy Clydesdale, David S. Cunningham, and Erin VanLaningham for their review of the manuscript at a very busy time in their lives.

A warm thank-you to the staff of the Orcas Island Library, particularly Rhett Ariston, who acquired several useful texts for me by the authors above.

I'm most grateful to the editorial and production team at Rowman & Littlefield, particularly Thomas Koerner, vice president/senior executive editor, education division, whose interest, encouragement, and advice were crucial to completing the manuscript. Thanks also to Carlie Wall, managing editor, for her gentle reminders in helping me navigate and complete several important supporting R&L materials; and Andrew Yoder, assistant editor, for working with me through the manuscript proofing and final production phase; and Jasmine Holman, assistant editor, for her help finishing the project.

On a more personal note, no words can express how beholden I am to my father, Charles "Bud" Hohn, who impressed upon me the importance of finding something that you love to do that will form the basis of your life and place in the community. Finally, my deepest love and gratitude to my wife, Lynda, for her proofing and composition advice, as well as her patience and sacrifices; and that of my children, Sam, Bryce, and Deah, in support of the time I spent working on this project.

Preface

I have a prospective student in my office, a forty-year-old man, who expresses both enthusiasm and trepidation. His age isn't surprising as my program attracts the oldest group of students on campus. Most are career changers seeking to learn more about the art and science of horticulture—an expertise and skill they practice as a hobby. Others have been working in lesser positions without degrees and come seeking knowledge for advancement.

This meeting is a pivotal moment for both of us. For the prospective student, this introduction could be a turning point in his life. For me, it is a test of credibility and building relationships. This beginning to our relationship is built on mutual enthusiasm for a subject we love and, perhaps, a vocation we share. I begin our conversation with a question that I ask all prospective students: "Why are you interested in the practice of horticulture?" The student pauses to think a moment. I suspect he notices a twinkle in my eye, which provides encouragement for the ensuing conversation.

"You know," he begins, "I've always loved working in the garden; planting new things, pruning, digging in the soil." He pauses here with a contemplative look on his face. "It's such a peaceful way for me to spend my time, especially after a hard day at work. Summer evenings I'm often out puttering around in the garden as a way to relax, and the next thing I know, it's dark. It finally dawned on me that my hobby could be a career." Typical of many prospective students, an epiphany has led him to pursue an avocational interest as a profession, maybe even a vocation.

For me, this shared excitement and understanding are the best part of these meetings. Then he says, "I realize that I'm unlikely to make the kind of salary that I'm paid now, and I hope that isn't an issue for me. I just want to be outdoors, working with plants, in the fresh air where I can breathe and be a part of nature." I explain that good salaries are not mutually exclusive to a career in horticulture; it all depends on what part of the work brings the greatest satisfaction—what part of this practice really feeds his heart as well as his head and hands, and his wallet.

In the end, we both recognize that this has been a powerful meeting, one that creates an important bond between us. I know that he is leaving my office with confidence and enthusiasm for a successful start down a new educational path. Our meeting also gives me pause to appreciate my vocation in horticulture and education.

I think back to my original vocation as a botanical garden curator when the idea of becoming a full-time teacher was the farthest thing from my mind. Well, the best laid plans of mice and men. . . . An unexpected budget cut meant finding another job, if not a new vocation. I accepted a faculty position in the horticulture department of a local community college assuming that my knowledge of the subject matter would provide the necessary competence to be an effective teacher—a common and often mistaken assumption. It didn't take me long to realize that being a good teacher would be the most challenging occupation of my life.

I was fortunate to work with a mature group of students whose eagerness to learn made my job as a neophyte instructor easier. Still, I spent most of the first decade of my teaching career struggling to develop teaching competency and helping my students meet program learning outcomes. A focus on helping them find greater purpose, meaning, and vocation wasn't yet in the picture.

Over time, as I became more confident in and relaxed with my teaching skills, the power of my students' dedication and enthusiasm for horticulture reignited my personal love of the subject, a love buried in my struggle to teach. As we shared personal and professional enthusiasms for our discipline, I became more aware of the incipient notion of a vocation, a distant calling, in my students' vision for their futures in horticulture. Talking with them during breaks and after class about their progress, special interests, and professional goals, my appreciation for the vocational significance of our program grew deeper and took on greater definition. At the same time, I was discovering my own vocation in education.

Soon, the informal conversations with my students about finding meaning, purpose, and vocation in our study spilled over into the classroom. Those opportunities came in the form of questions I posed or comments I made that triggered vocational thinking and responses from my students, just like during our informal conversations. Timing is important, and these questioning intervals came at the conclusion of a compelling concept or practice—a natural point of reflection.

These broader explorations of our subject helped build a vocational narrative within the curriculum. With this approach, I also became aware of the importance of how a particular vocabulary contributes to the vocational narrative, such as the word "practice."

I was amazed at how responsive students were to narratives about meaning, purpose, and exploring vocation. Much discussion revolved around how students perceived and felt about what they were learning, and how it contributed to their vision of a career and a life in horticulture. In addition to comprehensive study, our time together now included real fun, energy, and commitment.

My experiences with these wonderful students over twenty-two years inspires and informs this text. It was their perceptions of a career in horticulture in the larger context of vocation that shaped my awareness and appreciation for its importance in collegiate professional and technical education.

Some believe that vocation is of such a personal nature that it cannot be taught. In this text, I describe an approach to teaching to inspire vocation by building an intentional vocational framework within the curriculum—to help students hear a "calling" in their education. As you implement the approach put forward in the following chapters, your pedagogy will naturally evolve to carry these attributes forward with less effort and growing competency.

My hope is that this book will serve as a primer on teaching to inspire vocation for instructors, faculty, and administrators in collegiate professional and technical programs, as well as those studying for these vocations.

I have organized the text around what I consider to be the important instructional elements of a framework of teaching to inspire vocation: instructor *authenticity* and *mentoring*; *multimodal pedagogies* (cognitive, kinesthetic, affective) using *intentional vocabulary* and *narratives*; *contemplative practice* and *personal knowledge*; developing *learning communities* and *community-engaged learning* opportunities.

Teaching to inspire vocation involves influential narratives and frameworks to encourage and support the *discernment* of vocation or *hearing* a calling. It is not an instrumental pedagogy, or stepwise process, that leads students directly to a vocation. No force of will on the part of students or teachers will bring about the discovery or discernment of vocation.

You will encounter scenarios and examples throughout the text taken from my experiences as a college student and as a horticulture instructor. It is my intention that you will find them relevant and broadly applicable to your educational context. I have also included examples and cases from other disciplines within professional and technical education.

Finally, I don't pretend that this volume is the final word on teaching to inspire vocation, only that it is a beginning and a contributor to a growing literature on the subject. Glancing through the bibliography, you will see the many shoulders that I have stood on in order to gain a better understanding of the place of vocation in higher education and how we might help our students discover it. May you find inspiration and resource within these pages to expand the context of your program and help your students discover what they are looking for.

1

Answering Mary Oliver's Question

Tell me, what is it you plan to do
With your one wild and precious life?[1]

—Mary Oliver

Each year, students graduating from Harvard Business School are asked to answer the compelling question posed in the last two lines of Mary Oliver's iconic poem, *The Summer Day*. Imagine this: Rather than ending the student experience with this question, why not begin it this way? This inspirational question can serve as a guide for a holistic education that addresses humankind's purpose, the meaning of our lives, and all the necessities of life and career.

If we are to ask our graduates to answer such an important question, then colleges and universities need to serve their students accordingly. By that I don't mean simply helping them choose a major topic of study or a professional career, but a *life*. The values, practices, and vision presented at convocations about how students should go forward to discern their vocation and live their lives—answering Mary Oliver's question—should be embedded across the curriculum. By graduation, students could then answer Mary Oliver's question with confidence, competence, and vision. Isn't that what education is all about?

> When it comes to guiding students toward future paths that they will find rewarding and meaningful, our schools fall short. Students learn bits and pieces of knowledge that they may see little use for; and from time to time someone at a school assembly urges them to go and do great things in the world.[2]

One could make the case that our entire education system should be organized around Mary Oliver's question. Our current model of education starts down that path in primary school where the necessities of life and learning are first explored. However, as students proceed through the school system, explorations of purpose, meaning, and livelihood are replaced by compartmentalized studies in academic and abstract topics or the skills and technologies required for specific jobs. Eventually, students reach high school and college graduations presented with far-reaching philosophical questions and recommendations at their convocations about how they should live their lives with nary a clue to such considerations provided during their years of study.

> The thing being made in a university is humanity. . . . that is, a fully developed human being.[3]

The conclusion expressed in the above quote by Wendell Berry isn't new. In fact, it was a goal of the early academies of Axial Age Greece. It was the educational foundation of Plato's academy through an extensive curriculum in philosophy. Early models of Western education were based on Plato's academy with comprehensive studies in philosophy as part of a more extensive query into purpose and meaning.

One of the more important philosophical traditions that we inherited from the Greeks relative to explorations of purpose and meaning is contemplative practice. The contemplative focus of the Greek educational tradition allowed students to achieve deeper awareness of their emotions, perceptions, and learning. Similar to Eastern spiritual traditions, this practice develops deep mindfulness of internal and external identity. Contemplative practice engages both brain hemispheres for a complete cognitive cycle that is integral to a curriculum of wisdom. Over time, especially since the beginning of the industrial age, we have lost the philosophical and contemplative part of our educational legacy.

Most high school and college students are looking for something to care about. These schools need to be more than centers for credentialing, socializing, and employment. Most important, colleges can provide transformative experiences and be centers for students to discover for themselves a larger purpose in life. Studies show that—as the ancient Greeks knew—when institutions of higher learning engage their students in explorations of purpose and meaning, the result is greater commitment by students to academic goals and clearer visions for lives of significance and impact after graduation.[4]

What little current concern there is for incorporating explorations of meaning and purpose in college and university curricula resides at select traditional institutions: primarily liberal arts colleges founded by religious orders, such as the Jesuits, and some research universities. However, such an important segment of higher learning should be considered critical at every educational institution, especially those focused on developing job skills and professional competencies.

The purpose of this book is to reconsider and redefine collegiate and university professional and technical programs to support the discovery of vocation in the traditional and broadest sense. By that I mean a holistic vocational education that teaches a professional practice (law, medicine, architecture, accounting) or technical craft (construction skills, manufacturing skills, hand crafts) and assists in discovering purpose, meaning, and a life role for students through such practice.

Discovering a vocation is more than simply a process of learning a particular skill, technology, or practice, but a life-defining dedication to a clearly identified purpose, understanding of meaning, mode of self-expression, and role in the community. In his article "What Is Vocation," Roger Ebertz describes it this way:

> Vocation is one's response to a call from beyond oneself to use one's strengths and gifts to make the world a better place through service, creativity, and leadership.[5]

Returning to Plato's academy, in addition to philosophy, explorations of purpose, and studies in basic literacy, the curriculum also included an important segment devoted to learning a craft or practice: those skills and capabilities needed to produce a product or provide a service *for the community*. Practicing a craft, or crafting a practice, is an integral part of one's vocation. There is an important framing from this part of Plato's academy to achieve in the instrumental teaching of job skills common in today's professional and technical college programs.

Professional and technical education can be traced back to the trade guilds of Europe and their dependence upon apprenticeships as a core part of their programming. However, the employment needs of the industrial revolution gave birth to the manual training movement that evolved into specialized high-school and college training programs. These provided both manual and academic training to prepare students for a variety of career options targeted toward industry.

Current professional and technical training programs evolved from this early model. Many liberal arts colleges and research universities have expanded their curricula to include professional degree programs designed to train students for specific careers and professional practices, such as accounting, engineering, and architecture. With their narrow focus on skill development, today's professional and technical collegiate programs might best be characterized as "training" programs, rather than "education" programs. The decline of the Platonic academy model, the rise of professional training programs, and the resulting issues related to discovering vocation are presented in greater detail in chapter 2.

Three major elements of a more holistic vocational education are missing from the current model of professional and technical education. *First* is the cultivation of a contemplative mind, or mindfulness, to engage more fully in explorations of purpose, meaning, and the discovery of vocation. *Second* is an authentic vocational framework that includes intentional vocabulary and compelling narratives. With the necessary vocabulary, students can express and share the story-shaped reality of a vocation—a vocational narrative. *Third* is to cultivate student empathy and shift self-concern to others and the community through the integration of community service with academic studies.

Craftsmanship, and recognizing craft in vocation, is a powerful source of meaning, authenticity, and fulfillment. This is certainly true for professional practices such as architecture, law, and medicine as well as technical practices such as carpentry, metal fabrication, or HVAC technician. The same can be said of other professional disciplines involving products or services that are not traditionally considered as "craftwork"—for example, accounting. Consider Dorothy Sayers's broad interpretation of craftsmanship: "the full expression of the professional's faculties, in which one finds spiritual, mental, and bodily satisfaction."[6]

Vocational education as described here requires multimodal teaching involving head, hands, and heart pedagogies. Peter Korn describes the importance of the affective, or "heart," mode of learning to practicing craftwork in his book *Why We Make Things, and Why It Matters*: "They [craft work] may not lead to profound transfiguration . . . yet their satisfactions are well matched to the earthly nature of our spiritual appetites."[7] Craftwork, and the application of craft in vocation, has much to offer in the way of rewards in our shared search for personal and professional gratification and fulfillment. Sir Ken Robinson equates vocation with being in your element and describes it this way:

> Discovering your element is allowing yourself access to all the ways in which you experience yourself in the world and discovering where your own true strengths lie.[8]

An expanded vocational education involves inspiration and pedagogies from the Waldorf School and community-engaged learning playbooks. Their focus on "multiple intelligences" involving our heads, the cognitive domain; our hands, the kinesthetic domain; and our hearts, the affective domain, is an important part of teaching to inspire vocation. These multiple intelligences can be synthesized and synergized through contemplative practice (contemplation, introspection, reflection). Daniel Barbezat and Mirabai Bush make the case in their book *Contemplative Practices in Higher Education*:

> creative, synthetic thinking requires more . . . ; it requires a holistic engagement and attention that is especially fostered by the student finding him or herself in the material. No matter how radically we conceive of our role in teaching, the one aspect of students' learning for which they are unambiguously sovereign is the awareness of their experience and their own thoughts, beliefs, and reactions to the material covered in the course. In addition, students need support in discerning what is most meaningful to them—both their direction overall and their moral compass. Without opportunities to inquire deeply, all they can do is proceed along paths already laid out for them.[9]

Restoring the contemplative element of Plato's Academy can enhance students' cognitive abilities in learning their craft or practice and discerning their vocation.

Affective modes of learning, enhanced by contemplative practice, reveal and include personal knowledge. Unfortunately, most colleges and universities assiduously avoid a subjective, personal knowledge approach to learning. Michael Polyani's research on how knowledge claims rely on personal judgments—he elaborates on it in his *Gifford Lectures* and his book *Personal Knowledge*—is an important part of teaching to inspire vocation.

Polyani's work dovetails with the teachings of Parker Palmer, who makes the case that the research university's wholly objective approach to education shuts out the experiences and relationships of students and the impact of those on their interpretation of what is important in life.[10] Teaching to inspire vocation involves personal interpretations and responses of teachers and students derived from contemplative practice as part of the overall process.

Life experiences are usually an integral part of professional and technical education. In fact, they form the basis for laboratories and field experiences where students can obtain hands-on experience learning their craft. As educators in the Waldorf School system and others that incorporate community-engaged learning in their curriculum know, there is great resonance and synergy between contemplative practice and these real-life experiences. Holistic teaching practices assist students to identify key concepts and principles and then apply and test those concepts, principles, and theories in real-life situations. Many consider community-engaged learning the most powerful experiential pedagogy for connecting knowledge and skill to real-life expectations.

Alexander Astin and his colleagues revealed the impact of community-engaged learning when they examined thirty-five measures of student outcomes concerning civic responsibility, academic development, and life skill development. Here is an excerpt from their findings:

> The most remarkable finding of this . . . study was that all 35 student outcome measures were favorably influenced by service participation. In other words, participation in volunteer activities during the undergraduate years enhanced . . . academic development, civic responsibility and life skills . . . as a consequence of service participation, students became more strongly committed to helping others, serving their communities, promoting racial understanding, doing volunteer work and working for nonprofit organizations. Despite the additional time for service participation, students who engaged in volunteer service actually spent more time with studies and homework than did non-participants.[11]

The following chapters describe and detail the central elements of a framework for teaching to inspire vocation. The principal elements of that framework are instructor *authenticity* and *mentoring*; *multimodal* pedagogies (cognitive, kinesthetic, affective) using a vocational *vocabulary* and *narrative*; *contemplative practice* and *personal knowledge*; *learning communities*; and *experiential learning*. Teaching to inspire vocation involves influential narratives and frameworks to encourage and support the *discernment* of vocation or *hearing* a calling. It is not an instrumental pedagogy involving a stepwise process that leads students directly to a vocation. No force of will on the part of students or teachers will bring about the discovery or discernment of vocation.

Regarding the contents of each chapter, chapter 2 provides a short history of Western education and the place of vocation from Plato's Academy to the current incarnation of professional and technical education. The subject of vocation and the elements of teaching vocation are described in greater detail and within an educational context in chapter 3. Chapters 4 through 7 explore the individual elements of a framework for teaching vocation starting with authenticity and mentoring, vocabulary and narrative, through contemplative practice and community-engaged learning. Chapter 8 brings these elements together as you might implement them in a course or curriculum revision to include explorations of meaning, purpose, and discerning vocation. Finally, a brief conclusion contains parting thoughts on the elements of teaching vocation and their place in professional and technical education.

Textbox 1.1 Teaching Takeaways

- Students are looking for something to care about.
- Studies show that explorations of purpose and meaning result in a greater commitment by students to academic goals.
- Our purpose is to reconsider and redefine collegiate professional and technical programs to assist students in discovering purpose, meaning, and their vocation.
- Acquiring a vocation is a life-defining dedication to a clearly identified purpose, understanding of meaning, mode of self-expression, and role in the community.
- Explorations of purpose, meaning, and vocation transform professional and technical education from "training" programs to "education" programs.
- Three elements necessary for framing vocational education are cultivation of a contemplative mind, intentional vocabulary and narrative, and integration of academics and community service.
- Craftsmanship, and recognition of craft in vocation, is a source of meaning, authenticity, and fulfillment.
- Teaching vocation requires multimodal pedagogy involving head, hands, and heart pedagogies.
- Studies show that community-engaged learning is the most powerful experiential pedagogy for discovering vocation.
- Spend time during course orientation to discuss with your students their concept of vocation and what their expectations are for the possibility of discovering vocation in their studies.

NOTES

1. Mary Oliver, "A Summer Day," *House of Light* (Boston: Beacon Press, 1990).
2. William Damon, *The Path to Purpose* (New York: Free Press, 2008), xii.
3. Wendell Berry, "The Loss of the University," *Home Economics* (San Francisco: North Point Press, 1987), 77.
4. Tim Clydesdale, *The Purposeful Graduate* (Chicago: University of Chicago Press, 2015), xvii.
5. Roger Ebertz, "What Is Vocation?," University of Dubuque, dbq.edu, August 17, 2015, http://www.dbq.edu/CampusLife/OfficeofStudentLife/VocationalServices/WhatisVocation/.

6. Dorothy L. Sayers, "Why Work," in *Letters to a Diminished Church: Passionate Arguments for the Relevance of Christian Doctrine* (Nashville, TN: W. Publishing Group, 2004), 126.

7. Peter Korn, *Why We Make Things and Why It Matters* (Boston: David R. Godine, 2013), 10.

8. Ken Robinson, *The Element: How Finding Your Passion Changes Everything* (New York: Penguin, 2009), 51.

9. Daniel Barbezat and Mirabai Bush, *Contemplative Practices in Higher Education* (San Francisco: Jossey-Bass, 2014), 10.

10. Parker J. Palmer and Arthur Zajonc, *The Heart of Higher Education: A Call to Renewal* (San Francisco: Jossey-Bass, 2010), 31.

11. A. W. Astin and L. Sax, "How Undergraduates Are Affected by Service Participation," *Journal of College Student Development, 39* (1998): 255, 256, 259.

2

Vocation in the History of Education

The antebellum college was a landmark of American civilization.[1]

—Anthony T. Kronman

A good case can be made that formal education had its birth during the Axial Age, some twenty-two hundred years ago. The little-known Axial Age was an unprecedented era of transcendence in the evolution of human understanding and is often ignored in examinations of Western history.

A compressed period from 800 to 200 BCE named by the German philosopher Karl Jaspers, the Axial Age was the time of origin for most of the major world spiritual theologies and religions—Buddhism, Daoism, Hinduism, Islam, Judaism, Zoroastrianism—as well as Greek philosophies of reason. This period is also the first in human history to produce thinkers who are still a source of inspiration today: Buddha, Confucius, the Hebrew prophets, Lao-tsu, Plato, Pythagoras, Socrates, and Zoroaster.[2]

In the Axial Age, we have a segment of human history defined by reference to modern theologies, philosophies, and modes of intellectual inquiry. It may also be considered the birthplace of both intellectual and spiritual philosophy. This was the beginning of intense human reflection on the foundations of reality and the meaning and purpose of life.[3] As the new and developing philosophies were discussed, debated, and shared in ever-widening circles, schools were formed to support these activities—the most notable from this time period being Plato's Academy.

An immodest Plato characterized himself as an educator "full of resources . . . in order to speak about virtue—to say what kind of things a good man ought to think about, and with what he ought to busy himself."[4] Plato's Academy was a place where students spent a good deal of their academic time in philosophical discourse toward an understanding of their purpose, the meaning of their lives, and the pursuit of wisdom. There were other schools of philosophy during Plato's time, but "throughout the subsequent history of philosophy, we will encounter the memory and the imitation of this institution [Plato's Academy], as well as of the discussions and debates which took place there."[5]

It was Plato's original intention for his academy to train skillful statesmen, but in a larger sense and more importantly, the development of what was considered at the time as a complete human being.[6] The basic educational context and pedagogical approach that Plato imposed on his students was partly derived from his mentor, Socrates. Socrates had a different concept of education from most of his peers: he felt that education should take place in the community as opposed to a separate, artificial context removed from society—the original proponent of what we now call "community-engaged learning."[7]

For Socrates and Plato, the overall academic goal of training students as philosophers served the goal of developing complete human beings. As part of that overall goal, geometry and other mathematical sciences were also important, as were a mastery of speech and reasoning. As part of a comprehensive training in both intellectual and spiritual philosophy, reasoning was taught as a spiritual exercise more than a purely logical one. As such, the Academy taught the practice of how to create and conduct a true dialogue, one in which the participants put themselves in each other's place and thereby transcended their own point of view. Here then, was an integral part of the Academy's idea of philosophy: "philosophy consists in the movement by which the individual transcends himself toward something that lies beyond him."[8]

Plato's Academy set a standard for holistic education aimed at helping the individual answer questions of meaning and purpose through, in the words of Luc Brisson, "learning to live in a philosophical way."[9] To live in a philosophical way meant to live an intellectual *and* spiritual life that involved one's entire soul contributing to a moral life. Plato also believed that knowledge of an intellectual *and* spiritual kind is a prime virtue, a belief that Socrates also shared.

Plato characterized the Academy curriculum as a "wonderful path," one that involved spiritual exercises to complement intellectual training. The core of these exercises were contemplative practices of various kinds. This inspiration also came from Socrates and his famous dictum, "The unexamined life is not worth living."

In the final pages of Plato's dialogue, the *Timaeus*, he affirms that we must exercise the superior part of the soul, the intellect, in such a way that it achieves harmony with the universe.[10] This notion of harmony and wholeness is a philosophical axiom common to the Axial Age as a whole, particularly Eastern philosophical traditions. Plato's Academy and other emulating Greek schools were a spiritual community concerned with a radical transformation using philosophy as a method to teach people how to live and look at the world in a new way.

The educational concept was something they called "Paideia." The goal of education is the mastery of one's person; subject matter is simply the tool. In summary, these schools focused on the pursuit of wisdom and the discovery of vocation.

The spiritual, as well as intellectual, authority of Plato's Academy, and its subsequent modern incarnations, persisted for millennia but, regarding today's colleges and universities, is long gone. Plato and his peers in ancient Greece felt strongly that a complete education involved showing students how to think and how to choose. Through reflection and other contemplative, thought-provoking practices, they taught their students how to take stock of their passions and capabilities in identifying their true vocation. Plato's Academy formed the basis for what has come to be known as a "liberal education," one that is broad, open, and inclusive.

After the acceptance and spread of Christianity throughout the Western world, the academy model began to change. In twelfth-century Europe, the seven liberal arts taught in the cathedral schools were, according to Alain de Lille, intended to produce "the good and perfect man," with a new objective: one worthy of the spiritual journey to God.[11] This was the prevailing form of education—with some further evolutionary changes—in the Western world up to the industrial revolution.

This begs the question; how did Western education move away from a dynamic integration of intellectual and spiritual education toward a secular pluralism that puts wisdom at odds with education? David Levy has three explanations:

> One explanation is the ease with which we turn away from real inquiry to the safety and security of abstraction. Another is that Christianity borrowed these contemplative practices, made them their own, usurping a significant portion of philosophy for their practice and dogma. And finally, medieval scholasticism focused philosophy on Socratic argument and debate leaving out the contemplative aspect.[12]

The upshot of these long-term changes was the dissolution of a holistic education aimed at educating fully developed human beings toward the training of specialists in specific disciplines. While the elements of a liberal education were evolving from the model established by Plato's Academy, a parallel educational universe was also evolving to provide training in various crafts. We may construe this craft training parallel as the root of vocational or professional-technical education.

Immediately we come to a quandary of meaning about the word *craft*. Peter Korn, a furniture maker and director of the Center for Furniture Craftsmanship, explains:

> Premodern craft was made to satisfy culturally prescribed, functional purposes. Contemporary craft, being economically marginal, is created primarily to address the spiritual needs of its maker. As a result, it often lacks utility and its practical disposition may be left to the whim of the purchaser. . . . when it comes to definition, craft is a moving target.[13]

Regarding the premodern crafts, the Livre des Métiers of 1268 lists about a hundred of these divided into six groups: foods, jewelry, metals, textiles and clothiers, furs, and building.[14] Craftsmen working in one of these six groups maintained their own workshops that also served as their family home. These early craftsmen were trained by the leading craftsmen of the time in that particular locale who, as likely as not, were also their fathers/mothers, uncles/aunts, or other close relative. The craftsmen of the age were almost exclusively male, but this changes over time with the evolution of craftsmenship.

During the rise of cities and city-states in the Middle Ages and thereafter, craftsmen began to work collectively in what came to be known as "guilds." This collective form of organization helped to leverage bargaining power in the community and set standards for craft work. Guilds existed as a three-tiered hierarchy of ability and authority with the masters at the top, journeymen below them, and apprentices at the bottom. The historian Robert Lopez describes a guild as "a federation of autonomous workshops, whose owners [the 'masters'] normally made all decisions and established the requirements for promotion from the lower ranks."[15]

It should be pointed out that through the development of guild craft in the Middle Ages no distinction had been made between what we now might call the "fine arts" and the "applied arts." Sculptors belonged to the same guilds as stone masons, while painters of all sorts, from those working with canvases to those coloring walls, participated in the same guild. This is to say that the fine arts and applied arts carried equal merit. A dichotomy began to form between these two worlds of craft during the Renaissance period when the elements of the mind began to rise above those of the body in social consciousness.

One can easily blame the bane of Cartesian dualism for dividing mind over matter into separate and unequal categories. What we now consider fine art, or simply "art," is considered a practice of the mind whereas other types of object making are associated with the body, or applied art, and rank in a lesser category of endeavor.[16]

Regarding academics, the legacy of Plato's Academy in the history of American higher education evolved, along with its European forebears, based on the dominant role of Christian churches in shaping both European social and political institutions along with those of the "colonies." Colleges and, later, universities founded by Christian churches were institutions for both learning and the promotion of Christian values and morality.

Regardless of their denominational orientation, and in keeping with Plato's Academy, the religious elements of American colleges were those of piety and moral discipline more than religious theology. Explorations of purpose and meaning persisted in these decidedly Christian academic environments, albeit with a somewhat more dogmatic inclination.[17]

American colleges of the nineteenth century, no matter their religious creed, were focused on the development of sound character in their students along with academic training. This focus was capped by a senior-year course in moral philosophy, harkening back to the emphasis on philosophy from Plato's time, that usually was taught by the college president. In essence then, it's accurate to portray education from the time of Plato's Academy through the nineteenth century as principally an exercise in self-examination, self-discipline, and self-abnegation. From the early Middle Ages onward, the academic portion of the curriculum was based on what is known as the trinity of studies: language and literature, science, and philosophy.[18]

In colleges of the early nineteenth century, the entire curriculum was fixed. Students were required to take specific courses in a set sequence, and the reading for each course was generally prescribed for the whole student body. Today we refer to this now-rare approach, in various historical incarnations, as the "great books curriculum." The distinction between faculty and administration that we now take for granted didn't exist.[19] The changes that were to come in the twentieth century stem from, among other forces, Andrew Carnegie's harsh comments—shared by many of his peers—from the 1890s that "college education as it exists today," with its focus on antiquated ideas and "dead languages," is suitable only "for life on another planet."[20]

Perhaps the single most influential change in the Western model of education began in the early part of the nineteenth century with industrialization. Industrialization is the principal impetus for the rise of the modern university in a world, as David Levy bluntly states, "that emphasizes speed, production, and efficiency based on a philosophy of more, faster, better."[21] Further emulating the philosophy of industry, the modern university began to organize itself and its pedagogy in a mechanized way as if people and organizations could function together like machines.[22]

The end of the Civil War serves as a benchmark for when industrialization's spread and influence began to firmly grip broad aspects of American life, including our education system *and* the practice of craft. By this time, great controversy had erupted among the craft guilds and their craftsmen regarding the impact of mechanization and homogenization of production in industry. Demand was also growing for a different kind of worker training focused on specific types of manufacturing, construction, and technology skills that were in demand by industry and formed the foundations for various new and "acceptable" careers.

At the forefront of resistance to the perceived dehumanizing and devaluing impacts of mechanization, and the resulting poor-quality products of the industrial revolution, were two men: John Ruskin (1819–1900) and William Morris (1834–1896). These early British socialists were the principal founders of the Arts and Crafts Movement and, as part of the movement's foundation, wove together three important concepts—the applied, or decorative arts; the vernacular trades, or local handicraft; and the politics of work—into a compelling, counter-industrial narrative that they labeled simply *craft*.

The Ruskin and Morris conception of craft was intended to counteract the evils of industrial capitalism, in particular a perceived decline in standards along with a dehumanizing impact on workers. Our current notion of craft, whether as a form of production or a type of object, has its origins in the work of Ruskin and Morris, perhaps most particularly William Morris.[23] In short, the Arts and Crafts Movement stood for traditional, high-quality craftsmanship using simple forms. It advocated economic and social reform and was essentially anti-industrial.[24]

The social, cultural, and economic forces of industrialization came to bear on American education in dramatic ways in the aftermath of the Civil War. Pressure to conform to the needs of industrialization on college curricula, pedagogy, and administration were the impetus for all sorts of reforms, including the development of separate vocational training, otherwise known at the time as manual training programs and "trade schools."

You could make the case that trade schools evolved from craft guilds and their associated apprenticeship programs—organizations that began to dissolve at the beginning of industrialization as an impediment to capitalization and free markets. Such an assertion would be vigorously opposed by the leaders of the Arts and Crafts Movement on grounds similar to their opposition to industrialization in general. Nevertheless, skills training schools in Germany were being evaluated for their utility in this country just after the Civil War and receiving positive reviews.

The first trade schools to appear were private and of three types: "(1) schools that offered only trade training, (2) schools that offered a combination of trade training and general education, (3) schools that apprenticed their students to the boards of trustees in addition to offering trade and general education."[25] One of the first of these, which conformed to the second category, was the Hampton Institute in 1868 responding to a need for theoretical and technical training to supplant and/or streamline the need for an apprenticeship.

Manual training programs began to spring up with shops and laboratories as venues for providing the hands-on training necessary to replace apprenticeships. This trend wasn't completely ignored in public schools of the time, and some of them began to develop manual training programs in commercial, domestic, and agricultural practices. Because many graduates from the manual training programs were using their skills to acquire jobs, a special form of this training developed that focused on what was then termed "vocational education."

Collegiate involvement in trade and technical training really began with the passing of the federal Morrill Act of 1862 in support of trade and technical training at public colleges in agriculture. The second Morrill Act of 1890 supported the development of land-grant colleges. These colleges were created to provide knowledgeable and skilled workers in agriculture, home economics, and engineering. In order to "extend" the services of the land-grant colleges, the Smith-Lever Act of 1914 was passed to support the creation of the Agricultural Extension Service as a public outreach arm of land-grant college programs and expertise.

Throughout this period of change toward training schools, the concept of apprenticeships was always held in high esteem and considered an important part of skills training, despite the fact that some programs and schools created laboratories to replace them. An issue surrounding apprenticeships was the lack of standardization for their length and the particular skills required. This wasn't addressed until the 1930s when various federal and state laws and regulations were passed. Recommendations included in these legal frameworks were:

1. written agreements showing the terms of the agreements and the terms of the apprentice's relationship,
2. learning schedules in various aspects of the trade,
3. a scale of wages with periodic increases,
4. attendance in classes for related instruction,
5. continuous employment, and
6. approval by joint committees of employers and employees.[26]

The changes that took place between 1860 and 1910 eventually brought about a near-total break with the old order in education—theologically based colleges that descended from Plato's Academy—which had prevailed from the Puritan migration of the 1630s to the Civil War and set American higher education on a different path that we are still following today.

The new land-grant colleges, preparing students for modern careers, began to move beyond prescribed curricula centered on theology and the classics, to professional training. The number of elective courses in specialized subjects multiplied, students were assigned to recitation sections according to their proficiency as demonstrated by examination or by passing a prerequisite course, and instruction was increasingly organized through academic departments.

Here is the beginning of a new institutional template modeled on the Cartesian and industrial view of the world as machinelike and composed of autonomous parts. Out of this model evolved the research university, a new institution already conceived and renowned in Germany at the beginning of the post–Civil War period.

Harvard's president at the time, William Charles Eliot, was quick to adopt the German model of the research university, where academic freedom prevailed, research laboratories as well as graduate seminars first attained their modern form, and "professors could function exclusively as scholars and researchers."[27] Eliot believed that "society is best served when every man's peculiar skill, faculty, or aptitude is developed and utilized to the highest possible degree."[28]

By the end of the nineteenth century, American higher education had been completely transformed with the rise of research universities. Their major feature, different from traditional colleges of the previous era, was the focus on research in specific fields of endeavor siloed in their own segments of the institution, rather than on teaching. Regarding the rise of the research university, Andrew Delbanco's assessment seems apt:

> it created a context in which ambitious academics regarded teaching undergraduates as a distraction and a burden. In retrospect it all seems a predestined process that led inexorably to the educational hierarchy we take for granted today, in which the word "college" has been reduced from an honorific denoting high educational attainment to a kind of diminutive—a baby step in the credentialing process.[29]

The new American university wasn't only about research. As mentioned earlier, some broke away from the strict research paradigm by offering instruction in "practical" and what were considered vocational subjects such as business management and electrical engineering. These career-based subjects had no place in the classical curriculum of the pre–Civil War college. Manual training programs were also on the rise along with research universities, in public schools as well as designated colleges.

The Baltimore Manual Training High School was opened in 1884 as the first stand-alone manual training secondary school. Its mission was to provide both manual and academic training for students. A great deal of support for the push for more manual and vocational (used in the applied and strictest sense) training programs came from businessman and, later, labor unions that wanted to address skilled labor shortages and unemployment in an industrializing society.

As the manual and vocational training movement grew alongside the rise of the research university, members of the craft movement conceded some of their support. They saw this type of training as an opportunity to inculcate the moral value of work, something they feared was being eroded by mechanization and other attributes of modern society.

Moving into the twentieth century, so-called vocational education became more widespread among public school systems and at specialized colleges, taking on new titles such as "career and technical education" and "professional-technical education" common today. Even though business, manufacturing, and trades associations have been important supporters of professional and technical education throughout its developmental history, federal support has been the key legislative and financial ingredient in the development of this form of education.

American higher education at the beginning of the twenty-first century reflects the educational evolution of our society over the past two centuries. This evolution is most evident in a tripartite of institutions: the large, research university focused on grant-supported research projects and associated graduate education, subdivided into a dizzying array of specialties; small colleges that to one degree or another mimic elements of the research university while holding onto the elements of a liberal arts education; and professional-technical schools focused on career and trade skills.

Anthony Kronman, in his provocative book *Education's End: Why Our Colleges and Universities Have Given Up on the Meaning of Life*, reflects on an important element and narrative of American life that was reflected in college missions and programs during the first half of our nation's history but now seems to be forgotten:

> The colleges that sprang up everywhere in America in the eighteenth and nineteenth centuries were and remain one of the enduring expressions of the peculiarly American belief that everyone is educable, even up to the highest levels of intellectual ambition. Colleges, it was said, "break up and diffuse among the people that monopoly and mental power which despotic governments accumulate for purposes of arbitrary rule, and bring to the children of the humblest families of the nation a full and fair opportunity" for higher learning—a conviction that combined democratic and aristocratic ideas in a distinctly American way.[30]

In the coming chapters, we will reexamine the lost elements of Plato's Academy, the liberal arts education, and craftwork for their utility and contribution to developing a new vocational education through revised and amplified professional and technical education practices that serve and empower that goal.

Textbox 2.1 Teaching Takeaways

- The Axial Age was the time of origin for most of the major world spiritual theologies and religions as well as Greek philosophies of reason and formal education. This was the beginning of intense human reflection on the foundations of reality and the meaning and purpose of life.
- Plato's Academy formed the basis for what has come to be known as a "liberal education," one that is broad, open, and inclusive in the pursuit of purpose, meaning, and, ultimately, vocation.
- The twelfth-century cathedral schools of Europe intended to produce "the good and perfect man" through self-examination, self-discipline, and self-abnegation. This was the prevailing form of education in the Western world up to the industrial revolution.
- The onset of the industrial revolution marked the dissolution of a holistic education toward the training of specialists in specific disciplines.
- John Ruskin (1819–1900) and William Morris (1834–1896) were the principal founders of the Arts and Crafts Movement, one that pushed for the preservation of craftmanship and the discovery of vocation in education.
- Emulating industry and the tenets of Cartesian research, the modern university began to organize itself and its pedagogy in a segmented, mechanized way resembling a machine.
- Professional and technical education was born out of demand for industrial worker training in the latter part of the nineteenth century.
- American higher education has evolved into a tripartite of institutions: the large, research university focused on research and subdivided into a dizzying array of specialties; small colleges that mimic some elements of the research university while holding on to the elements of a liberal arts education; and specialty professional and technical two-year colleges and university programs focused on career and trade skills.

NOTES

1. Anthony T. Kronman, *Education's End: Why Our Colleges and Universities Have Given Up on the Meaning of Life* (New Haven, CT: Yale University Press, 2007), 52.
2. K. Jaspers, *The Origin and Goal of History* (New York: Routledge Revivals, 2010), 2.
3. N. Baumard, A. Hyafil, and P. Boyer, "What Changed during the Axial Age: Cognitive Styles or Reward Systems," *Communicative & Integrative Biology 8*, no. 5 (2015): e1046657.
4. Plato, *Symposium*, 209 b-e.
5. Pierre Hadot, *What Is Ancient Philosophy?*, trans. Michael Chase (Cambridge, MA: Harvard University Press, 2002), 57.
6. Hadot, *What Is Ancient Philosophy?*, 59.
7. John P. Lynch, *Aristotle's School: A Study of a Greek Educational Institution* (Berkeley: University of California Press, 1972), 63.
8. Hadot, *What Is Ancient Philosophy?*, 63.
9. L. Brisson, "Presuppposes et consequences d'une interpretation esoteriste de Platon," *Les Etudes Philosophiques*, 4 (1993): 480.
10. Hadot, *What Is Ancient Philosophy?*, 66.
11. Alain de Lille, *Anticlaudianus: The Good and Perfect Man*, trans. James J. Sheridan (Toronto: Pontifical Institute of Medieval Studies, 1973).
12. David Levy, "Head, Heart, and Hand: Cultivating the Contemplative in Higher Education," Annual Conference of the Association for Contemplative Mind in Higher Education at Amherst College, April 2009, https://vimeo.com/5187656.
13. Peter Korn, *Why We Make Things and Why It Matters* (Boston: David R. Godine, 2013), 30.
14. Richard Sennett, *Flesh and Stone: The Body and the City in Western Civilization* (New York: Norton, 1993), 201.
15. Richard Sennett, *The Craftsman* (New York: Norton, 2008), 57.
16. Korn, *Why We Make Things*, 34.
17. Arthur W. Chickering, Jon C. Dalton, and Liesa Stamm, *Encouraging Authenticity & Spirituality in Higher Education* (San Francisco: Wiley, 2006), 66.
18. Andrew Delbanco, *College: What It Was, Is, and Should Be* (Princeton, NJ: Princeton University Press, 2012), 73–74.
19. Kronman, *Education's End*, 53.
20. Carnegie quoted in Frank Donohue, *The Last Professors: The Corporate University and the Fate of the Humanities* (New York: Fordham University Press, 2008), 4.
21. Levy, "Head, Heart, and Hand."
22. Levy, "Head, Heart, and Hand."
23. Korn, *Why We Make Things*.
24. "Arts and Crafts Movement," https://en.wikipedia.org/wiki/Arts_and_Crafts_movement#cite_ref-king_1-1, April 13, 2019.

25. Howard R. D. Gordon, *The History and Growth of Career and Technical Education in America* (Long Grove, IL: Waveland, 2008), 1.
26. Gordon, *The History and Growth of Career and Technical Education*, 7.
27. Michael Rosenthal, *Nicholas Miraculous: The Amazing Career of the Redoubtable Dr. Nicholas Murray Butler* (New York: Farrar, Straus & Giroux, 2006), 75.
28. Delbanco, *College*, 84.
29. Delbanco, *College*, 81.
30. Kronman, *Education's End*, 52.

3

Vocation in Context

Seem like we're just set down here and dont nobody know why.[1]

—gas station attendant, *Pilgrim at Tinker Creek*, Annie Dillard

There is an intense hunger among today's students . . . : for a larger sense of purpose and direction; for an experience at school that speaks to them as human beings, not bundles of aptitudes; for guidance in addressing the important questions of life.[2]

—William Deresiewicz

The statement above by a musing gas station attendant in Annie Dillard's *Pilgrim at Tinker Creek* is ancient and eternal. And yet, within our scholarly institutions, little attempt is made to come to grips with such a statement. William Deresiewicz's observation makes it clear that today's students are ready and waiting for such considerations. The question of what current-day colleges and universities should do to assist students in pursuit of an answer to the bereft attendant's musing was answered long ago in several places at once during the Axial Age. In the West, answering this question was integral to the curriculum of Plato's Academy.

It's time we turned back to the lessons of Plato's Academy and the cathedral schools of the antebellum United States, where discovering one's meaning and purpose for discerning vocation were the raison d'être of the institution. It's frustrating to realize that we had the key to an important way forward in education and the betterment of ourselves so long ago and turned away from it. A study of human intellectual progress is fraught with similar circumstances illustrating that the progress of human understanding can be glacially slow. Here's a startling example:

> The Flat Earth Society mans the guns against oppression of thought and the Globularist lies of a new age. Standing with reason we offer a home to those wayward thinkers that march bravely on with REASON and TRUTH in recognizing the TRUE shape of the Earth—Flat. (The Flat Earth Society, 2020)

Pythagoras and Parmenides both proposed during the Axial Age in the sixth century BC that the Earth is round based on several observations. This has since been validated in myriad ways, the most compelling being decade's worth of images and personal observations associated with the space program. Fortunately, most of us recognize that the Earth is, in fact, round, although we find it much harder to come to grips with the purpose of collegiate education.

Many graduates from our colleges and universities go on to dwell in the pantheon of their disciplines and careers, likely remaining in those rarefied positions to the end of their lives, still questioning its purpose and meaning. It's also quite possible that many of these professional luminaries will reach the end of their work lives dreaming about that job or position that got away, the one they suspect answered their real calling.

Clearly something was missing from the education of those described above that has left the most important questions unanswered and created a cognitive blindness to their own condition. The reason, in professor and Noble laureate Elie Wiesel's words, is, "It [education] emphasized theories instead of values, concepts rather than human beings, abstraction rather than consciousness, answers instead of questions, ideology and efficiency rather than conscience."[3] The remainder of this chapter will explore concepts and ideas that are closely allied and/or impact vocation helping to provide greater context for understanding vocation.

COGNITION AND VOCATION

Educator and education researcher Sir Ken Robinson shares an important observation in his humorous and provocative 2006 TED presentation, "Do Schools Kill Creativity?":

> Truthfully, what happens is, as children grow up, we start to educate them progressively from the waist up. And then we focus on their heads. And slightly to one side.[4]

The "one side" that Robinson refers to is the left side, our brain's left hemisphere. He's not alone in his remarks; many other education analysts note that our education system, and our society, are increasingly driven by left-hemisphere cognition. This deserves more attention as a contributor to the changes in education we see leading to our current insufficient models.

A growing dependence on an incomplete, and some neurologists would add, handicapped cognitive process focused on the left hemisphere impedes our perception of larger questions and issues of purpose, meaning, and wholeness, not to mention a host of other critical perceptual and behavioral issues. In fact, this tendency may actively steer us away from such inquiry as Iain McGilchrist alludes to in observations from his neurological tome *The Master and His Emissary*:

> The right hemisphere needs not to know what the left hemisphere knows, for that would destroy its ability to understand the whole; at the same time, the left hemisphere cannot know what the right hemisphere knows. The left hemisphere cannot deliver anything new direct from "outside," but it can unfold, or "unpack," what it is given [by the right hemisphere]. . . . that is also its weakness. The clarifying explicitness needs to be reintegrated with the sense of the whole, the now unpacked or unfolded [analysis] being handed back to the domain of the right hemisphere, where it once more lives. This turns out to be a problem.[5]

Dr. McGilchrist provides a stark synopsis in that quotation of how the right and left hemispheres of the human brain relate to one another. This is still an evolving science and the subject of an entire literature but worth a very brief review here as a means of understanding our current relationship with explorations of purpose and meaning in education.

Most of us likely approach the subject of the interaction of our brain's two hemispheres from the common standpoint that the left hemisphere is in charge by making sense of and giving order to our perception of the world. The right hemisphere, on the other hand, is the subordinate one, focused on the aesthetic and metaphysical aspects of our perception as an ancillary part of our neurological function.

McGilchrist's research indicates that the relationship of the two hemispheres of our brain is quite the opposite. Fully functional human brains first perceive the world through the right hemisphere, which establishes a general context of perception. The right hemisphere then shares this information with the left hemisphere for select perceptual analyses and organization, the result of which is then sent back to the right hemisphere for a fully synthesized, holistic perception of the world that contains both a broad and detailed picture of what is going on at any one time.

The full potential of the human brain is realized when both hemispheres function together as they should. The right hemisphere as the master of activity provides context, connection, and continuity. The left hemisphere supplements the right by examining focal points of what is perceived, finding their organization, providing any necessary calculations, and assisting in putting language to their narrative. The right hemisphere is intuitive and implicit; the left, literal and explicit.

To contrast the two hemispheres in different terms, the left hemisphere's function and reality are starkly Cartesian, while the right hemisphere's is broadly and collectively Daoist. The left hemisphere is calculating, unemotional, and robotic. The right hemisphere is fluid, exploratory, and empathetic. The final reality produced by a complete cycle of perception, with both hemispheres cooperating in the centrality of the right hemisphere, is greater and richer than the sum of the two hemispheres alone.

The history of Western civilization has included periods of high emphasis on the functions of the left hemisphere as well as the right. However, since the beginning of industrialization, and more particularly in the current postmodern world, we have chosen an intensifying mode of cognitive function dependent upon the limited attributes and capabilities of the left hemisphere. In doing so, we are also creating a world that enhances that mode of being in what has become a positive social, cultural, and educational feedback loop reinforcing left hemisphere cognitive pathways. McGilchrist prefers to call it a left hemisphere "house of mirrors."

Looking back on the recent history of education in the United States outlined in the previous chapter, it's hard to resist identifying some parallels with the attributes of hyper-left hemisphere processing. At the level of the needs of individual students, incomplete left-hemisphere cognition handicaps the development of a key ingredient of critical thinking: the self-authoring mind. The self-authoring mind is the capability of an individual to internalize divergent points of view and author their own independent viewpoint.[6]

We will come back to this subject in later chapters regarding educational approaches and teaching pedagogies that encourage a complete cycle of cognition involving both hemispheres, a critical condition for explorations of purpose and meaning for discerning vocation.

SPIRITUALITY AND PERSONAL KNOWLEDGE

Studies show an unmistakable searching by college-age young people for purpose and meaning in a quest for spiritual fulfillment. Our left-brained concentration on objectivity and empirical rationality, in addition to a focus on utility education and job training, works against this pursuit. This observation helps us answer the question asked in chapter 1: How did Western education move from a dynamic integration of intellectual and spiritual education toward a secular pluralism that puts wisdom at odds with education? The answer: hyper left-hemisphere cognition and habits of mind.

The pursuit of purpose and meaning for discerning one's vocation is most successful and important within an expansive educational framework, one that places student discoveries in a broader picture of understanding facilitated by a complete cycle of cognitive engagement. A broader framework will also include spiritual and subjective explorations of value and meaning. Key ingredients for this framework are educational contexts and pedagogies that include modes of self-understanding and reflection.

Before going any further, let's define purpose and meaning in a professional context. According to Dr. Bryan J. Dik and Dr. Ryan D. Duffy, finding meaning in work depends on comprehension and purpose. Comprehension is how you make sense of your work experience and your place in the world. People with high career and work comprehension understand how it fits into the larger context and makes a difference.[7] They describe purpose as "a stable and generalized intention to accomplish something that is at once meaningful to the self and of consequence to the world beyond the self."[8] Within these two definitions of comprehension and purpose, comprehension is about understanding whereas purpose is about action.

A compelling, data-driven work on college student interest in self-discovery, purpose, and meaning comes from *Cultivating the Spirit: How College Can Enhance Students' Inner Lives* by Alexander Astin, Helen Astin, and Jennifer Lindholm. The book's core involves a series of student surveys, including a group of those just entering college. The authors found:

> Today's entering college students report high levels of spiritual interest and involvement. Many are also actively engaged in a spiritual quest, with nearly half reporting that they consider it essential or very important to seek opportunities to help them grow spiritually. Moreover, three-fourths of the students say that they are searching for meaning/purpose in life. . . . About two-thirds consider it essential or very important that their college enhance their self-understanding, prepare them for responsible citizenship, develop their personal values and provide for their emotional development. Moreover, nearly half say that it is essential or very important that college encourage their personal expression of spirituality.[9]

Based on these results, we can see that college students often have a vision and expectations for spiritual enrichment and explorations of purpose and meaning that, by and large, go unfulfilled in today's colleges and universities. Without a collegiate avenue to pursue these interests, many students take it upon themselves to satisfy these expectations through independent reading, seminars, and spiritual meetings. Other students have taken it upon themselves to create an entire venue for this activity at several institutions.

One of the most successful of these early endeavors is the Self-Knowledge Symposium (SKS) founded at three North Carolina college campuses in 1999. This is a campus community for the positive spiritual transformation of college-age students and adults looking for further spiritual support. Spiritual transformation as practiced by the SKS consists of:

- The quest to be a genuine or authentic person.
- The discernment of vocation.
- The spiritual search for truth.[10]

A key emphasis in each of these areas is leadership, character, and integrity, virtues important to a vocational professional and technical education. Weekly meetings are the foundation of SKS programming; there participants discuss books, films, and other media or activities that bring out provocative questions related to gaining self-knowledge.[11]

For the most part, the question of one's purpose, the meaning in our education and our life, and hearing our calling often lie in the unnoticed background of the many smaller questions one faces each day. We may go through long stretches of our lives without thought of it, but on occasion, we know it's there; we hear that faint calling. Part of the point of a purposeful education is to give that background a stronger presence and clarity in the foreground of our lives to make them more fulfilling.

Answering questions of purpose and meaning is inherently and intensely personal. Educational institutions and educators can only supply poignant contexts, conversations, and case examples to help students discover their answers. Students can't answer these questions with personal relevance simply by following someone's instructions or reading the right books. This is what makes Woody Allen's line from the film *Annie Hall* so poignant and funny: "I was thrown out of college for cheating on the metaphysics exam; I looked into the soul of the boy sitting next to me."

Despite the disappointing trajectory of Western education and the current challenges described above, several good examples of explorations of purpose and meaning in collegiate education are described in Tim Clydesdale's book *The Purposeful Graduate*. Here's a common finding from Dr. Clydesdale's research:

> when colleges and universities meaningfully engage their organizational histories to launch sustained conversations with students about questions of purpose, the result is a rise in overall campus engagement and recalibration of post college trajectories that set graduates on journeys of significance and impact.[12]

The revision of professional and technical education programs and courses described in this text is right in line with the core missions of most colleges and universities. You might even say that it is a call to draw closer to their goals and amplify their abilities to meet them. A tremendous boost toward this end was provided in 1999 by the Lilly Endowment's Programs for the Theological Exploration of Vocation (PTEV) initiative that spanned the years 2000–2007.

In May 1999, the Lilly Endowment invited a group of outstanding colleges and universities to design programs for this initiative. Schools were asked to establish or strengthen programs that

- assist students in examining the relationship between faith and vocational choices,
- provide opportunities for gifted young people to explore Christian ministry, and
- enhance the capacity of a school's faculty and staff to teach and mentor students effectively in this arena.

In total, three rounds of grant opportunities resulted in 138 college and university participants receiving a total of $176.2 million in awards.

Most of the work by the Lilly Endowment grantees focused on explorations of meaning and purpose for discerning vocation resulting in permanent programs, curricula, and learning objectives focused on these outcomes. One might conclude that the Lilly Endowment initiative has been the principal motivator of a reinvigorated focus on purpose, meaning, and discerning vocation in postsecondary education in this country.

The Lilly Endowment was a timely and forceful initiative that garnered the participation of colleges and universities with a programmatic focus on "theology," "faith," and "Christian ministry." One might expect that such language would certainly drive away the typically hyper-secular research universities and those colleges not founded by religious denominations. But no; the participants must have recognized that modes of inquiry in theology reveal metaphysical assumptions about purpose and meaning that spark deep, moving conversations about life and vocation. As several education researchers argue, and others have demonstrated through surveys, a blend of spiritual, social, and academic programming creates a synergy for broader and deeper learning that includes natural contexts for the exploration of purpose and meaning.

For his book *The Purposeful Graduate*, Tim Clydesdale investigated and surveyed many of the participating institutions in the Lilly PTEV initiative, their administrators, faculty, and students to ascertain the impact of their explorations of purpose, meaning, and discerning vocation. His findings and results are very compelling and, within a historical perspective, predictable. Here is one of his important conclusions:

> I recommend campus-based programming for exploration of purpose, therefore, because I have observed firsthand that these programs contribute to more mission-effective campuses, and present evidence regarding their broad appeal, organizational adaptability, and ability to supply nourishment and refreshment.[13]

William Damon, in *The Path to Purpose*, describes the dedicated lives of select young people who have found a purpose that sustains their interest and motivation. He makes the point that such intrinsically curious and motivated students are uncommon. Based on his studies at Stanford University, he typically finds "What is too often missing—not altogether absent but evident only in a minority of today's youth—is the kind of wholehearted dedication to an activity or interest that stems from a serious purpose, a purpose that can give meaning and direction to life."[14] The good news from Damon's work and the outcomes from many of the programs born of the Lilly Endowment's initiative is that students without the innate ability can, nevertheless, learn how to develop a sense of purpose, meaning, and vocation.

Clydesdale's conclusions about the impact of the PTEV grants initiative can serve as a developmental outline for any college or university wishing to include explorations of purpose and meaning in their programming:

> First, virtually all students welcome self-knowledge and will connect that with their future plans. Second, a sizable minority of students will embrace the self-transcendence, seeking to express their sense of life purpose through service now and in the future. Third, this sizable minority will generate a pro-vocational community that spans campus sectors and occupies pockets of student life. Fourth, faculty members will not only value mentorship, but generate new courses and academic programs to prepare students for the worlds they will enter and the complexities they will confront. Fifth, staff will eagerly restructure nonacademic programs, finding in exploration programming an affirmation of the commitment they have long sought to express. Sixth, senior administrators will enjoy greater consensus about organizational mission and operative strategies, and may even explore ways to reengage with elements of the educational experience that fueled their interest educational leadership.[15]

As previously mentioned, the Lilly PTEV grants initiative garnered a surprising number of academic participants for a program with a significantly spiritual aspect. Obviously, the participating institutions must have recognized that the spiritual vacuum among colleges and universities is a growing liability.

Among those grant recipients where a vigorous dialogue had begun centered on examining personal values, meaning, and purpose, the subject of religious and spiritual values also came to the fore as part of the educational experience. It seems only natural that it would, as the eminent sociologist Max Weber points out, because all systems of meaning stand on metaphysical assumptions that cannot be proven by rational empiricism and must be taken on faith as part of an important recognition of human limitations.[16]

This nuanced understanding of the world and the place of spirituality in the moral and character development of students inherent in explorations of purpose and meaning was integral to Plato's Academy and the antebellum American colleges of two hundred years ago. It seems we might be coming back to the future in this amalgam of academic and spiritual studies taking place at some postsecondary institutions, and with good reason.

Still, in a great majority of colleges and universities, along with others in the education support network, the language of spirituality and theology threatens the purported objectivity of their mission, programs, and curricula. In addition, they do not want to be associated with anything that smacks of proselytizing or indoctrination. However, a heavy concentration on objectivity and empirical rationality works against encouraging authenticity, identity, integrity, and spiritual insightfulness.[17] This is also further evidence of a hyper-left-brained orientation to education.

One of the best ways to address this issue begins with a broad, inclusive definition of "spiritual" and "spirituality." Consider the definition provided in Wayne Teasdale's *The Mystic Heart*:

> Spirituality is a way of life that affects and includes every moment of existence. It is at once a contemplative attitude, a disposition to a life of depth, and the search for the ultimate meaning, direction, and belonging. The spiritual person is committed to growth as an essential ongoing life goal. To be spiritual requires us to stand on our own two feet while being nurtured and supported by our tradition, if we are fortunate enough to have one.[18]

Teasdale's interpretation has a useful distinction between the dogmatic theology typical of church authorities and the personal experience of a spiritual life. The spirituality found in contemplative experience is available to everyone and is open to thoughtful study. In this light, spiritual practice often leads to a knowledge-based experience that revolves around values, meaning, and purpose.[19]

A distinction can also be made between what Parker Palmer and Arthur Zajonc describe as a cognitively oriented spirituality and a faith-based religious life. In a cognitively oriented spirituality—one that is advocated here to further our educational purpose—empirical knowledge and imaginative insight dwell side by side.[20]

In their students' search for purpose, meaning, and a calling, colleges and universities will need to give greater importance to issues of contemplative practice, mindfulness, and spiritual growth; these elements are part of the foundation of teaching to inspire vocation. Simply adding a course on these subjects to an otherwise orthodox curriculum or scheduling periodic extracurricular student seminars and activities isn't sufficient. The most impactful solution, short of a required series of courses that accompany students through their undergraduate curriculum, is to embed these elements in the curriculum. This will enhance student learning of the course material, not detract from it, and help students find meaning in their education.

Ideally, such efforts also need to be embedded in the governance and curricula of these institutions, but that is the subject for another text. Good examples of contemplative practice in the curriculum exist within the network of Jesuit colleges and universities scattered around the country. Checking the missions of any of these institutions you will see "liberal arts education," "critical thinking," "spirituality," and "community service" prominently displayed. The Association for Contemplative Mind in Higher Education is a good resource.

LIBERAL LEARNING AND VOCATION

The current standing of liberal arts education in the United States is in peril. It seems that literature, history, philosophy, and the arts are the current stepchildren of postsecondary education. The impact of this growing academic void is well described by Andrew Delbanco:

> This is a great loss because they are the legatees of religion in the sense that they provide a vocabulary for formulating ultimate questions of the sort that have always had special urgency for young people. In fact, the humanities may have the most to offer to students who do not know that they need them—which is one reason it is scandalous to withhold them. One of the ironies of contemporary academic life is that even as the humanities become marginal in our colleges, they are establishing themselves in medical, law, and business schools, where interest is growing in the study of literature and the arts as a way to encourage self-critical reflection among future physicians, attorneys, and entrepreneurs.[21]

The conditions that Delbanco describes within some STEM (science, technology, engineering, and math) education programs has generated some recent pushback. The acronym STEAM has arisen at some institutions, the "A" derived from art having taken its place among the other subjects as a means to accomplish what Delbanco encourages: the development of a vocabulary for self-critical reflection in a search for purpose, meaning, and vocation.

The components of a liberal arts education—particularly history, literature, and philosophy—help us formulate eternal questions and reformulate answers that have been contemplated since the beginning of time. This is the principal purpose of such "old-fashioned" liberal arts curricula as a Great Books Program. As Delbanco wonders,

> Does Achilles' concept of honor in *The Iliad* retain any force for us today? What would it mean truly to live according to Thoreau's ethic of minimal exploitation of nature, or by Kant's categorical imperative? Is there a basis in experience for the Augustinian idea of original sin? Such questions do not admit of verifiable or replicable answers because the experiment to which we must subject them is the experiment of our own lives.[22]

The point here is not a return to a classic liberal arts education for every postsecondary student. But many aspects and elements of a classic liberal arts education engage both our left and right hemispheres, triggering a full cognitive cycle of perception and processing that spills over into the most analytical of studies, including professional and technical programs, giving them a richness of connection to purpose and vocation that they might not have otherwise.

Reformulated STEM programs containing an art component (STEAM) are an example of liberal arts connections that encourage guided self-discovery: a blend of knowledge and skill; the synergy of inspiration and discipline; and the wonder of insight. Student self-discovery also leads to relevant and grounded information and, ultimately, the pursuit of knowledge for its own sake as well for the utility associated with a dedicated profession.

Answers to the big questions surrounding truth, justice, meaning, and purpose should not be restricted to those students studying the classics in the few remaining liberal arts programs. They are relevant and should be part of all collegiate programs no matter whether a student studies accounting, computer science, engineering, or business management. These questions once occupied the center of a college education, and they should again.

The challenge of helping students find personal relevance in their education is a function of integrating objective and subjective interpretations of the curriculum. The research university's wholly objective approach to education shuts out an important element: the experiences and relationships of students and the impact of those on their interpretation of what is important in life.

Parker Palmer and Arthur Zajonc put this into perspective in their book *The Heart of Higher Education*:

> we focus on the primacy of the participating observer.... This emphasis on the lived experience of the scientific "observer" links the power of scientific knowing with the feelings we have before a work of art and the compassion we feel for those who suffer, a shift of perspective whose implications are pivotal for higher education. In this view, the relationships and experiences of our lives—and the lives of our students—are not dismissed as irrelevant or inconsequential but are fully granted their own standing as building blocks of reality; they are not secondary qualities or adaptive strategies but primary dimensions of our humanity.[23]

VOCATIONAL VOCABULARY AND NARRATIVE

Perhaps we might find it easier to approach the weighty questions of purpose and meaning by reframing them into something more accessible, such as, "What should I care about?" Using this question helps to answer other questions because we make a connection between our life's purpose and meaning through what we care about at the highest level—something worth caring about in the ultimate way. What we care about at this level is certainly worth protecting and preserving such that it conveys powerful purpose and meaning.[24] Let's put this educational challenge in a slightly different context, one borrowed from Neil Postman:

> [When it comes to schooling ourselves]we have two problems to solve. One is an engineering problem, the other, a metaphysical one. The engineering problem . . . is one of by what means we will educate or school ourselves; the means—how learning is supposed to occur. But to become a different person because of something you have learned—to appropriate an insight, a concept, a vision, so that your world is altered—that is a different matter. For that to happen, you need a reason. And that is the metaphysical problem.[25]

Without a reason to be in the classroom, to listen to the teacher, to do the required work, schooling doesn't work. In this light, it's easy to assess the academic struggles of many students: lack of reason. Here we return to the question of *why*, not just *how*. For school to make sense, everyone involved must have a higher purpose to serve; otherwise, school is pointless. Nietzsche understood the problem: "He who has a *why* to live can bear almost any *how*."

Postman makes the case that a relevant narrative—preferably multiple narratives—offered in school will provide the answers to the question of why we are learning what we are learning. Such educational narratives are meant to supply guidance and inspiration for everyone involved in education: the administration, faculty, staff, and students. Address the need to recognize purpose, meaning, and vocation—Postman's metaphysical problem—by creating programs and curricula based on shared narratives with the capacity to provide an inspired reason for education.[26]

VOCATION AND COMMUNITY SERVICE

Perhaps one of the most important and powerful trends to redirect education to address the bigger questions in life is the incorporation of community service in the curriculum. The explicit connection of coursework with service work is important for helping to make learning more relevant to community need and, therefore, build a sense of purpose and vocation within our students. It's the connection to the "public good" that is so lacking and necessary today, instilling in students a devotion not just to personal advancement but also to community.

A powerful means of instilling in students a sensitivity to the public good is finding opportunities to incorporate community-engaged learning projects in a course or courses. Community-engaged learning is a wonderful way for students to connect what they are learning in school to the realities of work, professional life, and service in the community. A deep and relevant connection to the concept and reality of discerning a vocation is available to students engaged in community-engaged learning activities.

The instructor's role is vital in establishing an academic context as a bridge to community-engaged learning projects at both ends of the experience. Instructors need to establish connections of relevance to the community-engaged learning experience at the beginning of the project. You then need to check in with students throughout their experience to make sure that they are well grounded and the project is progressing smoothly. Finally, you will need to provide debriefing time to ensure that students recognize important connections available through the community-engaged learning experience.

A large part of the academic/community-engaged learning connection is for students to recognize their service to the common good through the knowledge and skills they are learning in class. A sense of serving the common good is one that is often paramount to hearing a calling or discerning a vocation. Chapter 7 is devoted to the community-engaged learning element of teaching vocation. The next section describes the close and analogous relationship between the concepts of vocation and calling and why the concept of "calling" is important to vocation.

Chapter 3

VOCATION AND CALLING

> Some time when the river is ice
> ask me mistakes I have made.
> Ask me whether what I have done is my life.[27]

Parker Palmer uses this segment from Stafford's poem *Ask Me* to define what it means to find a calling. He explains it this way:

> the poet's words. . . . They remind me of moments when it is clear—if I have eyes to see—that the life I am living is not the same as the life that wants to live in me. In those moments, I sometimes catch a glimpse of my true life, a life hidden like the river beneath the ice. And in the spirit of the poet, I wonder: What am I meant to do? Who am I meant to be?[28]

The use of the term "calling" is a way of describing the *discernment* of vocation, a word derived from the Latin term "Vox," or voice—a voice that "calls" to you about your purpose and livelihood. These two important and inseparable terms, "vocation" and "calling," have come to be used traditionally in association with a calling to a particular role or vocation within a narrowed religious context, or church, such as the Catholic Church. This is unfortunate due to the religious baggage associated with the use of these terms in a broader, secular context. As you can see from Palmer's interpretation, a calling is inextricably linked to a deep sense of what you do. The pursuit of your calling, or vocation, gives you a feeling that you fit within the larger scheme of things, and you have a distinct purpose.[29]

The concept of finding your true vocation and hearing your calling is not prevalent in our culture. The blare of messaging and advice all around is about what should be important in your adult life, most of it related to product advertising and consumption. The common threads are money, security, and status: how much does a particular form of work and career pay, what are its other security related benefits, what sort of class-based stature does such a job and career possess? The idea of choosing to do something that you feel called to do for its own sake and the sake of the community, something that will contribute to the common good and your own satisfaction, is not often discussed.

Many of us have experience with career-changing, older students who have returned to college for a second degree. That path often stems from the experience of having pursued a prior college degree based on the advice and wishes of family members and other influential people in their lives. However, after taking this advice, finishing their degree, and obtaining gainful employment, the students realized that they had made the wrong choice. What you may also notice about these students is their welcome level of enthusiasm and zeal for an education more in line with discerning a vocation or hearing a calling.

Consider the old Quaker saying, "Let your life speak." Instead of listening for their life to speak, many students originally choose to adopt the ideals of a mentor, a hero, or family members and friends. Although well-intended, they often do not fit who that student is; they are a distortion of their true self. It's like reading from someone else's script. Yes, it is possible to find a noble way to live by emulating inspiring people instead of letting your own life speak to you.

Too often though, the message of others about what one is supposed to do drowns out the messages that come from inside us. Many career-changing students let that happen and get off on the wrong track in college, then must repeat that experience with the additional investment in time and money that it requires. Fortunately, we can help our students discover their true vocation, or at least a sense of it, before becoming too vested in someone else's vision.

The concept of letting your life speak to you can be traced much further back than the Quakers. As first pointed out in chapter 2, Socrates, Plato, and their peers put great emphasis on identifying a calling for their students and in their philosophies. The life voice that the Quakers listened for was considered by the Greeks to be their "daimon." Their daimon could also be an urge that pushes you in a certain direction. Socrates described his daimon as "a voice which, when it makes itself heard, deters me from what I am about to do and never urges me on."[30]

Students face at least two significant challenges in identifying a vocation: the lack of attention to such concerns in our everyday lives, particularly at school; and the inability to hear your life speak, or identify your daimon, through all the surrounding cultural noise prescribing your life and career choices that schools often emulate. Meeting the first challenge is the focal point of this book. Meeting the second challenge is a personal one for all of us no matter the messages, dictates, and pressures of the surrounding social, cultural, and academic environment.

Many young people approach the matter of discovering their vocation or hearing their calling as an act of will. It's as if it can be puzzled out from a mixture of factors of social, cultural, and personal origin, which often results in borrowed or fractured visions that come from somewhere or someone else. Palmer puts this point into sharp relief:

> Vocation does not mean a goal that I pursue. It means a calling that I here. Before I can tell my life what I want to do with it, I must listen to my life telling me who I am. I must listen for the truths and values at the heart of my own identity, not the standards by which I must live—but the standards by which I cannot help but live if I am living my own life.[31]

Certainly, our students have had early life experiences that made important permanent impressions on them. As they get older, some of these experiences continue to guide their personal interests, becoming hobbies and/or avocational interests that suggest elements of a life's work. They are now in one or several of your classes and have reached a point of reckoning regarding their education, career, and life path amid a cacophony of voices full of direction. It can be difficult for them to hear that inner voice reminding them of those earlier, meaningful life experiences and their relationship to the choices they now face. The returning, career-changing students heard that voice late and are now acting upon it.

We must help our first-time students get in touch with their past and their inner voice speaking to them about their vocation. Stories from career-changers may help in this discovery. Careful contemplation of their past and thoughtful reflection on their experiences may yield several clues to the vocations of less-experienced students based on lasting positive experiences—their life (daimon) will speak to them. Vocation is all about achieving a deep congruence between one's inner life and one's outer life.

A "way" to identify vocation may not open in front of someone, but a lot of the "way" may have closed behind them—their personal history—and that may have a guiding effect. In other words, as much guidance comes from what does not and cannot happen in one's life as in what can and does—maybe more.

Let's say that you have a great deal of dislike for and difficulty organizing things. This has immediate implications for the kind of profession that will ultimately work for you. Any professional and/or personal endeavors that require good organizational skills will be troubling and stressful. In another example, someone with a geometric dyslexion has great difficulty with perceptual geometry. This will be a serious impediment for them working in design, building trades, or architecture, among other things. Discerning vocation is as much about recognizing one's fallibilities as one's capabilities.

Helping students discern their vocation is also about helping them be creative in their learning and in their lives. We all have that capability as evidenced by young children who are not afraid to be wrong. Fear of being wrong is a hard lesson all too prevalent in our culture and our schools, and it kills creativity.

Sir Ken Robinson tells the story of a six-year-old girl who was so engaged in an art project that her teacher was impatient to see what she was working on. When asked, the little girl said, "I'm drawing a picture of God." Concerned, the teacher replied, "Well, no one knows what God looks like." The little girl confidently responded, "In a minute they will!" He also tells of a little boy playing one of the three kings in the nativity play who stepped forward with his gift and, forgetting what it was called (frankincense), simply blurted out, "Frank sent this!" Funny and endearing to adults, the fortitude and creativity evident in these examples is partly the result of a lack of fear about being wrong. Dr. Robinson sums it up this way: "If you're not prepared to be wrong, you're not likely to come up with anything original."

These examples of creative thinking in children goes to show what C. G. Jung knew when he wrote that creativity is an instinct, not an optional gift granted to the lucky few. Finding and having a true vocation is a catalyst for creativity that energizes students' spirit, empowers their sense of self, and provides fulfillment in their work and life.

It may take time for a calling, or callings, to be fully revealed. Students may head down the wrong path, dabble with several possibilities, and make a host of other mistakes in their pursuit. We must help them recognize that it's possible to discover several equally compelling vocational possibilities that speak to them. It's not necessary to narrow these down to one in the mistaken assumption that discerning a vocation is concluded with a commitment to a single one. In these cases, such fortunate people may pursue one compelling vocation as a profession and the others as avocations.

A calling that one pursues will likely evolve and change over time. It's important that students attend to the gravity of their calling and vocation as they move forward in their lives so that if they are called in a new direction, they will be able to evaluate it carefully. This book emerged from an evolved calling in education. The call to education arose as an offshoot of a vocation in horticulture. The new calling didn't eclipse the old one; it simply emerged alongside it in a synergistic relationship. A calling to a particular life's work is a critically important and precious thing. A multiplicity of these is a rare treasure.

Some people hear other potential callings on a regular basis. Those potential callings create a useful tension in their lives. This is good for two reasons:

1. It creates a tension that repeatedly draws their attention to their primary calling, or vocation, for reaffirmation, a process that reinvigorates their dedication; and
2. It adds creative diversity in their life.

We may all possess a multiplicity of interests in addition to our principal vocation as mutually empowering aspects of our lives. Convey to your students that their life and work are like feathers in a peacock's tail, having myriad facets. They must not put all the weight of their life's work on their career because many other facets of their lives also contribute to who they are: spouse, parent, family, community, avocational pursuits—the feathers in a peacock's tail.

In putting vocation in context, this chapter makes a case for a new approach to professional and technical education with a focus on purpose, meaning, and discerning vocation based on a reexamination of old models, practices, and explorations of a new epistemology. There is not only a desperate need for the conveyance of purpose and meaning in education, but several broad avenues in which to bring this to fruition following ancient and long-established forms of education and practice combined with new perspectives on a purposeful epistemology.

If we're successful, then we will help our students achieve a learner's state of receptive engagement that will persist throughout their lives. We will also have moved the exploration of purpose and meaning beyond traditional areas of liberal arts into all aspects of professional and technical curricular and cocurricular life. In the words of the University of Washington's David Levy, "Receptive engagement may be taught and practiced in a way to redirect and transcend our current instrumental trajectory and bridge the liberal versus professional education divide resulting in a thoughtful hybrid approach."[32]

CONCLUSION

Teaching to inspire vocation is most effective when embedded within the academic and technical elements of the education program. To reiterate from chapter 1, the important elements of a framework for teaching to inspire vocation are instructor *authenticity* and *mentoring*; *multimodal* pedagogies (cognitive, kinesthetic, affective) using an intentional *vocabulary* and *narrative*; *contemplative practice* and *personal knowledge*; *learning communities*; and *experiential learning*.

Teaching to inspire vocation is a somewhat indirect, often oblique, and influential process. In teaching to inspire vocation, you are cultivating an orientation and perspective on your discipline using intentional vocabulary and narratives that frame it as a worthy vocation. As you progress through the curriculum and apply these elements, students will better comprehend the information, achieve proficiency with skills, and find meaning in their scholarship.

A common issue surrounding teaching to inspire vocation is the specter of instructors imposing their personal ideologies on students. Paths to learning developed around self-discovery make it possible to teach the elements previously described openly and with discretion. We will take up this concern again in the upcoming chapters. For now, Thomas Moore's observation is pertinent:

> We no longer educate young people to be open to the daimonic force that would give them their life work. Instead, we tell them what work they should do and

help them adapt to it. Today, we have surrendered to a view of the human being as a mechanical being ruled by a brain, and we see education as instilling skills and facts with the purpose of having a successful career and making as much money as possible. We ignore the education of the heart and the revelation of a deep power and direction within the person.[33]

As we all know, attempting to implement change within your small area of influence at an educational institution is an uphill battle. Tim Clydesdale's recommendation constitutes sound advice:

> developing purpose exploration programs requires honest conversation among a wide pool of stakeholders, occurs over many weeks and months, and is rooted in the organization's history and culture keyed to its specific needs.[34]

If you have an opportunity and/or the discretionary time in your busy schedule to adopt the role of institutional advocate for explorations of purpose and discerning vocation, then be that person. If not, seek out someone among the administration, staff, or other faculty to partner with you in this endeavor. Otherwise, use what works best for you among the examples provided in this text to incorporate in the portion of the curriculum for which you are responsible.

Moving forward as an independent entity on this subject in an otherwise unwelcoming institution may be risky and difficult. Still, if this work is part of your calling, it cannot be ignored. In this case, you will do what is known as "job crafting"—that is, looking for ways and opportunities to augment and embed explorations of purpose and meaning for discerning vocation in your curriculum, course outlines, and lesson plans.

The rest of this text will focus on instructional methods and practices to help individual faculty and instructors craft a learning environment that includes explorations of purpose, meaning, and teaching to inspire vocation. For examples of broader applications that involve aspects of the entire institution, I refer you to Tim Clydesdale's excellent book *The Purposeful Graduate*.

Before concluding this chapter, here are a few basic recommendations that serve as a preliminary to the rest of this text. An important and underlying recommendation implicit in all the elements of teaching to inspire vocation is this: professional and technical faculty and instructors must view their students and provide for their education as *whole persons*. Another broadly applicable recommendation alluded to already is that you establish a compelling and consistent vocabulary for all programs and pedagogies pertaining to explorations of purpose, meaning, and the discovery of vocation. This may seem implicit or even incidental, but it's very important to remember that language shapes thought, attitude, and an impactful narrative.

A carefully chosen vocabulary goes a long way toward helping students internalize and remember important concepts. For example, be careful to nest the relational terms "purpose," "meaning," and "vocation" together. Throughout this text, the term "vocation" and "calling" are used in a particular vein to help make their meaning clearer. Chapter 6 is dedicated to this subject.

If you have older, career-changing students who made compelling personal and professional discoveries related to discerning vocation on their own, you may be surprised at how responsive they are to the vocabulary, narratives, and reflections about their choices and new learning experiences as they relate to hearing their calling. When exposed to these teaching to inspire vocation elements, they resonate in a very powerful way and elevate their dedication and resolve to their scholarship and the program.

Another advantage of older, experienced students is their capacity to assist as mentors, tutors, and instructional aides, particularly regarding finding meaning, purpose, and discerning vocation in the curriculum because they are farther along in this process. These students have the potential to be helpful, credible guides lending validation to these explorations. Consider them partners in the education process.

Modifying the existing curriculum and your instructional technique to include the elements for framing teaching to inspire vocation involves careful adjustment. More specifically, it involves intentional changes to standard language you use surrounding career choice, references to career work and technologies in the field, professional paths in that field, and reflection on the connections between work and personal-professional goals.

This brings us to a particular point of importance and challenge: a concept known as the "purpose gap." Students of color and other disadvantaged students often face a purpose gap. For these students, after they have discerned their purpose, they often face impediments to pursuing that purpose and realizing their vocation. A good example is a first-generation student of color facing a host of obstacles in a system of education not designed for them. The purpose gap is most obvious and widest for the most marginalized of our students. Closing the purpose gap means, in the words of Patrick Reyes: "creating the conditions for future generations to achieve meaningful and purpose-filled lives. It means removing the barriers, generating the resources, building the power, and imagining the future where those who are most marginalized thrive." (Note: Patrick B. Reyes, *The Purpose Gap* [Louisville: Westminster John Knox Press, 2021] 12.) Closing the purpose gap begins with your awareness that it exists for some of your students. For a more thorough examination of the purpose gap and how you help those students facing it, I refer you to *The Purpose Gap* by Patrick B. Reyes.

When we help our students discover their vocation, we help them find a life's work that they love. They will love it as much for the process as the product. They will love doing the work for its own sake as well as the product or service it provides to others. That doesn't mean that they love every aspect of their vocation. However, the challenging parts of their profession are usually more than compensated for by their overall sense of dedication and vocation to their work and life.

One last and very important point. By reading this book and implementing its recommendations, you are fulfilling your own vocation as educators. To help your students fulfill their vocation, in turn, you need to bring the full force of your authenticity to this work.

In the remaining chapters, we will explore different concepts, pedagogies, and classroom techniques for embedding the elements of teaching to inspire vocation in your courses and curriculum.

> Textbox 3.1 Teaching Takeaways
>
> - Research shows that people of college-age are searching for purpose and meaning in a quest for spiritual fulfillment.
> - A purely objective and empirical approach to education works against the pursuit of purpose, meaning, spiritual fulfillment, and vocation.
> - Being spiritual suggests a personal commitment to a process of inner development, a key to discerning vocation.
> - Spiritual practice often leads to a knowledge-based experience that revolves around values, meaning, and purpose.
> - Having a vocation means choosing to do something that you feel called to do for *its own sake* and the sake of the *community*.
> - Teaching vocation relies on shared narratives with the capacity to provide an inspired reason for education.
> - Ancient wisdom and sociological research show that people's lives are fuller, richer, and happier when they revolve around a true vocation that defines and guides who they are and how they serve others.
> - Teaching vocation is most effective when it goes hand in hand with the academic and technical elements of education.
> - In teaching vocation, you are cultivating an orientation, perspective, and gestalt on your discipline using intentional vocabulary and narratives that frame it as a worthy vocation.
> - Set aside discussion time in an introductory course to share your story of how you became interested in the discipline and ask students to do the same.

NOTES

1. Annie Dillard, *Pilgrim at Tinker Creek* (New York: Harper Perennial, 2013), 2.
2. William Deresiewicz, *Excellent Sheep* (New York: Free Press, 2014), 73.
3. David Orr, *Earth in Mind: On Education, Environment, and the Human Prospect* (Washington, DC: Island Press, 2004), 8.
4. Ken Robinson, "Do Schools Kill Creativity," TED, https://www.ted.com/talks/sir_ken_robinson_do_schools_kill_creativity?language=en.
5. Iain McGilchrist, *The Master and His Emissary* (New Haven, CT, and London: Yale University Press, 2009), 208.
6. Robert Kegan, *In Over Our Heads* (Boston: Harvard University Press, 1998), 188.
7. Bryan J. Dik and Ryan D. Duffy, *Make Your Job a Calling* (Conshohocken, PA: Templeton Press, 2012), 68.
8. Dik and Duffy, *Make Your Job a Calling*, 68.
9. Alexander W. Astin, Helen S. Astin, and Jennifer A. Lindholm, *Cultivating the Spirit: How College Can Enhance Students' Inner Lives* (San Francisco: Jossey-Bass, 2010).
10. Arthur W. Chickering, Jon C. Dalton, and Liesa Stamm, *Encouraging Authenticity and Spirituality in Higher Education* (San Francisco: Jossey-Bass, 2006) 32.
11. Chickering, Dalton, and Stamm, *Encouraging Authenticity and Spirituality in Higher Education*, 31–33.
12. Tim Clydesdale, *The Purposeful Graduate* (Chicago and London: University of Chicago Press, 2015), xvii.
13. Clydesdale, *The Purposeful Graduate*, xix.
14. William Damon, *The Path to Purpose: Helping Our Children Find Their Calling in Life* (New York: Free Press, 2008), 7.
15. Clydesdale, *The Purposeful Graduate*, 70.
16. Max Weber, https://en.wikipedia.org/wiki/Max_Weber.
17. Chickering, Dalton, and Stamm, *Encouraging Authenticity and Spirituality in Higher Education*, 29.
18. Wayne Teasdale, *Mystic Heart: Discovering a Universal Spirituality in the World's Religions* (Novato, CA: New World Library, 1999) 17.
19. Parker Palmer and Arthur Zajonc, *The Heart of Higher Education* (San Francisco: Jossey-Bass, 2010), 119–21.
20. Palmer and Zajonc, *The Heart of Higher Education*, 121.
21. Andrew Delbanco, *College: What It Was, Is, and Should Be* (Princeton, NJ: Princeton University Press, 2012), 99.
22. Delbanco, *College*, 101.
23. Parker, *The Heart of Higher Education*, 11.
24. Anthony Kronman, *Education's End: Why Our Colleges and Universities Have Given Up on the Meaning of Life* (New Haven, CT, and London: Yale University Press, 2007), 23–24.
25. Neil Postman, *The End of Education* (New York: Knopf, 1995), 4–5.
26. Postman, *The End of Education*, 18.

27. William Stafford, "Ask Me," *Stories That Could Be True* (New York: Harper & Row, 1977).

28. Parker Palmer, *Let Your Life Speak: Listening for the Voice of Vocation* (San Francisco: Jossey-Bass, 2000), 1–2.

29. Thomas Moore, *A Life at Work* (Easton, PA: Harmony Press, 2009), 24.

30. Moore, *A Life at Work*, 121–22.

31. Palmer, *Let Your Life Speak*, 4–5.

32. David Levy, "Head, Heart, and Hand: Cultivating the Contemplative in Higher Education," Annual Conference of the Association for Contemplative Mind in Higher Education, April 24–26, 2009, Amherst College, Amherst, Massachusetts. https://vimeo.com/5187656.

33. Moore, *A Life at Work*, 134.

34. Clydesdale, *The Purposeful Graduate*, 23.

4

Authenticity, Mentoring, and Learning Community Elements

> To make any progress at all in this kind of education, we must possess an appropriate sense of humility, which is only fitting for those who have a lot to learn.[1]
>
> —John Neafsey

From here forward we will take a closer look at the principal framing elements for teaching to inspire vocation that you will use to revise and amplify a course and/or curriculum to help your students find meaning, purpose, and discern their vocation. As a reminder, those elements are instructor *authenticity* and *mentoring*, *multimodal pedagogy* (cognitive, kinesthetic, affective), *vocabulary/narrative/framing*, *contemplative practice* and *personal knowledge*, *learning community*, and *experiential learning*. In this chapter we will focus on the importance of authenticity, the role of faculty and instructors as mentors, and organizing classes and groups of students into learning communities.

AUTHENTICITY

> The true self is grounded in our personal emotional truth, our true feelings, what we actually think and feel about things.[2]

Teaching to inspire vocation requires that our efforts, first and foremost, be authentic. Having your attention up to this point in our exploration of the subject at hand is certainly evidence of an authentic interest in this goal. Still, taking the information from these pages into the classroom, laboratory, field site, and any other educational context will test your authenticity, not only on this subject but in your teaching and pedagogy as a whole. If you have self-doubt on this score, the good news is, your authenticity will reveal itself as you work through the other practices prescribed in this text.

Just to be clear what is meant by "authenticity"; being authentic requires psychological and emotional honesty with yourself and your students. What you believe, what you say, and what you do are consistent. To put it in more vernacular terms: being authentic means that what you see is what you get. It also means being able to say that you teach because it is your vocation.

Some of you may have come to education inadvertently after starting as a professional practitioner in your subject matter specialty. Such circumstances can put a strain on educational authenticity, particularly during early years of instruction when you are struggling to keep up with large course loads and correspondingly large preparation requirements. At the beginning, students may question your credibility, competence, and authenticity. With patience and dedication, career-changing faculty and instructors new to higher education may find a new vocation in their role as educators through the inspiration provided by students who see the vocational potential in their education.

The point of that narrative about finding authenticity is that it comes naturally to whatever we do if we find meaning, purpose, and discern our vocation in it. In addition, we may all live out our lives within multiple vocations, the source of a life full of richness and variety.

It can be difficult to maintain a consistent level of authenticity as we encounter new experiences, new information, and new generations of students. We must constantly deconstruct and reconstruct our cognitive and emotional connections to our work to strengthen our vocation and, in turn, our authenticity, just as previously described for someone starting a teaching career. As many of you already know, technique alone will not generate deep, lasting learning unless it is appropriate and authentic.

Authentic teachers have an innate capacity to connect with their students and assist them in connecting with the subject matter and to each other in forming learning communities.[3] When this happens, students are more likely to experience deeper learning and a strengthened sense of purpose and meaning. Your connection to your students, particularly in learning communities, is crucial to your authenticity. As Charles Taylor points out in "The Ethics of Authenticity," "modes that opt for self-fulfillment without regard (a) to the demands of our ties with others or (b) to demands of any kind emanating from something more or other than human desires or aspirations are self-defeating, that they destroy the conditions for realizing authenticity itself." (Note: Charles Taylor, "The Ethics of Authenticity" in *Leading Lives That Matter*, ed. Mark R. Schwehn and Dorothy C. Bass [Grand Rapids: Wm. B. Erdmans, 2006], 55.) The bottom line: before we can help our students discern their vocation, we must know ours. More on authenticity related to contemplative practice in chapter 5.

MENTORING

Authentic teaching naturally leads to varying degrees of mentorship. Being a mentor for your students is often a natural and important by-product of good teaching; it's a difficult relationship to construct because it often occurs spontaneously. A key is to develop and find opportunities to work more closely with students. Advising time is an obvious opportunity, albeit often too rare and too brief. More on intentional advising later.

Mentors, as Hannah Schell so aptly defines them, "help students ascertain what is important and of value to them at the current moment, to derive what underlying ideals and values inform their lives, and then to begin imagining what those ideals and values might look like when expressed over the longer arc of their lives."[4] During your career, you might work for long periods of time without thinking of yourself as a mentor even though, in the eyes of some of your students, you are serving as one. Sharon Daloz Parks comments on how this happens:

> When the locus of authority shifts from outside the self, inward, it does so most solidly by moving first from dependence on a given authority to dependence on a chosen authority—still external, but one that I now choose in accord with my own observations and lived experience. . . . the transition into emerging adulthood occurs most gracefully and with optimum potential when the emerging self is recognized and invited into a wider arena of participation by wise and trusted adults.[5]

Parks is describing an important evolution in student learning and the development of self-hood and self-authoring adults that progresses from a chosen authority (e.g., teacher/mentor) to greater self-reliance. The idea of a *chosen* authority is an important aspect and element of an educator/mentor—this is someone attended to, respected, and emulated when elevated to the position of a "spirit person," to use the vernacular of John Neafsey from his book *A Sacred Voice Is Calling*.[6] A spirit person is a source of vocational inspiration and guidance—a personal and professional hero.

As good teachers, we naturally have both a cognitive and affective appeal and impact on our students, offering both insight and emotional support. We should recognize our role as mentors and spiritual guides and carefully nurture it as a critical part of assisting our students in finding meaning, purpose, and a calling. As a mentor to your students, you provide inspiration, as Sharon Parks says, "for the long haul."[7]

Regarding teachers and professors as "spirit persons" or "spiritual guides," any such labels are certain to make some educators and administrators uncomfortable. This is a good point to reiterate Wayne Teasdale's definition of "spiritual" and "spirituality" from his book *The Mystic Heart*: "Spirituality is a way of life that affects and includes every moment of existence. It is at once a contemplative attitude, a disposition to a life of depth, and the search for the ultimate meaning, direction, and belonging."[8]

Given this interpretation, spirituality is a quality with a natural affinity to holistic education, if not education in general. In this regard, it doesn't seem far-fetched to consider affective educators as spiritual guides. We should recognize the important and appropriate role of teachers and professors to the meaning-making and spiritual lives of students.

In addition to relevant and compelling new information, good teachers provide for student recognition and support. At the same time, they must also challenge their students in ways that assist in developing critical thinking, holding multiple perspectives, and applied knowledge in multiple contexts. Supporting *and* challenging is a fine balancing act. By doing this well, teachers provide a guiding wisdom and become an inspiration, the final ingredient of a teacher as mentor. To sum up, teacher-mentors provide four key elements to their relationship with student "protégés": recognition, support, challenge, and inspiration.[9]

Mentoring, at the most basic level, involves dedicated office hours and intentional advising. "Intentional advising" means advising sessions that go beyond recommendations of good study habits and new courses to include a dialogue about the student's overall college experience and career aspirations. Dialogue is a way of being in conversation that is at risk in the age of sound bites and Twitter.

As teacher/mentors, we need to cultivate a dialogue with our students that involves good listening, a desire to understand our students, and a willingness to be moved and informed—in other words, a conversation that is essential to relationship. A dialogue also requires an authentic discussion by both parties, and this likely will involve sharing personal details of your own college and career development with your students. It is within a dialogue with your students where your recognition, support, challenge, and inspiration are made plain and reinforced.

Recognizing and supporting students often must be paired with challenges that will motivate them to move forward. This requires that you recognize and assess your students' readiness to respond to new information, ideas, opportunities, solutions, and relationships and then gently challenge them in those areas. These challenges—often in the form of questions about student progress, and so on—are born out of and occur within the context of recognition and support. With the right balance, you become a steady, inspiring point of orientation and success for your students—an inspiration.

Given your interest in the subject of this text, it's likely that you already work intentionally to mentor your students, or that through your natural proclivities as an effective teacher you are an unintentional mentor. You might also be effective as a mentor by taking advantage of "mentoring moments" before and after class, during office hours, and during other spontaneous encounters with students.

When asked, students invariably cite office hours as the time when the most valuable faculty interactions take place.[10] Students and faculty often feel less constrained during office hours to discuss the big questions about academics, careers, and life events. This is the context in which students are most likely to gain a more compelling understanding about concepts discussed in class.

The mentoring rapport that can develop during office hours and the intentional advising provided there create greater involvement in the classroom and allow students to feel a more personal connection to faculty typical of a mentor. Office hours are your best opportunity to create a personal dialogue with students for intentional advising and mentoring.

Best Practice 4.1: Office Hours

Here are some recommendations for the best use of office hours from *Putting Students First* by Larry A. Braskamp, Lois Trautvetter, and Kelly Ward:

- Stay true to office hour postings.
- Have students sign up for office hours so you have plenty of time to address their concerns.
- Give examples of the types of concerns students bring to office hour discussions and help provide insight on how to address common concerns.
- Some office interactions can bring up personal issues that are beyond faculty expertise. Faculty familiarity of boundaries in helping students and knowledge of the resources to direct students to more personalized professional help is useful.
- Faculty should be aware of proper etiquette and the appropriateness of office hour topics, given what can be viewed as an intimate setting between faculty and students.[11]

In addition to office hours, some unexpected and vital dialogue may occur, as I alluded to above, as part of a "mentoring moment." These often present themselves in passing between classes or when students happen to pop in your office at an opportune time. We need to be present to these opportunities for a meaningful and meaning-making dialogue with students. In fact, one of the most impactful elements of your relationship with students may be your willingness to listen and be present to them whenever you're on campus—particularly students with special needs. Sharon Parks puts the importance of dialogue into perspective very simply: "Dialogue tills the soil for the growth of critical thought and inner-dependence."[12]

As mentors, we bring to this role a basic sense that students can relate to their own experience. Our dialogues with students show mutual respect and make sense within the experience of our students. In this way, we are drawing out the students' own experience and distinctive voice to speak with greater integrity and confidence about what they are learning, what it means and how it contributes to their purpose and, eventually, their vocation. Daniel Levinson concludes that the most critical function of a mentoring relationship is to help the protégé develop and articulate a dream, an ideal that is intimately linked to a deep sense of purpose and an orienting vision for one's life—the stuff of vocation.[13]

Unfortunately, the objective/subjective dichotomy in higher education suppresses the notion of teachers and faculty sharing their personal lives and professional development experiences with their students. Often the resistance to having what might be construed as too much personal—nonobjective—influence over students is conscious. For the most part, this is nonsense and unfortunate. We owe it to our students to share the story of our discipline, including the practitioners, professors, and other luminaries in the discipline who have influenced our trajectory.

Providing course content is our first obligation and, if provided in compelling and creative ways, can open minds. But the right story can transform them. As Shirley Showalter points out, "The purpose of telling these stories is not to create clones of the professor, but rather to make invisible influences more visible—and therefore to make one's theoretical grounding more transparent. Undergraduates often have little or no comprehension of what forces go into the making of the subject before them."[14] Good stories and good questions can reveal elements of themselves previously hidden in students; they can also energize a classroom as a community of learners begins to form. More on learning communities later in this section.

As a mentor, your impromptu conversations with students between classes, during advising sessions, and in classroom dialogues may contain personal/professional anecdotes related to your training, experiences, and vocation. This is an effective means of helping students make practical sense of what they are learning and how it may apply to their careers and lives. This is also a critical part of mentoring.

As we become mentors through our work as good teachers, a whole new avenue of communications opens between our students and us. The dialogues we enter with our students provide us with greater insight into their needs as learners and seekers of meaning and purpose. We build into our curriculum and pedagogy big questions of consequence that require probing dialogues about our subject of study within a larger frame of issues.

Having done this, we've entered a new dimension of sharing and understanding with our students in a process of mutual challenge and discovery. As William Deresiewicz notes,

> one of the rewards of being a professor is the chance to learn from fresh young minds as well as teach them. You have to get to know your students as individuals—get to know their minds, I mean—and you have to believe completely, as a fellow student wrote about my own professor, Karl Kroeber, in each one's absolute uniqueness.[15]

This familiarity invariably will lead to more relevant and effective pedagogical shifts in your approach to teaching, making everyone's experience more satisfying. Then you're in position to facilitate what might be a teacher/mentor's most important job: helping students understand themselves. David Schoem underscores what I mean in his essay "Honoring the Humanity of Our Students,"

> I have learned first-hand from many wonderful university colleagues who bring a long-standing and dedicated commitment to good teaching. These teachers emphasize building strong relationships that often extend throughout a student's undergraduate years and beyond, and they prioritize mentoring students to help them realize their potential and lead informed lives of purpose and fulfillment.[16]

Intentional mentoring does not always culminate in wisdom and light in the minds of students. Few teacher-mentors get it right all the time. It is important not to push, or attempt to "inspire," too hard. It is not the place of mentors to guide and inspire carbon copies of themselves. Our purpose as teacher-mentors is to recognize, support, challenge, and inspire our students to find their own true path in discerning a vocation. In so doing, we may help them develop vital habits of mind that make it possible to parse diversity and complexity, moral ambiguity, strengthen critical thought, encourage holistic awareness, and develop a deeper sense of meaning and purpose. That is no small achievement.

The subject of critical thought has come up several times and is the subject of an entire educational literature. Critical thinking is lauded as a principle of effective education. Therefore, let's take a moment to make sure we understand what critical thinking is. Consider Sharon Daloz Parks's definition: "critical thought is the capacity to step outside of one's own thought and reflect on it as object. It is the ability to recognize multiple perspectives and the relativized character of one's own experience."[17] Teacher-mentors encourage and nourish critical thought with compelling questions and encourage a challenging milieu of differing perspectives in dialogue with individual students and their classes as a whole.

Critical thinking requires a fully cognitive awareness involving both our right and left hemispheres. A vital element of critical thinking requires the thinker to perceive the systemic and dynamic connections among things—a perceptive ability of the right hemisphere. Thinking about our thinking is the first stage of critical thought. The second stage is the ability to see the relationships of these thoughts to one another for the purpose of making our thinking whole.

The complete cycle of critical thinking requires processing time. The necessary time and focus may best be found in contemplative pause. A contemplative mind is fully cognitive and best prepared for critical thought and the challenge of big questions, all of which serve our purpose in helping our students discern their vocation. More on the subject of contemplative practice in chapter 5.

Finally, and perhaps most important, teacher-mentors are passionate about their discipline, scholarship, and teaching. Inspired by Samuel Taylor Coleridge on the subject of passion in poetry, Parks writes, "Mentoring educators are . . . professors whose spirits so infuse their subject matter that the spirit of the student is beckoned out and discovers fitting forms in which to dwell."[18] Passionate teacher-mentors make their subjects come to life; the student, in the words of Professor Diana Eck, "must recreate Lincoln, must feel like Wordsworth at Tintern Abbey, must visualize the pressure of the atmosphere on a column of mercury."[19] Passion inspires vocation.

LEARNING COMMUNITIES

The benefits of mentoring may extend beyond the dynamic between a teacher and student to a group of students or an entire class that then responds as a learning community. As Parker Palmer points out, "No matter how you slice it, the basic mission of the academy—knowing, teaching, and learning—is, at bottom, communal."[20] And yet, in today's academy, the value of the individual high performer, be it the faculty member or student, too often takes precedence over the learning community.

Helping students come together as a learning community is essential for discovering meaning, purpose, and discerning vocation. The Harvard Assessment Seminars of 2001 found that students not only benefited from individual mentoring relationships with faculty, but also experienced highly valued learning experiences with teachers and students in small groups.[21] William Damon in *The Path to Purpose* underscores that "in the formation of purpose two conditions must apply: 1) forward movement toward a fulfilling purpose and 2) a structure of social support consistent with that effort."[22] That support structure is a learning community of peers sharing their challenges and new knowledge together in your courses.

Studies show that our relationship with others is a powerful influence on discerning vocation. It comes through the sharing of stories, accounts of fulfilling work, and professional experiences that others echo. Something else related to the college environment: the learning community counters what may seem like a fracturing experience, especially for freshman who feel their lives attended to by differing elements of the academy. The mentoring environment of learning communities can help to mend this perception.[23] It is vital to recognize that a network of belonging within your classes that serves your students as a learning and mentoring community is a powerful educational context for deep learning and making meaning. The mentoring role doesn't need to fall solely to you.

Knowledge, ideas, and possibilities take hold in the imagination of your students most profoundly within a learning community. Learning communities are intentionally created by faculty who provide a vocational framework in which a new, more adequate imagination of life and work is explored, created, and anchored within the group. A learning/mentoring community provides an educational environment of greater trust, confidence, and positive self-reflection.

Learning communities also open more possibilities for academic risk taking and broader, deeper inquiry into the subject matter, its meaning and relevance for professional practice and personal identity. In addition, learning communities reinforce and diversify the important mentoring elements of recognition, support, challenge, and inspiration. All of this makes a transforming learning environment possible, one in which the process of a search for vocation can be directly connected to intellectual development.

Learning/mentoring communities are of particular importance to professional and technical education because those careers are defined, and their operations are, to a significant degree, guided by shared knowledge, standards of practice, and norms that they enforce on themselves and their members. Of particular importance to learning communities for this type of education is the specific expertise and intrinsic values around which the professions are organized.[24] These are strong, vocationally oriented elements that create useful intellectual and vocational bonds among students within the learning community and serve as additional mentoring forces for academic success and vocational discernment. As William Sullivan points out,

> This is an important reason education at all levels so often works through cohorts, small platoons in which personal connection and shared history can be expected to generate loyalty and engagement. Communities educate by mentoring. As individuals participate in learning activities at the center of the community's concerns, they gain personal recognition, becoming more closely bonded with the group and committed to its common aims.[25]

The confidence and trust with which learning communities of students approach their education makes them more capable of wrestling with and processing multiple perspectives. As such, they evolve into a community of confirmation and contradiction that culminates in a broad and deep academic and life-affirming commitment to shared truths. Their education becomes greater than the sum of their individual academic experience.

The learning community also becomes a powerful source of positive feedback and self-affirmation of an equal or greater impact than grades and awards. A classroom learning community may convey a fitting correspondence between students' aspirations and a positive reflection in the eyes of their trusted and valued peers.[26]

Self-selected majors who come to you with a growing sense of their vocation in their field of study and professional practice will probably form dedicated cohorts almost immediately. Because of this, they naturally form a class learning community that you and fellow instructors can adeptly build upon. These natural cohort/learning communities can be incredibly synergistic in their overall impact on everyone's enthusiasm, dedication, and commitment to study, activity, and mutual support. In addition, a mutual sense of vocation is reinforced and amplified as you work together. As teachers, our relationship with such cohorts can bring *our* vocation into sharper focus helping us to move forward with greater dedication.

William Campbell emphasizes what other authorities previously quoted point out: that vocational discernment is best negotiated in the community of others.[27] You may find that the mentoring communities that arise in your classes often persist after graduation as professional cohorts or small, mutually supportive guilds. This is reminiscent of the communes and guilds that existed in the past for centuries to nurture the creative talents and curiosity of their members.

Several teaching practices and pedagogies will assist in transforming classes into learning/mentoring communities. Three principal methods are of such broad importance to the subject of this book that they have separate chapters dedicated to them as elements of framing for teaching to inspire vocation—contemplative practice, intentional vocabulary and narrative, community-engaged learning. In addition to those, other strategies to encourage the transformation of your classes into learning communities are listed below.

Best Practice 4.2: Learning Communities

- Give students opportunities to share stories, narratives, and anecdotes about personal experiences with and interpretations of classroom subjects.
- Acknowledge student thinking, creativity, sharing, and insightful responses. In other words, look for opportunities to acknowledge what students say and do that is good.
- Set the tone for learning community evolution by underscoring shared learning and aspirational goals as well as shared frustrations and difficulties. Always use inclusive language and supportive methods of assessment.
- Use small-group and cohort pedagogies.
- Engage in experiential and community-engaged learning opportunities (more on community-engaged learning in chapter 7).

Parker Palmer summarizes the importance of learning communities with a different and helpful perspective:

The ontology and epistemology I have explored here . . . lead to a pedagogy of carefully crafted relationships of student to teacher, student to student, and teacher to student to subject. . . . a pedagogy shaped by relational principles and practices requires a virtue not always found in university classrooms: hospitality. . . . hospitality supports rigor by supporting community, and the proof is found in everyday classroom experience.[28]

Textbox 4.1 Teaching Takeaways

- Being authentic—a critically important attribute for teaching vocation—requires psychological and emotional honesty with yourself and your students.
- Authenticity means recognizing your vocation.
- Basic requirements for mentoring are four key elements to your relationship with student "protégees": recognition, support, challenges, and inspiration.
- Student learning and the development of self-hood and self-authoring adults progresses from a chosen authority (e.g., teacher/mentor) to greater self-reliance.
- The most critical function of a mentoring relationship is to help the protégé develop and articulate a dream.
- The Harvard Assessment Seminars of 2001 found that students experienced highly valued learning experiences with teachers and students in small groups—a simple and common classroom "learning community."
- Studies show that vocation is most often discerned through our relationship with others (a learning community): it comes through the sharing of stories, accounts of fulfilling work, and professional experiences that are echoed by others.
- Learning communities are intentionally created by teacher/mentors who provide a context in which a new, more adequate imagination of work and life is explored, created, and anchored within the group.
- A network of belonging within learning communities is a powerful educational context for deep learning and the formation of meaning, purpose, and vocation.
- Learning/mentoring communities are of particular importance to professional and technical education because those careers are defined, and their operations are to a significant degree guided by, shared knowledge, standards of practice, and norms of practice that they enforce on themselves and their members.

NOTES

1. John Neafsey, *A Sacred Voice Is Calling* (Maryknoll, NY: Orbis Books, 2011), 11.
2. Neafsey, *A Sacred Voice Is Calling*, 54.
3. Arthur W. Chickering, Jon C. Dalton, and Leisa Stamm, *Encouraging Authenticity and Spirituality in Higher Education* (San Francisco: Jossey-Bass, 2006), 129–30.
4. Hannah Schell, "Commitment and Community," in *At This Time and In This Place*, ed. David S. Cunningham (New York: Oxford University Press, 2016), 249.
5. Sharon Daloz Parks, *Big Questions, Worthy Dreams: Mentoring Emerging Adults in Their Search for Meaning, Purpose, and Faith* (San Francisco: Jossey-Bass, 2011), 105.
6. Neafsey, *A Sacred Voice Is Calling*, 11.
7. Parks, *Big Questions*, 165.
8. Wayne Teasdale, *Mystic Heart: Discovering A Universal Spirituality in the World's Religions* (Novato, CA: New World Library, 1999), 17.
9. Teasdale, *Mystic Heart*, 167.
10. Larry A. Braskamp, Lois Trautvetter, and Kelly Ward, *Putting Students First* (Boston: Anker, 2006), 148.
11. Braskamp, Trautvetter, and Ward, *Putting Students First*, 150.
12. Parks, *Big Questions*, 186.
13. Daniel J. Levinson, *The Seasons of Man's Life* (New York: Ballantine, 1978), 91–93.
14. Shirley H. Showalter, "Called to Tell Our Stories: The Narrative Structure of Vocation," in *Vocation across the Academy*, ed. David S. Cunningham (New York: Oxford University Press, 2017), 73.
15. William Deresiewicz, *Excellent Sheep: The Miseducation of the American Elite and the Way to a Meaningful Life* (New York: Free Press, 2015), 176.
16. David Schoem, "Essay 24: Honoring the Humanity of Our Students," in *Well-Being in Higher Education*, ed. Donald Harward (Washington, DC: Bringing Theory to Practice, 2016), 22.
17. Parks, *Big Questions*, 185.
18. Parks, *Big Questions*, 218.
19. Diana Eck, *Encountering God: A Spiritual Journey from Bozeman to Banaras* (Boston: Beacon, 1993), 37.
20. Parker Palmer and Arthur Zajonc, *The Heart of Higher Education* (San Francisco: Jossey-Bass, 2010), 43.
21. Richard J. Light, *Making the Most of College: Students Speak Their Minds* (Cambridge, MA: Harvard University Press, 2001), 45–50.
22. William Damon, *The Path to Purpose: Helping Our Children Find Their Calling in Life* (New York: Free Press, 2008), 38.
23. Cynthia Wells, "Finding the Center as Things Fly Apart," in *At This Time and In This Place*, ed. David S. Cunningham (New York: Oxford University Press, 2016), 68.

24. William Sullivan, *Liberal Learning as a Quest for Purpose* (New York: Oxford University Press, 2016), 122.

25. Sullivan, *Liberal Learning as a Quest for Purpose*, 121.

26. Parks, *Big Questions*, 196.

27. William D. Campbell, "Vocation as Grace," in *Callings!*, ed. James Y. Holloway and William D. Campbell (New York: Paulist Press, 1974), 279–80.

28. Palmer and Zajonc, *The Heart of Higher Education* (San Francisco: Jossey-Bass, 2010), 29.

5

Contemplative Practice Element

Contemplative pause is integral to the intellectual life, and to the formation of trustworthy meaning. . . . The contemplative moment is under siege in contemporary society, where life is shaped by the unexamined demands of an economy running on digital and brittle time.

—Sharon Daloz Parks[1]

To listen for the still, small voice is a countercultural enterprise, for much in our lives works against the patient labor of attentiveness.

—Margaret Guenther[2]

A popular culture celebrating quick results and showy achievements has displaced the traditional values of reflection and contemplation that once stood as the moral north star of human development and education.

—William Damon[3]

Sharon Parks is correct about the importance of the contemplative pause when it comes to teaching, learning, and finding meaning and purpose in life. Decades of research and study show that contemplative practices are nearly without peer for helping students achieve a broad and deep understanding of their subjects of study at colleges and universities. This is also a pivotal part of helping students find purpose and meaning for discerning vocation.

But, as Parks, Guenther, and Damon also point out, engaging in contemplative practice cuts across the grain of modern life in Western culture. This shouldn't be, given the ancient lineage of the academy and its traditional curriculum. You'll recall from earlier chapters, and as David Levy points out in his provocative article "No Time to Think,"

Today's universities trace their origins to Plato's Academy and, more immediately, to the medieval universities that emerged from the monastery schools. Both Plato's school and the medieval universities took contemplative inquiry as central to their mission. In the extreme, a loss of allegiance to this dimension of academic life would reduce universities to training institutes, largely preparing people to become efficient multitaskers in a world of "total work." And it would reduce faculty to trainers and coaches, rather than scholars demonstrating and communicating the beauty and power of mature, creative thought.[4]

Be that as it may, and as some of you may already know from classroom experience, one can't ignore the potential rewards of expanding your pedagogy and bolstering the impact of your curriculum with contemplative practice. To frame this importance another way, Dan Siegel, in *The Mindful Brain*, calls reflection "the fourth R of education," the skill that embeds self-knowing and empathy in the curriculum.[5]

Before delving into an exploration of the various kinds of contemplative practices that contribute to this element of teaching to inspire vocation, the first section of this chapter outlines aspects and elements of cognition that impact and facilitate these practices, followed by cultural forces and norms that work in a synergy with those cognitive elements. The challenging elements of our cognitive/cultural environment are alluded to in the referenced quotes by Parks and Guenther. To summarize the nature of these challenges in a single word, it would be "attention"—the building block of intellect, wisdom, intimacy, and cultural progress. It's antonym, distraction, is a fact of modern human life and the proclivity of an important region of our brain.

VOCATION AND COGNITION

If we are going to explore cognition, we need to start with a short review of how our brain works. Because we all have one, and it has been the subject of intense study, you would think we would be intimately familiar with our brain's workings. But no. Our understanding of what the brain is made of is good, but how it thinks and where consciousness comes from is poor, if not in some cases completely unknown. Even more interestingly, websites of interest about the brain often have the least to report about the left and right hemisphere structure of the brain and the asymmetry between those two halves.

However, the cognitive challenges we face in helping our students find purpose, meaning, and discern vocation in their education is tied to the workings, connection, and relationship between our brain's two hemispheres. Let's consider the decades-long work of psychiatrist, writer, and former Oxford literary scholar Dr. Iain McGilchrist, first introduced in association with studies of the brain's two hemispheres in chapter 3. The subject of the divided brain is explored and interpreted in his tour de force on the subject, *The Master and His Emissary*.

Any discussion about the purpose and function of the human brain's two hemispheres is often full of conjecture, myth, and false assumptions, as McGilchrist describes:

> There can be no question that it would be foolish to believe most of what has passed into popular culture on the topic of hemisphere differences. And yet it would be just as foolish to believe that therefore there are no important hemisphere differences. When people object that each hemisphere is involved in everything we do, they are right. When they assume that means there are no differences, they are wrong. It is not what each hemisphere does, but how it does it that matters. Each hemisphere is involved in everything, true enough; just in a quite different way.[6]

A general but graphic description of the hemispheric differences within the human brain is described by neuroanatomist Dr. Jill Bolte Taylor in her book *My Stroke of Insight*. In it, Taylor describes what she experienced when she awoke after having a stroke during the night. The stroke had occurred in her left hemisphere and impaired her ability to carry out all the specific and immediate elements of her morning routine getting ready for work. Simultaneously, she felt an unexpected and exhilarating connection to a larger context and found it difficult to separate her embodied self from her surroundings. She was immersed in a larger context of existence based on the perceptions of her unaffected and fully functional right hemisphere.

At the same time, she was having great difficulty with the immediate requirements—showering, dressing, and so on—of preparing herself to start her day, normally made possible by the functions of her left hemisphere. Of particular interest for a neuroanatomist, Dr. Taylor's experience made it clear to her how left-hemisphere oriented and dependent we've become in Western culture. Why is that relevant to the pursuit of meaning, purpose, and discerning vocation in higher education? Let's take a closer look.

Our brain's two hemispheres are joined together by the corpus callosum, a bundle of nerve fibers located in the middle of the brain. There is a lateralization between the two hemispheres; each hemisphere is responsible for different functions. Each function is localized to either the right or left side. Structurally, the hemispheres differ in size, shape, number of neurons, neuronal size, dendritic branching, and the ratio of gray to white matter.

Gray matter consists primarily of neuronal cell bodies, or soma, that house the neuron's nucleus. White matter areas of the brain mainly consist of axons, which are long relays that extend out from the soma, forming connections between brain cells. Neurochemically, the hemispheres differ in sensitivity to hormones, dependence on pharmacological agents, and neurotransmitters.

Before looking more closely at what the two hemispheres do, it should be reiterated that in a fully cognitive, normal brain, the two hemispheres work together most of the time at the everyday level.[7] Under those conditions, most people assume—many researchers included—that the left hemisphere is dominant. However, McGilchrist makes a compelling case that, in fact, the right hemisphere is dominant: the "master." It may be understandable that most people in the Western world assume the left hemisphere is in charge given the left-hemisphere nature of the modern world. More on this later and how it impacts the search for meaning, purpose, and vocation.

> The right hemisphere matures earlier than the left, and is more involved than the left in almost every aspect of the development of mental functioning in early childhood, and of the self as a social, empathic being.[8]

Based on McGilchrist's description, the right hemisphere plays a dominant role in early mental development and continues in that role as we mature. With our right hemisphere we first perceive and become conscious of our surroundings at any given time. Our right hemisphere contextualizes our reality. That information passes on to the left hemisphere for focused perception within that context.

Details from the left hemisphere pass back to the right hemisphere for setting perspective and further contextualization. This is an extremely general, oversimplified interpretation of how the two hemispheres relate to each other. To put it another way, one of equal generalization, the right hemisphere generates the big picture, and the left hemisphere fills in some of the details.

The right hemisphere's contextual, big-picture reality maintains a relational perspective of ourselves—how we connect to everything present in the big picture. The left hemisphere focuses on details as independent, inanimate "things" that are examined and quantified. I suggested at the beginning of this chapter that attention will be the most important beneficiary of contemplative practice and balanced cognition.

A major consideration in how the two hemispheres perceive the world is related to attention. In fact, McGilchrist might point to attention as the primary area of concern regarding our understanding of bi-hemispheric cognition. This concern aligns very well with that of educators hoping to enhance their students' learning and their search for meaning, purpose, and vocation.

Regarding your brain and attention, the right hemisphere is the source of alertness, vigilance, and sustained attention. Focused attention is the domain of the left hemisphere, and it is capable of and prone to rapid shifts in attention. As you can imagine, these different types of attention bring different aspects of the world into being. A more complete, more realistic picture of the world is generated by the combined and balanced application of both types of attention. McGilchrist elaborates on this relationship:

> the brain must attend to the world in two completely different ways, and in so doing to bring two different worlds into being. In the one [the right hemisphere], we experience the live, complex, embodied, world of individual, always unique beings, forever in flux, a net of interdependencies, forming and reforming wholes, a world with which we are deeply connected. In the other [the left hemisphere] we "experience" our experience in a special way: a "re-presented" version of it, containing now static, separable, bounded, but essentially fragmented entities, grouped into classes, on which predictions can be based. This kind of attention isolates, fixes, and makes each thing explicit by bringing it under the spotlight of attention. In doing so it renders things inert, mechanical, lifeless.[9]

The workings of the two hemispheres form a temporal hierarchy of attention that begins in the right hemisphere, then moves to the left hemisphere, and then back to the right hemisphere in a progression of attention that lies at the foundation of experience. The right hemisphere's global attention comes first not just in time, but also in precedence—if the cognitive sequence is in full working order. In this cyclic cognitive process, new information, new skills, and new experiences engage the right hemisphere more than the left hemisphere, but once these have become familiar (known), they become the concern of the left hemisphere.

The left hemisphere prefers what it knows and leans toward predictive modes of perception. On the other hand, the right hemisphere is more malleable to changing perspectives and new framing with greater flexibility and openness to an array of possibilities. For instance, our ability to play the devil's advocate when looking at possibilities is powered by the right hemisphere.

In contrast, our left hemisphere overlooks and avoids what it doesn't know and denies discrepancies in pursuit of a sharper focus. Both approaches, when brought together in our right hemisphere, elevate our cognitive abilities above those of our fellow creatures, but they also pull in opposite directions.

We are fully cognitive when the relationship between our two hemispheres is in balance. The cognitive cycle occurring at any moment begins with the holistic perceptions of the right hemisphere. The right hemisphere brings a broader world into being, from which the left hemisphere selects what to attend to—it makes the implicit reality presented by the right hemisphere more explicit.

The left hemisphere's choices have already been made for it by the initial, broad perceptions of the right hemisphere. When the focal points of the left hemisphere are made explicit, they are returned to the right hemisphere, leading to a cognitive result that is more complete and comprehensive coming forward in our consciousness. The left hemisphere is a crucial part of the creative process, but it needs to hand its work back to the right hemisphere.

Our two hemispheres present two ways of dealing with the world. The left hemisphere, directing specific attention to the overall picture the right hemisphere provides, is divisive and manipulative. If left to its own devices, it can also be acquisitive, competitive, and power hungry. The right hemisphere is cooperative, collaborative, and cohesive.

Although these two different ways of dealing with the world appear conflicting, the result is often creative if the hierarchical, cognitive rotation is completed back to the right hemisphere. A useful, overarching analogy is that the necessary tension that exists between unifying and separating forces in the universe also exists between our hemispheres.[10]

In short, as McGilchrist explains, "It [left hemisphere] is a useful department to send things to for processing, but the things only have meaning once again when they are returned to the right hemisphere."[11] The right hemisphere has temporal and ontological supremacy in bringing the world into being.

What happens when the cognitive cycle and hemispheric relationship described above is out of balance, and what does that mean for our purpose in helping our students discern their vocation? We must begin answering that question by recognizing that the structure and function of our brain have influenced the evolution of our culture, and the evolution of our culture has, in turn, influenced the function of our brain.

Cultural and social influences in the West, particularly since the beginning of the industrial revolution, encourage a cognitive rewiring and evolution of our brain's functioning toward left-hemisphere dominant cognition. One may also point to the general influence of a Cartesian approach to understanding the world and the nature of reality.

McGilchrist's take on a completely left-hemisphere dominated world sounds disturbingly familiar. It would be "relatively mechanical, an assemblage of more or less disconnected 'parts'; it would be relatively abstract and disembodied; relatively distanced from fellow-feeling; given to explicitness; utilitarian in ethic; over-confident of its own take on reality, and lacking insight into its problems."[12]

Jenny Mackness's summary of our industrial revolution world reflects in greater detail where McGilchrist leaves off:

> The Industrial Revolution created a world in the left hemisphere's likeness: urban environments which are increasingly rectilinear grids of machine-made surfaces and shapes; an increased proportion of the population living in these environments; an assault on the natural world, exploitation, despoliation,

pollution; excessive management; and increase in the virtuality of life, television, and the internet. Modernity is marked by social disintegration, drift from rural to urban life, breakdown of familiar social orders, loss of a sense of belonging, and advances of scientific materialism and bureaucracy. The culture of modernity is characterized by a hunger for certainty, and reflects a world increasingly dominated by the left hemisphere.[13]

Mackness's summary is only a partial list of perceptual attributes and behavioral tendencies associated with the hyperfunctioning and dominance of our left hemisphere. Accentuate these attributes and behaviors even further along their trajectories, and the result is mental pathology we see with increasing frequency, such as social- and psychopathy as well as schizophrenia.

A less severe but highly impactful left-brain dominant malady affecting student education and learning is the loss of sustained and vigilant attention, the domain of our right hemisphere. This has been replaced with fleeting, short-term focus favoring facts, sound bites, and the propensity for distraction associated with dominant left-hemisphere cognition. The preference and tendency toward a wide, contextual approach and meaning-making is the domain of the right hemisphere—a richer domain for deep learning and the discovery of vocation. A potent antidote to left-hemisphere dominance is contemplation, reflection, introspection, meditation, and mindfulness; the foundations of directed right-hemisphere engagement.

VOCATION AND ATTENTION

Attention is the rarest and purest form of generosity.[14]

—Simon Weil

A common denominator of the increasingly left-hemisphere world we live in is distraction. It seems that every force that comes to bear on us in our culture these days conspires to magnify inattentiveness. Perhaps the most powerful and insidious of those forces is technology, which has made distraction ubiquitous. Witness television screens on pumps at gas stations, or newspaper headlines, "Man plunges to his death while staring at device." This is now the air we breathe, so it's hard to notice what is happening to us until some rude interference from the "outside" slaps us in the face—although even that may not exert enough gravity.

> Amid the glittering promise of our new technologies and the wonderous potential of our scientific gains, we are nurturing a culture of social diffusion, intellectual fragmentation, sensory detachment. In this new world, something is amiss.

And that something is attention. The way we live is eroding our capacity for deep, sustained, perceptive attention—the building block of intimacy, wisdom, and cultural progress. Moreover, this disintegration may come at great cost to ourselves and to society.[15]

This quote from Maggie Jackson's provocative book *Distracted* is an accurate summary of the human predicament resulting from a culture derived from left-hemisphere dominant cognition. Increasingly, we are shaped by distraction, caught in a left-hemisphere feedback loop. The structure and function of our brain have influenced the evolution of our culture, and the evolution of our culture has influenced the evolution of our brain. As such, our culture of distraction is intensifying like images in an expanding hall of mirrors.

But wait, you might say, kids show themselves to be skilled multitaskers, the technologically fluent new breed that is better suited for the lightning-paced, many-threaded digital world. One might think that demonstrates a potent capability for the future. Think again. Fifteen-year-olds in the United States rank twenty-fourth out of twenty-nine developed countries on tests of problem-solving skills related to analytic reasoning.[16] Government studies show that many U.S. high-school students can't synthesize or assess information, express complex thoughts, or analyze arguments.[17] That's not a stellar assessment of high-school age critical thinking skills, something that higher education touts as a principal outcome.

Maggie Jackson describes attention as a cognitive process: "Attention is a process of taking in, sorting and shaping, planning, and decision making—a mental and emotional forming and kneading of the bread of life."[18] Under normal circumstances, attention begins in our right hemisphere with alertness and orienting, allowing us to sense and respond to our environment. Then, our left hemisphere's focused attention contributes an array of details that the right hemisphere edits using the highest form of executive attention for a final overall picture that makes ultimate sense of the world. In our left-hemisphere dominant culture, left-hemisphere pathways have hijacked a complete cognitive process to form a fractured, incomplete sense of the world based on shifting arrays of details.

When we rely on multitasking as a way of life, we sever and short-circuit our right-hemisphere cognition and, along with it, our opportunities and abilities to make big-picture sense of the world. This also disrupts our pursuit of long-term goals, suppressing or blocking the potential for students to discover a dedicated purpose and a vocation. We need to recognize that our right-hemisphere executive attention is a precious and necessary capability. Without it, we warp and dilute many of the essential qualities that make us human.

Our split-screen, multitasking lives interfere with the possibility of the unbroken attention and exclusive focus made possible by right-hemisphere cognition that results in "flow." Flow is that state often described by artists, athletes, and craft practitioners who may become so fully present to their endeavor they describe themselves as being "in the zone," or in a flow of performance and/or creativity that raises them to a higher state of being.

People experiencing flow get a deep sense of contentment working with both their mind and body, stretching themselves to meet a challenge.[19] Using Jackson's metaphor, "without the symphonic conductor [right hemisphere] of a great capacity for attention, the music of the brain disintegrates into a cacophonic noise."[20]

The concept of cognitive "flow" is crucially important to discerning your vocation and hearing your calling, especially as it relates to a particular practice and/or craft. Popularized in the work of Hungarian American psychologist Mihaly Csikszentmihalyi, his work has been influential in encouraging teachers to consider questions of motivation and how to fully engage their students in learning, goals important to finding meaning and purpose for discerning vocation.

Csikszentmihalyi's theory of flow, "the holistic sensation that people have when they act with total involvement,"[21] dates to 1975, when he noticed that artists could be completely immersed in their work for hours and hours, losing a sense of time passing, and completely focused on process rather than outcome. The question arises, why don't schools focus more on the importance of the process instead of on outcome and reward?

Csikszentmihalyi has described eight characteristics of flow:

1. complete concentration on the task
2. clarity of goals and reward in mind and immediate feedback
3. transformation of time (speeding up/slowing down of time)
4. the experience is intrinsically rewarding
5. effortlessness and ease
6. balance between challenge and skills
7. actions and awareness are merged, losing self-conscious rumination
8. a feeling of control over the task[22]

McGilchrist suggests that seeing the world as in a state of flow is to understand it as "live, complex, embodied," "a world of individual, always unique beings, forever in flux, a net of interdependencies, forming and reforming wholes, a world with which we are deeply connected."[23] This perspective avoids fragmentation of knowledge, something that Csikszentmihalyi also believes is necessary to experience flow.

Several physicists and cosmologists have expanded the concept of flow as it relates to quantum mechanics, ecology, and Eastern theologies into a new concept of reality: unbroken wholeness in constant flow, a concept most clearly defined in physicist David Bohm's groundbreaking book *Wholeness and the Implicate Order*.

Returning to the importance of right hemisphere cognition and teaching to inspire vocation, we must consider the importance of self-discipline. Self-awareness, insight, self-concept, and self-discipline are all more dependent on the right hemisphere. We rely on the right hemisphere for self-control and to resist temptation. Lacking self-control, a condition common to our left hemisphere world, we can have the strongest of motivations and set the highest of goals, yet we will invariably get sidetracked. A continuous shift of attention seeking instant gratification foils the pursuit of our aims in life.

Studies of 164 eighth graders over the course of a school year showed that their scores on measures of self-control proved twice as predictive as IQ of final grades and other predictors of academic success. Self-control, it seems, is the key attribute of high-performing middle schoolers, and this outcome likely extends to all students. Underachievement among students is most likely due to a failure to exercise an important function of our right hemisphere: self-discipline.[24]

On the flip side, self-controlled students manage their efforts at learning not only by suppressing distractions but by constantly evaluating their own thought and progress.[25] Jackson sums up the importance of attention to education and the life of the mind this way:

> Perhaps attention is the true missing key to better learning. Without the powers of focus, awareness, and judgement that fuel self-control, we cannot fend off distractions, set goals, manage a complex, changing environment, and ultimately shape the trajectory of our lives. . . . as individuals and as a society [we] should be concerned by the fact that many campuses are plagued by high dropout rates, lukewarm gains in critical thinking and reflective judgement, and low engagement with the life of the mind.[26]

VOCATION AND CONTEMPLATIVE PRACTICE

Contemplative practice engages and strengthens the cognitive pathways of our right hemisphere. If practiced regularly as part of our pedagogy, contemplative practice helps our students achieve a balanced and complete cognitive engagement with subject matter information and activities as well as the possibility of finding purpose and meaning for discerning vocation in what they are learning. Both the Montessori and Waldorf School models are good examples of right-hemisphere focused teaching and learning. Both models encourage a student-centered, holistic, place-based, experiential education, with a focus on a multimodal pedagogy—head, hands, and heart—an embodied mode of education.

Embodied learning provides a balanced approach to abstract learning (left hemisphere) and emotion, movement, and processes rooted in body-environment interactions (right hemisphere). At the collegiate level, a concern for embodied learning is part and parcel of the community-engaged learning model, another type of head, hands, and heart learning approach. All three of these models involve the affective domain of education, the core of a head, hands, and heart educational strategy.

This is the purpose behind the reflective intervals prescribed for community-engaged learning practicums. Paulo Friere observed that when we explore the act of service in the context of theoretical and other forms of knowledge, coupled with reflection on our perspective and position in the world, we can enhance and transform the quality of the service and of the learning.[27] In this way, and through this process, students often hear and/or recognize their calling. As Arthur Chickering, Jon Dalton, and Liesa Stamm point out in *Encouraging Authenticity and Spirituality in Higher Education*,

> Contemplation is the cerebral metabolic process for meaning making. It makes sense that the second step in Kolb's (1984) experiential learning cycle is reflection, after direct experienced and before abstract conceptualization and active application. Reflection is the necessary intervening activity that converts input—whatever the experiences are—into meaningful working knowledge that can then be tested in other settings. Without reflection, whatever new experiences we have, whatever new information and concepts we encounter in lectures and texts, end up like the residue from food we don't metabolize.[28]

Contemplative practice has a long history in intellectual inquiry, not to mention spiritual and religious traditions—most of which occurred in the West before the industrial revolution. Parker Palmer laments, "The mind is at the core of our human nature, our humanity. Yet its direct exploration by introspection has been off-limits for a century."[29] We've since lost sight of the integral place of contemplative practices in the academy.

As Robert Sullivan points out, "reflective activities helped students integrate academic learning and practical experience with important dimensions of meaning in their lives."[30] Perhaps now, more than ever, we need to restore this part of the curriculum and our pedagogy. Two more relevant and instructive excerpts on the importance of contemplative practice come from the writing of, first, Sharon Parks, and Daniel Barbezat and Mirabai Bush:

> It is enormously difficult to make meaning, to compose a faith, within the intensified complexity of today's commons, but it is particularly appropriate to

do so in the institution charged with teaching the value and practice of critical reflection.[31]

The university is well-practiced at educating the mind for critical reasoning, critical writing, and critical speaking as well as for scientific and quantitative analysis. But is this sufficient? In a world beset with conflicts, internal as well as external, isn't it of equal if not greater importance to balance the sharpening of our intellects with the systematic cultivation of our hearts?[32]

A cognitive parallel to the "cultivation of our hearts" above is the systematic cultivation of the pathways to and within our right hemisphere.

As we move forward in this review of contemplative practices, we will be looking primarily at forms of reflection, introspection, and mindfulness with some reference to meditation and other contemplative practices. You might be wondering what's the difference. Well, let's begin with mindfulness, a mental state of calm awareness that usually results from the practices embodied in the other four terms. Meditation is a practice to slow down and quiet our mind, cultivating a state of calm mindfulness ripe for introspection, contemplation, and reflection. Reflection and contemplation involve different levels of mindful attention.

Reflection is mirroring a thought or experience back to you; reviewing a thought or experience again for the purpose of seating feelings and/or meanings in place. Reflection adds a dimension of self-awareness to the learning activity taking place. Contemplation is a relaxed, gentle, careful, and considered look at thoughts and experiences from all sides and in all aspects; to view or consider with continued attention; to regard with deliberate care. Introspection often follows these states of mind and is a reflection on your own mental states: "I'm feeling mindful and contemplative; perhaps it's a good time to work on a new instructional unit."

As you can see, reflection, contemplation, and introspection are closely allied; in fact, they are often part of a continuum of attentive and mindful review. As William Sullivan observes, "A reflective posture lays the groundwork for expanding self-awareness toward directing one's own learning."[33]

For example, if you wish to write a short essay on a specific experience in nature, you might begin with a reflection on that experience to relive it and make it more vivid. You will then contemplate specific elements that stand out in your reflection for more extended contemplation as a subject for the essay. Your contemplation brings forth possible narratives for your essay. You might say, then, that contemplation is a deeper, more deliberate form of reflection. Finally, through introspection you identify and consider the role of reflection and contemplation in your perceptions of nature and your pleasure in writing about them.

A good general recommendation for the use of contemplative practices in your courses—one recommended by more experienced practitioners and researchers—is a mix of contemplation, reflection, introspection, and simple meditation. Susan Ambrose and others evaluated the research on effective teaching in *How Learning Works: Seven Research-Based Principles for Smart Teaching* and found that contemplative practices were one of the key elements. An important reason is that contemplative pedagogy uses forms of introspection and reflection that allow students to focus internally and find more of themselves in their courses.[34] This can make the course work profoundly relevant to them.

The contemplative practices discussed here all have an inward or first-person focus that creates opportunities for greater connection and insight. No matter the specific type of engagement, the focus is on the present experience, be it cognitive, kinesthetic, or affective. The most important aspect of this practice is for students to feel centered in the experience and to discover their internal reactions to the information, technologies, and other elements of what they are learning. Contemplative practice is a means for making what is presented in class personally meaningful for students and more deeply understood. At its root, contemplative practice is an experiment in silence.

By legitimizing students' experience, we change their relationship to the course material. Unfortunately, this practice cuts across the grain of most formal education where the goal is a purely objective approach, ignoring the fact that we all must find personal meaning in what we learn to internalize it fully. A direct, contemplative inquiry validates and deepens student understanding of the course material. It also gives students a deeper understanding of themselves, making the experience more holistic and, in turn, contributing to greater meaning, dedication to the subject matter, their education, and the discovery of vocation.[35]

By using contemplative practices in your pedagogy, you will achieve the following objectives with your students as Barbezat and Bush describe in *Contemplative Practices in Higher Education*:

- focus and attention building, mainly through focusing meditation and exercises that support mental stability
- contemplation and introspection into the content of the course, in which students discover the material in themselves and thus deepen their understanding of the material
- compassion, connection to others, and a deepening sense of the moral and spiritual aspect of education
- inquiry into the nature of their minds, personal meaning, creativity, and insight[36]

Contemplative exercises bring the power of our right hemisphere—to coordinate and to contextualize—to bear on the analytical attention of our left hemisphere and thereby help us make broader and deeper sense of the complete picture of a concept, issue, a challenge, and the world in general. The claim of higher education that we are teaching students to think is translated as teaching them to be fully cognitive using the unique powers of both hemispheres in a coordinated and broad perception of the world.

A key element of critical thinking and problem solving is attention. More specifically, two types of attention: persistent, and a diverse and variable attention. In this way, students will have the capacity to hold alternative possibilities in mind along with the ability to switch their attention between them. Sharon Daloz Parks points out another important aspect of critical thought: "Critical thought is the capacity to step outside of one's own thought and *reflect* on it as object."[37] Right-hemisphere reflection and mindfulness power these forms of attention and critical thought. Contemplative practices refine and hone these right-hemisphere capacities.

As the practice of meditation has become more prevalent in the West, there has been a great deal of research on its impact and effects. Studies done with students and teachers show that they achieve significant gains in attention and self-regulation even after short periods of mediation. Here is an example that Arthur Zajonc used:

> In a course on the history of science at Amherst College, Arthur Zajonc guides his students through the process of discovery that Einstein experienced as he developed his theory of relativity. It was a process very much like the Tibetan tradition of analytical meditation followed by calm abiding that allowed Einstein to make one of the greatest breakthroughs of the twentieth century. Zajonc guides his students through the complex examination of perspective and its impact on measurement. Students are guided to realize for themselves that they can hold contradictory positions in their minds at once [a critical capacity for Einstein in the discovery of relativity].[38]

Let's pause a moment to reiterate an important aim in the use of contemplative practices in our teaching. These pursuits are not meant to replace other effective means of learning and certainly not the disciplinary subject matter. Rather, consider them powerful complements to instruction and accelerants to learning of great significant to students during their education and for the rest of their lives. This brings us back to the importance of authenticity presented in the previous chapter. Educators intending to use contemplative practices in their pedagogies should be practitioners themselves to bring the necessary authenticity to this element. If not, consider what follows the start of your personal contemplative practice.

Using contemplative practices in your pedagogy is not an all-or-nothing proposition. However, like anything new and unorthodox, it is better to start slowly and work up to a routine over time. When starting a fitness program, one doesn't begin by spending all day, every day at the gym. Developing mental fitness requires the same consideration—work up to it gradually.

Begin your contemplative practice segments as informal, occasional, easy-going elements. That said, the effect will still be noticeable and, after some adjustment, positive. As Barbezat and Bush describe, "They [contemplative practices] should be thought of as structured improvisations rather than following rigid, fixed scripts."[39] "Structured improvisations" is an apt description for early forays into contemplative practice.

Thinking ahead to what we can expect from contemplative practice based on the current research, we can categorize the results of these practices into five broad groups:

- increased concentration and attention
- increased mental health and psychological well-being
- increased connection, generosity, and lovingkindness
- deepened understanding of the course material
- increased creativity and insight[40]

An online search will reveal that the research on the impacts of meditation on human cognition, psychology, and well-being is dense and compelling.

Note two important caveats at this point. First, as we apply contemplative practices, we must be sure to keep them separate from various ideologies, doctrines, and dogmas. Of course, contemplative practices are meant to explore our students' own beliefs and views so that a first-person, critical inquiry becomes an investigation of their academic study rather than an imposition of specific views. Second, allied to this concern is a sensitivity to the range of backgrounds from which our students come and that our contemplative practices are not alienating.

With these caveats in mind, and with a consideration of contemplative practices as "structured improvisations," start this work with a new group of students in a very benign, gentle way. For instance, the label "thoughtful moments" feels natural, is unobtrusive, and flows well within the larger course pedagogy. As such, don't concern yourself initially with explaining or drawing attention to the fact that everyone is engaged in a "contemplative practice." You're simply pausing for some momentary "consideration" and "reflection" on a point of attention in your course work.

Points of reflection and contemplation, when inserted at transition and other natural pause points in the pedagogy, become a more natural part of your practice. Later, when the protocol is better established, one may then be more deliberate about making contemplative practices obvious in your pedagogy and your goals for doing so clear to your students. I suggest you refrain from introducing any meditation until that time.

To reinforce and credit students for their participation in your contemplative practice, consider asking them to keep a journal or some other form of documentation about their experience. It could also be a hybrid documentation tool used as a place for them to record answers and observations to other course materials and activities. For example, lab records could also include reflections on the process and result. The combined purpose of the journal will make the requirement more familiar to your students than if it applies just to contemplative practice.

Brief and extemporaneous moments of reflection may come and go without documentation. Beyond this level, contemplative practices can form significant parts of more elaborate assignments when they are closely tailored to the subject matter of your course.

Other kinds of writing assignments may combine contemplative experience with the material from the course. Professor Judith Simmer-Brown at Naropa University explains,

> They may begin with anecdotes, but I guide them to reflect, in the present moment, on their insights rather than turning to plotlines to explain their views. Eventually they draw richly from the depths of their reflections, improving their ability to engage in first-person investigation and to trust themselves as participants in their own education.[41]

This approach has a significant impact on making more plain the relevance of their course of study and its personal meaning to each student. Such assignments, coming at the end of the course, also bring forth more sophisticated analysis and synergy between the course material and the students' life experience.

Before going any further on this subject, we need to address a common important concern. First, an acknowledgment: robust survey data show that many college and university students yearn for spiritual guidance. It's common knowledge that contemplative practices can contribute to the development of greater spiritual fulfillment as well as a deeper understanding of the course material—these often go hand in hand without any intentionality on your part. Nevertheless, we must strike a balance between this acknowledgment and the openness and tolerance of differing views. As Barbezat and Bush point out:

> One of the fiercest critiques of contemplative practices in the classroom is that religious views are being rolled in with the Trojan horse of secular ideas of "attention" and "mindfulness." We understand this concern, but the practices we

are suggesting require no particular belief by the participants; they are intended to allow students to experience, for themselves, their own inner processes.[42]

Best Practice 5.1: Openness and Tolerance

Barbezat and Bush also provide a useful checklist of steps we can take to ensure that we maintain an openness and tolerance.

- Construct our practices so that no element requires adopting or even role playing of a particular religious view.
- Become aware of our language so that we do not use a particular vernacular that implies specific religious worldviews.
- Allow our students to use their own language to express and understand their experiences while supporting them in being respectful to others.
- Include practices from a variety of backgrounds so that students do not perceive an underlying bias.
- Be grounded clearly in our own practice so that we are capable of mindful listening.
- Be open fully and aware of our judgments as they arise, letting them go to listen and connect deeply.[43]

An important element of these recommendations is a sensitivity to language and appropriation. Consider carefully using a language of pluralism that encourages students to share their own views. Also, you must be aware of your own limitations as a teacher while encouraging students to get in touch with their feelings about the topics of study. Some students may profess deep and disturbing feelings that you may have difficulty responding to on your own.

Seek out and consult with experienced colleagues who may have a better sense of the appropriate bounds of their contemplative practice in the classroom. Knowing one's own limits as well as the other resources available for students is essential. This concern also points out the importance of faculty having personal experience in contemplative practice.

You may use several different kinds of contemplative practice to initiate a thoughtful beginning to a period of instruction and learning. Chogyam Trungpa, of Naropa University and founder of the first U.S. contemplative center for higher education, noted that contemplative wisdom is "immediate and nonconceptual insight which provides the basic inspiration for intellectual study."[44] With this in mind, a good time to introduce a "thoughtful moment" is often at the beginning of classes and other educational activities to raise and inspire mindfulness for a new area of study.

Start with a concept or idea for student reflection connected to the previous class meeting or attached to the upcoming subject. Consider framing either the familiar concept or the upcoming one using language for reflection that will give your students a new or different perspective.

It is very important to establish the right context for introspective and contemplative exercises, particularly if you sense that your students have had little exposure to such practices. It's important to assess the attitudes and orientation of your students toward these practices and work to accommodate them in your preliminary activities. As recommended earlier, look for natural intervals in the flow of course work for contemplative moments. If none exist in your standard pedagogy, seek to create them in ways that are fitting and not disruptive. This is important for two reasons:

1. Students must be able to follow the instructions of the guided exercise; if they are too apprehensive, they will not gain from the exercises.
2. If you ignore the context for the students, they may not trust that their experience matters and may not believe the stated intention of the exercises. Recall that the motivation for the exercise is for the students to assert their agency along with the material in a meaningful way; students will quickly perceive a structure that contradicts the basic intent.[45]

Timing and attitude adjustment are very important, and so is the way you frame any given contemplative practice—the clearer and more familiar your language, the better. Depending upon how a contemplative practice is introduced may unconsciously impose an unnecessary order. This, of course, could preempt our students' ability to have their own, unique experience. Consider framing your transition to a contemplative practice as an invitation, being careful that you're not issuing orders.[46] Intentional vocabulary and narrative are principal elements of a framework for teaching to inspire vocation and are the subject of the next chapter.

Some of the more concerted and deeply engrossing contemplative practices, such as many forms of meditation, call for an understanding and appreciation of their origin and their traditional context of practice. Consider sharing this background and contextual information with your students. However, this doesn't mean that your students must adopt a larger tradition commonly associated with that practice. As you begin to use more varied forms of contemplative practice, you should provide some explanation about your goals and intentions so that your students are more likely to learn from the exercises.

Be sure that your use of these practices fits well with your pedagogy. The design of many contemplative exercises will help students discover how they personally react to inputs and experiences. The explanation or intent of the practice is best described after the experience. In fact, experiment with having students share their thoughts and feelings among themselves before explaining your intention. Their personal reflections, combined with those of other students, will help ground their experience and knowledge so that when they discuss the exercises, they have a better basis for applying their experience to the material they are studying.

Allow your students to recognize and acknowledge their unique experience in contemplative practice and its impact on their understanding of class material. To reiterate an earlier point, one of the shortcomings of higher education is that it remains heavily biased toward a Cartesian and third-person type of learning; a primarily left-hemisphere orientation. Students learn how to analyze, quantify, and memorize subjects as objects, something that exists separate and apart from us. We too often ignore the subjectivity of the learner as important to their learning. Michael Polanyi adeptly points out how misguided this is in his treatise *Personal Knowledge*:

> Personal Knowledge. The two words may seem to contradict each other: for true knowledge is deemed impersonal, universally established, objective. But the seeming contradiction is resolved by modifying the conception of knowing.[47] It goes without saying that no one—scientists included—looks at the universe this way, whatever lip-service is given to "objectivity." Nor should this surprise us. For, as human beings, we must inevitably see the universe from a center lying within ourselves and speak about it in terms of a human language shaped by the exigencies of human intercourse. Any attempt rigorously to eliminate our human perspective from our picture of the world must lead to absurdity.[48]

The value of contemplative practice is that it helps bridge this gap between "knower" and "known" with a focus on critical first-person learning. It helps the students engage directly with the information, material, and techniques studied and to evaluate their experience with openness and discernment.

As this process moves forward, our students will begin to trust in the process of using contemplative practice to help them better understand the course material and what it means to them. Allowing them to have their unique experience, and then helping them make sense of it in terms of the information they are studying, helps them integrate their experience and allows them to trust processes that will arise for them in the future.

As you know from your classroom experience, the best laid plans may still go awry. As you make plans to include contemplative practice in your pedagogy, be sure to include intervals to monitor and adjust. When obstacles to your plans arise, consider using them as a context for contemplative practice as a transition and/or solution. This may also be an opportunity to express authenticity on your part about how you will appreciate a contemplative moment to help sort out and resolve a situation or make a necessary change.

With this approach, we become learning companions with our students, if we allow ourselves to be.[49]

You may want to give some thought to arranging your classroom and other learning space to make it more conducive to contemplative practice. An easy, often effective change for promoting class cohesiveness, involvement, and sharing is the seating arrangement. Larger classrooms with spacious laboratory tables that accommodate several students around their perimeter are very useful for group work and student interactions of all kinds.

Adjustable lighting is also helpful for changing the classroom ambiance. Consider the use of contemplative and ambient sounds and music to accompany longer contemplative practice intervals. You will likely find other advantages related to these environmental changes regarding student attentiveness, involvement, and progress.

It must be reiterated that contemplative and introspective practices are complements to traditional teaching methods. Use them with a clear instructional purpose. With gradual and thoughtful application, these practices should become routine, and students should become more competent. It is important to recognize that contemplative practices have no wrong outcomes or responses. Whatever students experience *is* part of the outcome. In addition to developing an experiential sense of the material, contemplative and introspective practices can sharpen various kinds of analytical thinking, among other important cognitive advantages.

Before moving forward with specific suggestions for contemplative practice, let's review the basic preliminaries from Barbezat and Bush that we must have in mind as we begin to implement them below in Best Practices 5.2.

Best Practice 5.2: Contemplative Practices Prerequisites

- You are engaged in contemplative practice of your own, which allows you to plan their timing, adapt practices as needed, and process the students' experiences afterward.
- You pay attention to and have knowledge of the context from which the practices arise and the appropriate incorporation of the tradition into the classroom.
- You allow students the freedom to maintain their own beliefs while not requiring them to believe anything specific to engage in contemplative practices.
- You maintain humility, clarity, and authenticity when introducing and conducting these practices so that students new to them do not identify them exclusively with you.

- You are aware of the different backgrounds of the students so that practices can be introduced in the most open, accessible manner.
- You recognize that these practices are powerful complements to other forms of teaching and learning.[50]

Contemplative practices can have a wide range of benefits. Two that are common to all of them are greater focus and the development of mindfulness. "Mindfulness is both a process (mindfulness practice) and an outcome (mindful awareness). Mindfulness is being aware in the present moment, not judging but accepting things as they are. . . . This way of being, and it does become a way of being and thinking and acting, allows every moment to be fresh—a moment we can learn and grow from."[51]

"Being mindful means that we are showing up fully for each moment, paying attention with an open heart."[52] When we are fully present, fully in the moment, in the flow, we come closer to a clear comprehension of a situation, circumstance, or body of information. The cultivation of mindfulness through contemplative practice is a critical element for the academy in terms of the overall impact on learning as well as discovering meaning, purpose, and vocation.

Below is a condensed list of best practices described from *Contemplative Practices in Higher Education* by Daniel Barbezat and Mirabai Bush.

Best Practices 5.3: Contemplative Practices Guidelines

- Plan the structure of the exercise but hold it lightly, more like a structured improvisation, so that you can be present in the moment [mindfulness] with student responses.
- Frame the exercises skillfully. Choose appropriate language, timing, context, and other factors so that students are open to learn and have the space to discover their own responses.
- Have a clear pedagogical purpose for the practice, so that you can lead the session toward the goal and properly assess its impact.
- Provide an opportunity for students to opt out during any exercise so that they feel safe in exploring it.
- Allow students time after the exercise to reflect on and write about [and/or discuss] their experience.
- Explain the purpose of the practice in the course so that students understand how it is affecting their learning.[53]

Consider these additional guidelines from Gurleen Grewal of the University of San Francisco for augmenting your contemplative practices to further support and increase their efficacy:

- After a long period of discussion, provide an opportunity for some mindful movement. Have students get up and stretch or walk quietly.
- Appreciate gaps during the discussion. As you and others speak, allow spaces and gaps to occur.
- Appreciate the interplay of serious logical exchange with spontaneous playfulness and humor.
- Practice holding the questions posed by others or yourself without needing to supply an immediate response.
- Allow room for different textures in discussions: cool, careful, fiery, tender, intimate, bold, expansive. Think of diversity in discussion styles as analogous to biodiversity in a healthy ecosystem.
- Trust disagreement and doubt. Do not artificially work for agreement, but value nonaggressive differences and direct feedback.
- Let go of preconceived outcomes for the discussion or for your contribution. Notice your resistance to dissolving preconceived goals. Allow the discussion to emerge in ways that are original, creative, surprising, and adventurous.
- If you are generally vocal in class, allow space for those who are silent to speak. Practice courtesy and compassion as well as directness.[54]

MINDFULNESS

The concepts of "mindful teaching" and "mindful learning" are gaining traction in educational research and literature. Ellen Langer of Harvard University characterizes mindful learning as openness to novelty, alertness to distinction, contextual sensitivity, multiple perspectives, and present orientation. She concludes that the essence of mindfulness is flexible thinking.[55] Dr. Langer's summary of mindful learning reads like a laundry list of right-hemisphere cognition and pathways critical to explorations of purpose and meaning for discerning vocation.

Also of general interest, mindfulness instruction in the classroom is a secular activity and speaks to a basic human capacity. Mindfulness is an outcome of several types of contemplative practice, but it is also cultivated through several simple methods, such as "witnessing and welcoming" and mindful breathing.

Witnessing and welcoming is a perspective and mind-setting practice. In a sense, this is an approach to taking on new topics and challenging subjects, a regular part of instruction and student learning. The difference is that in this case we are taking care to frame our approach from a mindful perspective that begins with a fresh and unassuming focus, one without predetermined or stereotyped notions and judgments, one that is open-minded and provides space for new understanding—mindful. It is not uncommon to move from a period of witnessing and welcoming a new or difficult topic to a moment of pause to help fix this new information within a mindful perspective.

As an example, imagine you've just introduced the subject of genetic variation to a group of biology students. This can be a challenging subject that is fraught with common misunderstandings. After a mindful witnessing and welcoming approach to the subject, it might be useful to pause for a short period of mindful breathing followed by a short, guided reflection on the subject matter just presented:

> if emerging adults are going to learn to self-superintend the power of imagination, they need to be initiated into the power and practice of pause—the strength of the contemplative mind.[56]

Let's turn again to Gurleen Grewal and her instructions for mindful listening and breathing in her women's studies course.

- Sitting in your chairs, body relaxed and spine erect, eyes closed, follow the sound of the gong or singing bowl as it reverberates and hums in space.
- Follow the ebbing of the sound into silence.
- Rest in that silence.
- If thoughts arise, simply observe them.
- Do the same for any bodily sensations or emotions: simply witness [and welcome] them.
- If you find yourself getting caught up in your thoughts, return to the awareness of your breath. Anchoring your attention in your breath breaks the compulsiveness of thought.
- Witness and welcome, without getting caught in whatever arises.
- Simply notice the mental chatter, the resistance to what is.
- The meditation ends with the sound of the gong or the bowl. Gradually open your eyes.[57]

David Levy suggests a similar mindfulness practice in his book *Mindful Tech* called the "mindful check-in."

> In our rushed and production-oriented culture, we tend to be focused on "getting things done." This often means focusing more on the goal we're trying to achieve than on our moment-to-moment experience while we're working toward it. The mindful check-in practice is meant to counter this tendency, asking you to notice what is happening in your mind and body while you're online [or engaged in any other activity]. . . . it asks you to explore your breath and body, your emotional state, and the quality of your attention.[58]

As his students become accustomed to the mindful check-in, Levy notes that he is then able to abbreviate his approach by simply asking how they are feeling. Some of you may include a "reflective check-in" type interlude in laboratories or similar practicums. Taking time to reflect on laboratory work allows students to consider more fully their techniques, stumbling blocks, and areas needing further practice. It is also a time to consider more carefully how the technique relates to purpose and efficacy.

You may also have your lab students reflect on how they feel about a particular practice: accomplished, fulfilled, competent, inept, and so forth. Finally, you might have your students reflect on where this skill or practice fits in their discipline, practice, and discerning vocation. In other words, how does it fit with our conception of our future work, and more?

Some science courses are implicitly mindful and/or require an inherently mindful approach for success. A good, and perhaps unexpected, example is an introductory entomology course. Mind you, such a course may not deliberately incorporate mindful practice. However, some of the practice does require and benefit from mindfulness, such as insect identification. To excel in field identifications requires a significant degree of mindful attention.

Students spend long hours in the field searching for insects to collect and study. To do so, they must exert tremendous patience and prolonged focus on the search area, which will put them in very close contact with a range of insect habitats. As a result, students often become very mindful of plant and insect ecology, various kinds of mutualisms, and the mindful application of focus and search imagery over long periods of time.

Another element of an entomology course that fosters mindfulness is the search for anatomical details among the collected specimens for positive identification. The same degree of mindfulness is required in botany and plant identification, human anatomy, and other whole organism as well as ecological field studies, to name a few. Imagine the impact of such courses when the professors emphasize this aspect of the discipline?

Mindful breathing, a practice that some might call anchor breathing, is a basic contemplative practice for cultivating mindfulness. It is a simple practice, but it is not easy. Simple because you focus only on your breathing and when your mind wanders, you bring it back to your breath. Not easy because your mind (your left hemisphere) has a strong tendency to wander, especially at the beginning, and one must be gentle and patient with oneself in bringing attention back to their breath.[59] Mindful breathing is an effective practice for a moment of pause, attitude adjustment, and centering. See the simple best practices for mindful breathing below.

Best Practices 5.4: Basic Mindful Breathing

- relax into a comfortable sitting posture with a few deep breaths;
- close your eyes or allow them to come to rest on a benign point;
- breathe normally, then begin to focus on your breath as it enters your nose, fills your lungs, and then exits your nose;
- if you become distracted by thoughts and sensations, witness and welcome them and return to your breathing without effort.

The key is to allow yourself to flow with your breathing, noticing sensations and thoughts as they come and calmly turning your attention back to your breathing. As students become more accustomed to mindful breathing, have them begin to focus with greater attention on the four points of breathing: the inhale (particularly air entering their nose), the full point with their lungs expanded, the exhale (again at their nose), and the empty point between breaths. This exercise may be no more than a minute or two in length, or longer. It may be a prelude to a more involved meditation. Either way, with practice, your breathing becomes your only focus and with it a new calmness, self-awareness, overall sensitivity, and centering.

REFLECTION

The practice of reflection is one of the most prevalent and useful forms of contemplative practice in academia, particularly community-engaged learning programs. The important element of reflecting as "reseeing" is underscored in this excerpt from *Looking In, Reaching Out: A Reflective Guide for Community Service-Learning Professionals* by Richard Harris, Barbara Jacoby, and Pamela Mutascio:

> To reflect is to re-see, to respect. Respect is a continuous process of seeing a changing landscape of people, ideas, problems, and solutions; it is also participation in a community of others who are also considering their own roles in society. The notion of reflecting as respecting complicates common assumptions about reflection, explorations of purpose and vocation, and service-learning.[60]

We must be clear about what reflection is not: a simple recounting of experience, an emotional outlet for opinionating, or a way to terminate an experience. These behaviors, although not forms of reflection, may be useful preliminaries to reflection. As alluded to at several points earlier in this chapter, reflection (and contemplative practice in general) is not a practice easily accepted in academia—hence, some earlier recommendations about broaching the subject using a vocabulary that resonates more strongly in the academy, such as "critical thinking." We can borrow from this popular term to form a more comprehensive version of our subject as "critical reflection."

Critical reflection is not a semantic ruse in that reflection is a critical element of explorations in purpose, meaning, and discerning vocation. Critical thinking and reflection are linked in a fully cognitive (bi-hemispheric) approach to our scholarship, our craft, and our overall combined practice: important elements of framing for teaching to inspire vocation. You stimulate critical reflection with critical questions surrounding the nature of our cognitive, kinesthetic, and affective academic and community-engaged learning experience.

As we become more familiar and adept at reflection, we tend to progress through three identifiable reflective stages of competence. At the beginning, or *stage one*, participants can identify responses, impressions, and manifest behaviors but do little or no analysis of them. They tend to focus on a single aspect and perspective of the subject in reflection but often rely on unsupported personal beliefs as explanations.

With growing experience, *stage two*, participants' reflections become more detailed and nuanced but still lack context. At this stage, they can provide a useful critique of their experience from a single perspective, one that is more perceptive of different viewpoints and includes useful evidence.

Finally, having a good deal more practice, students at *stage three* will reflect from multiple perspectives, parse conflicting goals and variable factors affecting their experience, and assess the importance of different decisions they face within their academic circumstances. Each of these stages demonstrates a richer, more sophisticated ability for reflection. You will need to be aware of this evolution of the impact of reflective practice and help steer your students successfully through these stages—don't rush the process; encourage growth by offering more reflective experience and being supportive of the process.

As you and your students begin to pause and reflect more often as part of your pedagogy, you may notice and begin to encourage four different "rhythms," or forms of reflection: continuous, connected, challenging, contextualized. Continuous reflection occurs at several points from the beginning of an experience to the end. You may ask your students to reflect on introductory elements of a lesson or experience as a preparatory interval, followed by a reflection during the lesson or experience to invite evaluation of the experience, and a last reflection at the end to summarize and contextualize what they learned.

Connected reflection is common to community-engaged learning and other experiential learning opportunities to help connect the experience with the academic learning outcomes. As Jennifer Pigza explains, "Connected reflection bridges classroom learning, personal reflections, and firsthand experiences."[61] Through this process a sense of meaning, purpose, and vocation develops around the profession, craft, or practice learned.

Challenging reflection is what it sounds like: reflection that stems from probing and difficult questions, which, in turn, often raise new ones. Contextualized reflection, like connected reflection, provides a link between thinking and doing in a context of process, content, and location—a particularly pertinent form of reflection for experiential learning.

The above forms of reflection—known as the "four Cs of reflection"—are familiar to community-engaged learning providers and may take the form of informal conversations, structured journals, or small-group encounters in the classroom, laboratory, workshop, or community-engaged learning site. Out of these types of reflection, and then action, comes what may be called "praxis"; accepted or customary practice.[62] As we move through lessons and units of study, including laboratories, workshops, and community-engaged learning experiences, we should be inserting intervals of reflection to ground our students' understanding of concepts and praxis.

Consider opportunities for critical reflection associated with major or compelling themes or topic threads—sustainability, for example—in each segment of the curriculum. Identify the important components or building blocks of those themes and threads as subjects for reflective pause in your pedagogy. Place these reflective intervals along the continuum of study based on which of the four Cs of reflection you are using. Typically, experienced educators use a combination of reflective forms, depending upon where in the unit of study the reflection occurs.

As suggested earlier, it can be helpful practice to begin a new unit of study with a short reflection on student expectations regarding the new material. You may have students record these in a journal, log, or lab book. Reflective intervals that come after the presentation of major concepts and experiential learning segments are also helpful. The reflections may be a combination of short, quiet moments followed by group discussion or journal entries, and so on.

If you have experienced colleagues, ask them for advice on their favorite reflective activities. Otherwise, be patient with yourself as you experiment with different approaches. In the beginning, err on the side of making the intervals of reflective practice short. No matter what kind of reflection you choose or how often you insert a reflective interval, make reflections an intentional part of your pedagogy. A casual approach will lead to missed opportunities, slowed progress, and poor results. Outlined below are several different types of contemplative practice. Additional reflective practices are presented in chapters 7 and 8.

CONTEMPLATIVE READING, WRITING, LISTENING, SEEING

A collegiate education usually involves a great deal of reading and writing. Both modes of learning may be contemplative and mindful. Writing assignments are a good way to have students consider and report on what they have learned. Recall how pleasing and satisfying it is to receive a written work from a student who clearly inhabited what he wrote, and it spoke of a deep reflection and understanding of the subject material.

Contemplative reading and writing make that kind of inhabited experience possible. Contemplative reading and writing require students to slow down in the process and carefully attend to their work in a way that can fundamentally change their experience. Doing this also means that we need to consider more carefully our expectations of how much reading and writing they will do.

In various religious and spiritual traditions, the careful reading of sacred texts is part of a fundamental devotion reinforced by copying those texts as an exercise in careful interpretation. The Christian tradition of contemplative reading, known as *Lectio Divina*, recognizes four levels of meaning: literal, metaphorical, moral, and mystical. These are recognized as increasing levels of reading comprehension and complexity.

College reading requirements are often approached in a way humorously characterized by Woody Allen: "I took a speed-reading course and read *War and Peace* in twenty minutes. It's about Russia." Contemplative reading is the antithesis of Woody's experience, slowing down the reader and the reading, completely changing the experience. Contemplative reading makes time for reflection and contemplation.

Contemplative reading is more deliberate and deliberative, and as such, you must select your course reading carefully for maximum impact and reduced volume. Following the ancient tradition of *Lectio Divina*, students begin by becoming keenly aware of what is written, then ever more aware of deeper meaning leading to the realization of a multidimensional connection. The point is to increase students' engagement with and comprehension of their subject.

David Haskell, professor of biology and environmental studies at the University of the South, takes a modified and effective approach to *Lectio Devina* that he describes as" *Lectio* without too much *Devina*." His instructions to the students:

- Sit quietly and relax your minds and bodies for one minute.

- Read aloud, slowly, the entire text [article or excerpt], each person reading one or two sentences, passing along the reading to the left to the next reader.
- One minute of silence and reflection.
- One person reads aloud a short passage that is chosen in advance.
- Another minute of silence and reflection.
- Each person shares a word or short phrase in response to the reading—just giving voice to the word without explanation or discussion.
- Another person reads the short passage again.
- One minute of silence and reflection.
- Each person shares a longer response to the text—a sentence or two. All listen attentively to one another without correcting or disputing.
- Another person reads the short passage one last time, followed by another minute of silence.[63]

The process of reading aloud may seem juvenile, but rather than skimming over the surface, it can be very effective in immersing the students in the text to an extent that is unusual and meaningful. You will need to assure your students that their reading proficiency is of no concern, and they should take their time. Give them the option to pass to the next student if they are uncomfortable reading aloud.

Lectio Divina may not be well suited to technical literature. There are a few ways to approach textbook, handbook, and technical manual reading using contemplative practice. Consider a mindfulness practice as a preparatory exercise for technical reading. Then, assign short, contemplative missives or anecdotes related to the practice and/or subject at hand to accompany the drier technical writing.

Look for associated reading material that frames the technical information or activity as a "practice" or a "craft" with special attributes and unique assets. Share this piece with the students in class before sending them on their way with their homework. Also, review segments of technical reading homework during the following class meeting. If this is already part of your instructional routine, consider taking a more contemplative or quasi-*Lectio Devina* approach involving reflective moments followed by analytical discussions, giving students time to process and contextualize the new information.

A more difficult area to penetrate with contemplative practice is digital media. The challenge with digital media is the context, its raison d'etre being interconnectedness, a condition that makes contemplative use difficult. Digital technologies and media encourage multitasking, spreading the user's attention out horizontally but not vertically into what Nicholas Carr criticizes as "the shallows."[64] Managing this tendency is an exercise in self-discipline, a right-hemisphere capability that is strengthened with contemplative practice.

One of David Levy's students describes her experience with mindful tech and multitasking this way:

> I learned that there really is a way to be an efficient, mindful, and productive multitasker! . . . By setting manageable intentions before I engage in multitasking, I'm able to be kind to myself while also setting a goal. This creates a place where I am better able to focus on the tasks. By taking deep breaths, I remind myself of my intention and am able to kindly refocus and bring myself back to the task.[65]

That approach involves mindful interludes prior to going online and at intervals during online sessions to help restore one's focus on a goal. With focused multitasking, one may participate and take advantage of the interconnectedness of digital media without becoming lost and endlessly distracted.

The point is to stay focused on your goal by being able to observe and monitor your multitasking behavior and not let habitual and unconscious behaviors and choices take over. This involves recognizing choices and then choosing the best ones. In his book *Mindful Tech*, David Levy lays out a set of useful exercises for helping you observe your own multitasking behaviors and tendencies and for focusing your digital multitasking to fulfill specific goals. More on contemplative practice in digital technologies in chapter 8.

A more natural tendency toward a contemplative state of mind exists when it comes to writing, certainly among professional writers. Ask most writers, and they'll tell you that their writing time is spent in a solitary, quiet location, allowing for a contemplative approach to discovering their muse and inspiration. Creative writing, like reading, also falls within the domain of the right hemisphere, drawing from the capacities for mindfulness, reflection, contemplation, and introspection that also reside there. Writing helps to activate these capacities and give them greater strength toward coming to know one's own mind and purpose.

Contemplative writing emphasizes process rather than outcome and should be done freely and without weighty analyses. Journaling is a common and *affective*, as well as *effective*, form of contemplative writing.

The famous journals of the likes of Anne Frank, Virginia Woolf, Robert Falcon Scott, and Nelson Mandela illustrate how they can help one cultivate the ability to live in the present and to become deeply aware and appreciative of life. A journal is different than a diary in that it is a series of reflections on the experiences, thoughts, and emotions within one's life as opposed to a chronicle of events.

As Thomas Merton wrote in *Learning to Love*, "Journals take for granted that every day in our life there is something new and different."[66] From a contemplative and mindful standpoint, journaling is most valuable when done without self-conscious editing, when the writing flows like a musical improvisation. Well, that's easy to say, but it certainly takes some practice.

Some of you may already assign a simple journal that your students use to document their thoughts and reactions to class information and activities. Extend that practice to go hand in hand with other contemplative practices, such as contemplative reading and reflection. Collect those journals at least once during the term to see how they are shaping up and, if necessary, to offer advice on journaling. The initial results will likely be a mixed bag, and some will be disappointing.

Students who are new to journaling will tend to record activities and actions and/or stereotyped responses rather than mindful personal reflections. Checking their journals at a midpoint in the course gives you the opportunity to help students get in touch with the process. Providing your students with a mindful moment in association with a unit of information and/or practice usually yields more thoughtful journal entries and meaningful experiences.

Contemplative journal writing often pertains to student responses and feelings stemming from reflections on course material or skills practice. You will have to remind students to keep their journal entries simple, brief, and as uncalculated as possible—in other words, off the top of their heads and authentic. Field courses and laboratories often require journal writing to document observations and outcomes. These journals can do double duty in also being a record of reflections and introspections on these field experiences that help them become a more indelible and meaningful part of a student's education. Here's a wonderful prosaic example from Stephen Mitchell about his observation of bamboo:

> Sometimes I have spent hours face to face with a single stalk, watching for its essence, listening, waiting on the sheer edge of attention, until my arm begins to sway in the light wind, and my brush is blown across the page, along the branches, out to the tendrils and leaves, the last spray turns into calligraphy, moves down the lines of verse, and with one final half-dry flourish: signs my name.[67]

The idea of asking students to focus on one moment as the subject of a journal entry is epitomized by Allan Ginsberg when he was teaching at the Jack Kerouac School for Disembodied Poetics at Naropa University. His simple instructions:

- Stop in your tracks once a day, take account of the sky, ground, and yourself, write 3 haiku verses.
- Sit for 5 minutes a day and afterward, recollect your thoughts.
- Stop in the middle of a street or country, turn 360 degrees, write what you remember.[68]

Douglas Henry, dean of the Honors College at Baylor University, summarizes the benefits to students of contemplative writing, particularly as it applies to finding purpose, meaning, and discerning vocation:

> in selected courses we can guide students in writing—provisionally and fallibly, to be sure—their own memoirs. Especially when a structured, iterative process guides memoir-writing, and particularly when the assignment includes an invitation to vocational reflection, students may gain great insight into who they are, better understand the vocations to which they are called, think about why these things matter, and consider how they might "write ahead" a worthy narrative to enact. In the process of editing and revising their memoirs, students are also encouraged to explore alternative interpretations of the important episodes in their lives, seeing them as openings into (or foreclosures of) possible life callings.[69]

Good listening is a critically important requirement for gaining any benefit from contemplative practice. Listening is a rarefied skill in our left-brain dominant culture where constant vocalizing for attention is the norm. Studies show that we spend about 45 percent of our time listening, but we are distracted, preoccupied, or forgetful about 75 percent of that time. The average attention span for adults is about twenty-two seconds. Immediately after listening to someone talk, we usually recall only about half of what we've heard and within a few hours, only about 20 percent.[70] John Neafsey summarizes well the importance of really being heard:

> The capacity to really listen, to put aside our own concerns for the moment, to feel or imagine ourselves in the world of another person and then to communicate our empathic understanding to that person in such a way that he or she feels heard or understood is the foundation for all genuine relationships and solidarity between human beings.[71]

Listening mindfully and well to your students can be a challenge. Perhaps the biggest difference mindful listening can make is with challenged and special needs students. Often, the most valuable mentoring and counseling service provided to those students is undivided attention when they need help. Students quickly realize the difference when someone is listening to them and hearing them.

Remember that so much of contemplative practice is an experiment in silence. Mindful listening begins with one's own silence. Also, hearing your calling is dependent upon a silent mind, one that can best hear what calls out from deep inside. Notice that many of the contemplative practices already covered contain silent moments that allow for one to hear his own mind, his thoughts, ideas, and get in touch with his feelings.

Musicians recognize that contemplative practice helps with improvisation; this connection, by extension, also assists in improvisational thinking in a broad range of disciplines. Contemplative practice opens music students to a fuller range of musical understanding that encompasses sound *and* silence, a complete acoustic world. The same goes for contemplative practice and a broad range of practices, skills, and professions. In part, and by extension, this explains the improved academic performance of students who spend time listening to classical music before engaging in academic activity.

Right Listening by Mark Brady is a very helpful text on mindful listening practices. He provides the following best practices.

Best Practices 5.5: Mindful Listening

- Listen without agenda.
- Listen without "should'ing on people."
- Establish support for speaking truth to power.
- Stop when your energy flags.
- Avoid letting your story take over their story.
- Listen for feelings.
- Listen as caregiver.
- Ask for more information.
- Be curious as you listen.[72]

Looking through that list, notice your own listening faults and shortcomings. Notice that the list begins with suggestions on listening orientation and ends with suggestions on what to listen for. It may be Brady's intention to point out that listening orientation often gets in the way of what to be listening for. Listening only for opportunities to insert yourself is a left-hemisphere dominant tendency common in our culture. Contemplative practice engages more fully the right hemisphere's ability for patient self-control and focused listening.

Spending time with your students working on better listening habits through contemplative practice will contribute immensely to their success in class and in finding meaning and purpose in their scholarship. Mindfulness is a prerequisite for full and deep listening in that we require a contemplative, fully cognitive mind to be completely receptive. "Such listening not only increases retention of material but encourages insight and the making of meaning."[73]

Good listening habits and exercises in deep listening can be part of the contemplative reading and writing approaches just described. For example, when you intend to have students read aloud class material and/or their contemplative writing, this may also be an opportunity for contemplative listening. The same may be said for anything presented as part of your course work that will benefit from contemplative listening. In that case, you will need to provide guidance for your students on how they should listen and what they should listen for, borrowing from Brady's list.

The following is a set of instructions for a mindful listening exercise devised by Jack Himmelstein and Gary Friedman for their contemplative practices retreat with Yale Law School students.

> Everyone find a partner. One person speaks; the other listens. The listener listens as carefully as possible, letting go of interpretations, judgements, and reactions, as well as irrelevant thoughts, memories, plans. When the speaker finishes, the listener repeats as closely as possible what the speaker said, until the speaker feels truly heard. The following instructions are for the person who leads the exercise:
>
> *To both partners:* One partner will spend three to five minutes speaking [decide on the time before beginning the exercise], in response to a prompt about the class content [e.g., "What I learned from that lecture was . . . "] or about an aspect of his or her life ["Right now, I am feeling . . . "].
>
> *To the speaker:* This time is yours. If you run out of things to say, you can just sit silent, and whenever you have something to say, you may continue speaking again.
>
> *To the listener:* Your job is to listen in silence. When you listen, give your full attention to the speaker. Be curious, but don't ask questions while listening. You may acknowledge with facial expressions or by nodding your head. Try not to over-acknowledge, or you may end up leading the speaker. You may feel an urge to coach, identify, chime in, or interrupt: this is normal. Just notice when this occurs, resist the temptation to act, and refocus your attention on your partner. Listen with kindness. When thoughts or emotions come into your mind, simply notice them, then gently return your full attention to the speaker. If the speaker runs out of things to say, give them the space for silence, and then be available to listen when they speak again.
>
> *To the listener:* After your partner has finished telling the story, repeat what you have been told; don't worry about memorizing –paraphrase. Have your partner correct you if you misunderstood the story. Ask questions to be sure you understand, as closely as possible, what your partner intended to say.

To both partners: When the speaker is satisfied that she or he has been heard and comprehended, switch roles. Now it is the listener's turn to tell a story until she or he feels heard.

To both partners: Reflect on how it feels to be listened to so closely and what it felt like to listen deeply to another. Remember to listen to the words but also the tone, the emotional undercurrent. This is an important way to stay connected at times where it may be difficult to connect to the ideas or perspective being expressed.

To both partners: End by thanking each other for listening.[74]

This exercise may be modified to follow any number of course units of study, specific exercises, field trips, and so forth. The point is to provide a time for contemplation of the material or experience in a sharing, speaking, and listening format—an embedded contemplative practice within your pedagogy.

Not only do we need to relearn how to listen, but we need to relearn how to see. Seeing well and clearly, like listening deeply, is another way of being fully present in the world, another form of focused, vigilant attention. It is this capacity for seeing that Thoreau was talking about when he observed, "Wisdom does not inspect, but behold. We must look a long time before we can see."[75] Beholding, as meant by Thoreau and within contemplative practice, is about appreciation and relatedness rather than abstraction and distancing. Repetition and practice are important parts of learning to behold. As Thoreau said, "We must look a long time."

The seeing associated with beholding involves a revolving capacity for changes in contextual view, level of focus, and relatedness: a right-hemisphere capacity strengthened through contemplative practice. Composer John Cage describes the benefits of a beholding experience to later observations after viewing works of abstract expressionist painter Mark Tobey. Leaving the gallery, he happened to look down at the pavement "and—literally—the pavement was as beautiful as the Tobey. So the experience of looking at the Tobey was instructive about looking at the pavement . . . Art became identical with life."[76]

Thinking about beholding as a practiced and contemplative form of seeing may remind you of a puzzle that many young students looked forward to with each new copy of *Highlights* magazine. These seeing puzzles are known as "hidden picture" or "hidden object" puzzles. They are typically elaborate line drawings of trees or farmyard scenes with instructions to find a list of hidden objects within the drawings. Solving such puzzles is helped by a list of objects to find so that the looker will have a search image to look for.

Beholding, or contemplative seeing, provides you with a greater visual flexibility to see what is there without a particular search imagery. Advanced versions of these puzzles, available for adult observers, can serve as useful contemplative seeing and beholding exercises for your students.

Another approach to contemplative seeing, or beholding, is developing a "practiced eye," which leads to greater powers of observation, perception, and recognizing interconnection. Observation stations in nature are valuable contexts for these exercises. In many cases, this involves selecting an observation point in the landscape that is revisited several times over the course of weeks, months, or even years. Over time and with practice, it becomes clear that the observer is no longer seeing the same landscape even though looking in the same direction.

The observation station approach to the study of nature and contemplative seeing is exemplified by two studies. One is a photographic study by Rick Darke, a Pennsylvania-based consultant focused on the conservation, design, and management of living landscapes grounded in an observational ethic that blends art, ecology, and cultural geography. For more than a year, Darke photographed a segment of Red Clay Creek in southeastern Pennsylvania at weekly intervals. The resulting collection of images illustrates the dramatic changes in growth, color, depth, forest architecture, and mood that take place in a mature, eastern deciduous forest over the course of a year.

The other example of the practiced eye form of beholding, or contemplative seeing, in nature is George David Haskell's inquiry of one square meter of old-growth Tennessee forest as a window into the entire natural world, documented in his book *The Forest Unseen: A Year's Watch in Nature*. Visiting his tiny research plot on a weekly basis for a year, Haskell observes a universe of life and activity that leads to broad, sweeping exposés on forest ecology and natural history.

Haskell uses his observations to explain the science that binds together the tiniest microbes and the largest mammals in describing the ecosystems that have cycled for thousands—sometimes millions—of years. What is seen and learned from beholding the details within a square meter of forest is simply remarkable. Both of these examples may be duplicated in a range of modified versions to bring home powerful examples of what it means to look and see carefully.

Art historian Joanna Zeigler uses a similar contemplative seeing approach with her students who engage in repeated observations of great works of art to learn to behold and see them fully in their detail. She notes that her students went from an antipathy for these works to a love for them through beholding and developing a practiced eye. Then, in reporting and discussing what they have seen, Zeigler concludes that her students "discover that sense of connectedness with things that alone makes it possible to be connected with ourselves."[77]

CONTEMPLATIVE MOVEMENT

A kinesthetic approach to contemplative practice also has gained quite a bit of traction in our culture: contemplative movement. Local parks are filled with dedicated walkers, slow-motion tai chi practitioners, and contorted yoga afficionados. Unless you teach a practice or craft with a significant kinesthetic component, our students tend to spend a significant amount of time in their heads: thinking, studying, planning, and rehearsing. Their academic and life experience may be enriched with a more embodied approach to education. Contemplative movement integrates the workings of the mind with those of the body for a more holistic, more meaningful learning experience. Ann Cooper Albright of Oberlin College writes,

> the term "physical mindfulness" evokes for me the interconnected realms of embodied knowledge and critical thinking. I use it to underscore the psychic implications of one's physical being-in-the-world. I confront every day the paradigm of the separation of the mind and spiritual life from that of the body. For me, physical practice is the core of my contemplative experience.[78]

Many people enjoy a long walk around their neighborhood or town as a respite from everyday obligations and responsibilities. Some might recognize it as a necessary walking meditation with varying degrees of contemplative interlude, nature appreciation, and occasional social interaction. In an earlier period, these walks were referred to as engaging in or being out for your "constitutional." The word "constitutional" referred to one's constitution or physical makeup, so a constitutional walk is considered beneficial to one's overall well-being. The phrase is more common in British literature and parlance than in America.

Candid observations of people on their constitutional often reveal someone walking with her head slightly bowed, apparently lost in thought—contemplation, introspection, reflection, meditation. It's a way of using a common activity as a natural accompaniment to mindfulness. One might feel fully present to the surroundings during a constitutional, and this may be why they do them. I suspect they may result in moments of inspiration or resolution regarding various elements of one's life.

A simple exercise (probably born out of a party game) that brings together mindful approaches to body and mental function is moving a spoonful of water between two bowls. To do so, one needs to remain focused on what one's body is doing at a very specific level: holding and manipulating the spoon. At the same time, one must be aware of the general surroundings to move yourself without tripping, bumping, or falling. This multifunctional perspective is a good illustration of a combined left-brain/right-brain kinesthetic awareness, a parallel to left- and right-brain cognitive cooperation during complete mindfulness.

Practice walking meditations in unobstructed, simple locations free of human busy work. You and your students may pace back and forth over a short distance in- or out-of-doors; circumscribe a bounded space; follow an uncrowded path, trail, or walkway; or trace a labyrinth. You may begin by having your students stand still to notice the details and sensations of posture, then shift their weight from one leg to another, one side to another, in preparation for walking. Start walking slowly and deliberately to take note of all the mechanics of movement. This noticing may occupy your students for the bulk of their walking meditation as a focus, much like a mantra, for contemplation.

Vietnamese Zen master Thich Nhat Hanh suggests that the key to a walking meditation is that you know you are walking and to be in the present moment of that movement. Students may coordinate their breathing with their stepping, combining these two types of meditation and mindfulness. If students are trained in meditation, they may choose to invoke their mantra in time with their steps and walking. The emphasis of this choreographed walking meditation is to focus the moment to moment of one's being here, present to each moment. Ultimately, that sharpens one's attention.

Tai chi ch'uan is a more tightly choreographed type of contemplative movement and martial art. The focus is on slow, relaxed, but deliberate movements that teach the practitioner greater awareness of balance, energy flow, spatial projection, and the weighted use of one's body in space. Tai chi can be a wonderful contemplative movement discipline for students receiving training in various practices, crafts, trades, and physical arts, from surgeons to dancers, gardeners to carpenters—any field where maintaining a mind-body connection is of critical importance.

Closely allied to tai chi in cultivating a healthy mind-body connection is yoga. Like tai chi, yoga uses a prescribed set of movements to promote flexibility, balance, and strength of body and mind. Unlike tai chi, yoga also concentrates on breathing as additional focus toward these ends. Both practices, or disciplines, become a means for their practitioners of inquiry and self-knowledge, as well as physical well-being. Movement practices of all sorts, such as walking meditation, tai chi, and yoga improve sensitivity, concentration, mental clarity, and precision.

CONCLUSION

Don't miss an opportunity to bring in experienced practitioners to help establish contemplative practices in your course and classroom. Learning from an acknowledged expert will create a unique bond between you and your students as you work together to implement their recommendations. Also, an experienced practitioner will embody the qualities acquired through contemplative practice for all your students to see, hear, and sense.

Field trips to visit professionals, organizations, and businesses that incorporate contemplative practice in their work can be very a powerful example and illustration of benefit. Field trip providers will be able to draw direct connections to their contemplative practice and the positive outcomes in their professional practice or service to the community.

Mirabai Bush summarizes very nicely the cumulative benefits to professional and technical education of contemplative practices:

> contemplative development opens the mind to new possibilities, cultivates wisdom through deepening one's relationship to the world, and encourages compassion and empathy through an understanding of the interconnection of all life. And at the same time, scientific research is confirming that contemplation/ mindfulness develops such cross-disciplinary cognitive capacities as decision making, attention, intuitive understanding, and memory as well as emotional capacities such as self-awareness, self-management, and empathy.[79]

The attributes and capabilities conveyed by contemplative practice that she listed are the result of practiced, fully engaged right-hemisphere cognitive pathways, a mutually beneficial cycle. The analytic and objectifying capabilities of our left hemisphere, those cognitive traits that dominate current pedagogies and metrics of higher education, are insufficient for critical thinking, deep understanding, and making meaning. Contemplative practice helps our students to bring a fully cognitive attention to their education and discerning their vocation.

Contemplative practice in the form of reflection was a large part of the extensive Lilly Endowment's Programs for the Theological Exploration of Vocation (PTEV) that spanned the years 2000–2007 and involved 138 colleges and universities. William Sullivan summarizes the impact and importance of reflection to the success of those programs then, and those that continue today:

> The third common element of successful explorations in discerning vocation is the use in all learning communities of practices of group and individual reflection. Reflection made it possible for students to construct over time an understanding of life, encompassing connections between interests, immediate

goals, and longer life trajectories. Practiced in multiple settings, orally and in writing, both within and outside the formal curriculum, these activities provided ways for students to integrate academic learning and practical experience with important dimensions of meaning in their lives.[80]

Finally, a reminder and a parting word. Introduce contemplative practices in your pedagogy gradually and at natural intervals, characterized as improvisational moments of pause and reflection. If you find yourself questioning the relevance of this practice, remind yourself that deep understanding, making meaning, and learning are most likely to occur with students who are mindful and attentive. As Liz Coleman, former president of Bennington College likes to point out, "deep thought matters when you're contemplating what to do about things that matter."[81]

Textbox 5.1 Teaching Takeaways

- Reflection is the fourth R of education, the skill that embeds self-knowing and empathy in the curriculum.
- Contemplative practice is a means for making what is presented in class personally meaningful for students and more deeply understood.
- Introduce contemplative practices in your pedagogy gradually and at natural intervals, characterized as improvisational moments of pause and reflection.
- In a complete cycle of cognition, the right hemisphere generates the big picture and has temporal and ontological supremacy in bringing the world into being. The left hemisphere fills in some of the details.
- Contemplative practice activates and exercises right-hemisphere pathways to assist in finding meaning, purpose, and vocation.
- Contemplative practices encourage cognitive flow. The concept of cognitive "flow"—the holistic sensation that people have when they act with total cognitive involvement—is crucially important to finding your vocation.
- Contemplative practices cause students to slow down and carefully attend to their work, their understanding, and their feelings in a way that can fundamentally change their experience.
- Use a mix of contemplation, reflection, introspection, and simple meditation.
- Using contemplative practices in your pedagogy is not an all-or-nothing proposition.
- There are no wrong answers within contemplative practice: whatever students experience *is* part of the outcome.
- Mindfulness, a result of all contemplative practice, is both a process and an outcome.
- Review the general contemplative practices guidelines on page 79.
- Seek to begin each class session with a contemplative pause and end the session with a reflection on what has been presented in class.

NOTES

1. Sharon Daloz Parks, *Big Questions, Worthy Dreams: Mentoring Emerging Adults in Their Search for Meaning, Purpose, and Faith* (Hoboken, NJ: Jossey-Bass, 2011), 148.
2. John Neafsey, *A Sacred Voice Is Calling* (Maryknoll, NY: Orbis Books, 2011), 32.
3. William Damon, *The Path to Purpose: How Young People Find Their Calling in Life* (New York: Free Press, 2009), 105.
4. David M. Levy, "No Time to Think: Reflections on Information Technology and Contemplative Scholarship," *Ethics & Information Technology* 9, no. 4 (2007): 237–49.
5. D. J. Siegel, *The Mindful Brain: Reflection and Attunement in the Cultivation of Well-being* (New York: Norton, 2007), 309.
6. Iain McGilchrist, *The Master and His Emissary* (New Haven, CT: Yale University Press, 2009), x.
7. McGilchrist, *The Master and His Emissary*, 91.
8. McGilchrist, *The Master and His Emissary*, 88.
9. McGilchrist, *The Master and His Emissary*, 31.
10. Jenny Mackness, *The Master and His Emissary Wiki*, https://jennymackness.wordpress.com/2020/07/03/the-master-and-his-emissary-notes/.
11. McGilchrist, *The Master and His Emissary*, 195.
12. McGilchrist, *The Master and His Emissary*, 209.
13. Mackness, *The Master and His Emissary Wiki*.
14. Simone Pétrement, *Simone Weil: A Life* (New York: Pantheon, 1976), 462.
15. Maggie Jackson, *Distracted: The Erosion of Attention and the Coming Dark Age* (Amherst, NY: Prometheus Books, 2009), 13.
16. *Problem Solving for Tomorrow's World* (Paris: Organization for Economic Cooperation and Development, 2004), 47.
17. H. Persky, M. Daane, and Y. Jin, *The Nation's Report Card: Writing 2002* (Washington, DC: U.S. Department of Education, Institute of Edcational Sciences, 2003), 11, 19, 21.
18. Jackson, *Distracted*, 24.
19. Mihaly Csikzentmihalyi, *Flow: The Psychology of Optimal Experience* (New York: Harper Perennial, 1991), 84–85.
20. Jackson, *Distracted*, 23.
21. Karen Stansberry Beard and Wayne K. Hoy, "The Nature, Meaning, and Measure of Teacher Flow in Elementary Schools: A Test of Rival Hypotheses," *Educational Administration Quarterly* 46, no. 3 (2010): 427.
22. Mike Oppland, "8 Traits of Flow According to Mihaly Csikszentmihalyi," *PositivePsychology.com*, https://positivepsychology.com/mihaly-csikszentmihalyi-father-of-flow/#flow-types-characteristics.
23. McGilchrist, *The Master and His Emissary*, 30.
24. Martin Seligman and Angela Duckworth, "Self-Discipline Outdoes IQ in Predicting Academic Performance of Adolescents," *Psychological Science* 16, no. 12 (2005): 939–44.

25. Jennifer Fredericks, Phyllis Blumenfeld, and Alison Paris, "School Engagement: Potential of the Concept, State of the Evidence," *Review of Educational Research* 74, no. 1 (2004): 59.

26. Jackson, *Distracted*, 233.

27. Paulo Freire, *Pedagogy of the Oppressed* (London: Penguin, 1972).

28. Arthur W. Chickering, Jon C. Dalton, and Liesa Stamm, *Encouraging Authenticity and Spirituality in Higher Education* (San Francisco: Jossey-Bass, 2005), 143.

29. Parker Palmer and Arthur Zajonc, *The Heart of Higher Education* (San Francisco: Jossey-Bass, 2010), 71.

30. William Sullivan, *Liberal Learning as a Quest for Purpose* (New York: Oxford University Press, 2016), 15.

31. Parks, *Big Questions*, 17.

32. Daniel P. Barbezat and Mirabai Bush, *Contemplative Practices in Higher Education* (San Francisco: Jossey-Bass, 2014), xii.

33. Sullivan, *Liberal Learning as a Quest for Purpose*, 68.

34. Sullivan, *Liberal Learning as a Quest for Purpose*, 8.

35. Sullivan, *Liberal Learning as a Quest for Purpose*, 6.

36. Sullivan, *Liberal Learning as a Quest for Purpose*, 11.

37. Parks, *Big Questions*, 185.

38. Barbezat and Bush, *Contemplative Practices in Higher Education*, 17.

39. Barbezat and Bush, *Contemplative Practices in Higher Education*, 19.

40. Barbezat and Bush, *Contemplative Practices in Higher Education*, 23.

41. J. Simmer-Brown, "Training the Heart Responsibly: Ethical Considerations in Contemplative Teaching," in *Meditation and the Classroom: Contemplative Pedagogy and Religious Studies*, ed. J. Simmer-Brown and F. Grace (Albany, NY: SUNY Press, 2011), 116.

42. Barbezat and Bush, *Contemplative Practices in Higher Education*, 78.

43. Barbezat and Bush, *Contemplative Practices in Higher Education*, 79.

44. Barbezat and Bush, *Contemplative Practices in Higher Education*, xiii.

45. Barbezat and Bush, *Contemplative Practices in Higher Education*, 68.

46. Daniel Rechtschaffen, *The Mindful Education Workbook* (New York: Norton, 2016), 55.

47. Michael Polanyi, *Personal Knowledge* (Chicago: University of Chicago Press, 1974), vii.

48. Polanyi, *Personal Knowledge*, 3.

49. Polanyi, *Personal Knowledge*, 55.

50. Barbezat and Bush, *Contemplative Practices in Higher Education*, 84.

51. Barbezat and Bush, *Contemplative Practices in Higher Education*, 98.

52. Rechtschaffen, *The Mindful Education Workbook*, 3–4.

53. Barbezat and Bush, *Contemplative Practices in Higher Education*, 90.

54. Barbezat and Bush, *Contemplative Practices in Higher Education*, 90–91.

55. E. J. Langer, *The Power of Mindful Learning* (Reading, MA: Addison-Wesley, 1997), 22–23.

56. Parks, *Big Questions*, 149.

57. Barbezat and Bush, *Contemplative Practices in Higher Education*, 100.

58. David Levy, *Mindful Tech* (New Haven, CT: Yale University Press, 2016), 187–88.

59. Levy, *Mindful Tech*, 185.

60. Jennifer M. Pigza, "Developing Your Ability to Foster Student Learning and Development through Reflection," in *Looking In, Reaching Out: A Reflective Guide for Community Service-Learning Professionals*, ed. Richard Harris, Barbara Jacoby, and Pamela Mutascio (Boston: Campus Compact, 2010), 74.

61. Pigza, "Developing Your Ability," 80.

62. *Merriam Webster Dictionary* online, https://www.merriam-webster.com/dictionary/praxis.

63. Barbezat and Bush, *Contemplative Practices in Higher Education*, 115.

64. Nicholas Carr, *The Shallows: What the Internet Is Doing to Our Brains* (New York: Norton, 2011).

65. Levy, *Mindful Tech*, 111.

66. Thomas Merton, *Learning to Love* (London, UK: HarperCollins, 1999), xiii.

67. Stephen Mitchell, *Parables and Portraits* (New York: Harper, 1990), 63.

68. Barbezat and Bush, *Contemplative Practices in Higher Education*, 132.

69. Douglas V. Henry, "Vocation and Story: Narrating Self and World," in *At This Time and In This Place*: *Vocation in Higher Education*, ed. David S. Cunningham (New York: Oxford University Press, 2016), 187.

70. The Listening Center, http://www.sacredlistening.com/tlc_about.htm.

71. Neafsey, *A Sacred Voice Is Calling*, 12.

72. Mark Brady, *Right Listening* (Jordan Station, Ontario, Canada: Paideia Press, 2009), 10–11.

73. Barbezat and Bush, *Contemplative Practices in Higher Education*, 136.

74. Barbezat and Bush, *Contemplative Practices in Higher Education*, 144–45.

75. Henry David Thoreau, "Natural History of Massachusetts," in *Essays* (New Haven, CT: Yale University Press, 2013), 2.

76. John Cage and Joan Retallack, *Musicage: Cage muses on words *art* music* (Middletown, CT: Wesleyan University Press, 2011), 106.

77. C. A. Dustin and J. E. Zeigler, *Practicing Mortality: Art, Philosophy, and Contemplative Seeing* (London, UK: Palgrave Macmillan, 2007), 13.

78. Barbezat and Bush, *Contemplative Practices in Higher Education*, 159.

79. Mirabai Bush, "Uncovering the Heart of Higher Education: The Contemplative Practice Fellowship Program," in *The Heart of Higher Education*, Parker J. Palmer and Arthur Zajonc (San Francisco: Jossey-Bass, 2010), 163.

80. William Sullivan, *Liberal Learning as Quest for Purpose* (New York: Oxford University Press, 2016), 193.

81. Liz Coleman, "A Call to Reinvent Liberal Arts Education," TED, https://www.ted.com/talks/liz_coleman_a_call_to_reinvent_liberal_arts_education?language=en.

6

Vocational Narrative Element

Humans swim in a sea of talking, listening, planning, and reasoning.
—Steven C. Hayes, Eric Fox, Elizabeth V. Gifford, and Kelly G. Wilson[1]

Without a narrative, life has no meaning. Without meaning, learning has no purpose. Without a purpose, schools are houses of detention, not attention.

—Neil Postman [2]

As professional and technical faculty, instructors, and educators, we're invested in staying abreast of new developments and maintaining our subject matter competency, improving our pedagogy and instructional skills, and perhaps most of all, making sure that our students learn the subject matter, the associated skills, and meet our program outcomes. A concern for making connections between our field of study and its technical competencies to explorations of purpose, meaning, and vocation is not normally a part of our educational framework. If we think about vocation at all, we take the possibility of such connections for granted as an implicit, private part of our students' academic experience.

Some of you may take exception to that description, having realized this important oversight at some point in your career. You may have gone so far as to develop a framing pedagogy to help your students discern a vocation in the academic, professional, and technical subjects they study. Most of this effort likely revolves around a specific lexicon of terms with important meaning and connection to vocation as well as ongoing references to various affective elements of study that you know are important to your students. In so doing you probably have noticed how this approach has developed and girded your students' confidence and dedication to their chosen field or, conversely, made it abundantly clear early on that they might have made the wrong choice.

Chapter 6

The place of vocabulary, narrative, and framing is of critical importance to discoveries of meaning, purpose, and vocation in professional and technical collegiate education. This recommendation from Barbara Jacoby and Pamela Mutascio in *Looking In, Reaching Out* serves as a good introduction to an initial strategy for choosing a vocational vocabulary and using it to develop an instructional narrative and vocational framework:

> As you develop your vision, goals, and educational strategy for expanding your curriculum and pedagogy to include explorations of purpose and vocation, and with that, community service-learning, consider carefully the underlying assumptions and concepts pertaining to this vision, goals, and strategy. To do so will help you select and use the correct vocabulary to construct a helpful and compelling narrative in support of your vision.[3]

In the most basic terms, in this chapter we will cover how you are cultivating an orientation, perspective, and gestalt around your discipline using intentional vocabulary and narratives that frame it as a worthy vocation. In short, you want your students to perceive and envision making a life for themselves as a dedicated professional in their field of practice.

To begin, recognize that to weave explorations of purpose, meaning, and vocation together effectively in the curriculum and pedagogy as part of an instructional narrative and vocational framework, you must become more subjective and personal in communicating with your students. This connects directly to the contemplative practices discussed in the previous chapter.

Any discussion of these subjects is inherently personal, and some would say, spiritual. There's that word again, spiritual; when uttered in academia it may create troubling repercussions. As a reminder, here is a condensed version of the definition of "spirituality" first presented in chapter 3: "Spirituality is a way of life that affects and includes every moment of existence. It is at once a contemplative attitude, a disposition to a life of depth, and the search for the ultimate meaning, direction, and belonging." Consider Victor Kazanjian's experience with and interpretation of his interaction with his students at Wellesley College on "moments of meaning":

> As I listened to students tell their stories, the questions that were foremost on their minds were questions which I consider profoundly spiritual: "What is the purpose to all of this learning? What does it mean to be an educated person? What does my learning have to do with my living? How is my learning relevant to the lives of others?" Buried in these stories and these questions was a vocabulary that seemed to bridge the chasm between the language of spirituality and the language of scholarship. I settled on a definition of spirituality in education as that which animates the mind and body, giving meaning, purpose and context to thought, word and action or the meaning-making aspect of learning.[4]

Kazanjian's definition of spirituality in education is compelling, and his identification of a bridging vocabulary between the "language of spirituality" and the "language of scholarship" is helpful and important for framing this relationship. Another important consideration is that the students Kazanjian interviewed are liberal arts majors, an academic forte of Wellesley College.

The liberal arts—literature, history, philosophy, and more—has become a stepchild of our colleges and universities in a rush to emphasize a more instrumental science, technology, engineering, and mathematics (STEM) education. As Andrew Delbanco points out in his book *College: What It Was, Is, and Should Be*, "This is a great loss because they are the legatees of religion in the sense that they provide a vocabulary for formulating ultimate questions of the sort that have always had special urgency for young people."[5]

Picking up on Kazanjian's point again, we start bridging explorations of purpose, meaning, and discerning vocation to a pedagogy of scholarship with the understanding that there is no way to eliminate human subjectivity from human knowing. Put another way, based on Michael Polanyi's interpretation, "We must cross the logical gap between a problem and its solution by relying on the unspecifiable impulse of our heuristic passion, and must undergo as we do so a change of our intellectual personality."[6]

As teachers, we know we've made an important breakthrough when students begin to show evidence of a "heuristic passion" for their studies and what they are learning—they become self-motivated learners with a self-authoring capability. We know who these students are because we find them in a contemplative reverie for the subject and/or discipline they are learning or eagerly standing before us at the end of class enthusiastic with questions and comments.

Effective teachers strike a balance between objectivity and subjectivity in their pedagogy and interpretation of their subject and/or discipline. They range widely in their interpretations, making connections among subjects. They frame their subject and/or discipline broadly and inclusively. An effective teacher, then, is personal as well as professional.[7] Hence, two of the important elements of teaching to inspire vocation, first presented in the introduction, are *affective* pedagogies and *personal knowledge*.

FRAMING

Framing is an important concept for melding explorations of purpose, meaning, and vocation together into professional and technical education. Simply put in the words of linguist George Lakoff, "Frames are mental structures that shape the way we see the world."[8] Jack Mezirow, an educational theorist, has another simple take: "Frames of reference are the structures of assumptions through which we understand our experiences."⁹ A frame of reference may be a composite of several subframes of reference.

Our frames of reference involve both habits of mind and points of view. Habits of mind are simply habitual ways of thinking, feeling, and acting influenced by assumptions drawn from a frame of reference. Habits of mind become articulated in specific points of view that may be manifest in beliefs, value judgments, and attitudes that define a particular interpretation.[10] Habits of mind are more fixed and durable than points of view. Our work as professional and technical educators with the goal of revising and amplifying our curriculum to include explorations of purpose, meaning, and vocation involves transforming both habits of mind and points of view by reframing our students' educational experience.

Our frames of reference underpin our behavior and actions, our goals, and how we judge the results of our actions. Frames affect our reasoning and structure our common sense. Our language and the words we choose are defined by our conceptual frames. Frames provide mental structure for the way we interpret the world. Turning to Lakoff again regarding framing and education, "Reframing is changing the way the public [and students] see the world. It is changing what counts as common sense. Because language activates frames, new language is required for new frames. Thinking differently requires speaking differently."[11]

Most of you will be working with students of a traditional collegiate demographic and young-adult mentality who are entering professional and technical education, as Sharon Daloz Parks describes them:

> with only an interpersonal ethical frame. They have not yet been initiated into critical thought and a connective-systemic way of perceiving the world that would yield a more comprehensive understanding of the significance of their chosen profession and the broad, systemic reach of their own actions.[12]

On the other hand, you are just as likely to have older and/or career-changing students who come to you with a mental framework and supporting narratives around career and vocation already under construction. If so, then you have a leg up in this process and will simply need to recognize their orientation and support their continued search for meaning, purpose, and vocation through a pointed and relevant vocabulary that builds on their evolving narrative and mental framework. As a reminder, such a vocationally oriented group of students can be a helpful cohort in mentoring new students as they learn and use a new vocabulary, educational and professional narratives, and a vocational framework.

Reframing and creating new frames are about ideas. To reiterate, framing and reframing take place through a combination of experience, language, vocabulary, and narrative. The point here for teaching to inspire vocation is that we need to frame our programs within instructional narratives that combine acquiring knowledge and developing skills with discovering meaning, purpose, and vocation. This will require attention to vocabulary, language, and narrative in our pedagogy and other communications with students—in particular, using a shared, professionally relevant, and vocationally oriented language and style of communicating meaning-making narratives.

A point of clarification: it may seem that vocabulary and language are the same; however, vocabulary requires grammar to become language. The basic relationship among frames of reference, narratives, and language is described in the advanced text *Relational Frame Theory*: "a relational frame is the simplest unit that can describe the key elements of speaking with meaning and listening with understanding. Even a simple sentence is often too complex to be understood if any of the defining elements of a relational frame are left out."[13]

As Sharon Parks describes in her quote on the previous page, students usually come to us with a narrow, interpersonal frame of reference. They are then presented with professional and technical instructional narratives that contribute to the development of an equally narrow professional mental framework built around the requirements for a particular profession or job.

Two crucially important elements for assisting students in reframing their education to include discerning vocation are compelling instructional narratives *and* critical reflection. To reiterate an important attribute of contemplative practice and reflection from chapter 5, critical reflection on the assumptions upon which our interpretations, beliefs, and habits of mind or points of view are based most often leads to growth, change, and a deeper understanding of things—we reframe our cognitive orientation to an interpretation of the world.

To ground the connection between reflection and reframing requires reexamining the bi-hemispheric nature of our cognition. Contemplative practice opens and activates cognitive pathways in our right hemisphere. Research shows that the right hemisphere is the locus of mental flexibility and reframing. It is also more open to an array of possibilities and possible solutions to problems than the left hemisphere.

This suggests that activation of the cognitive pathways in the right hemisphere through contemplative practice may be the key to the positive relationship between reflection and reframing. A third element critical to framing professional and technical education is community engagement. We will take up this subject in the next chapter.

A gateway to helping students reframe their orientation to and interpretation of their professional and technical education begins with the valuing associated with their chosen field of study. Those of you who have already begun this process may have recognized that several values reveal themselves in your scholarship, skills training, and dialogue about professional practice. Faculty comments from teaching assessment studies at Alverno College underscored the importance of professional valuing frameworks and personal reflections:

> "I can use the valuing frameworks of a major field of study or profession to address significant issues in personal, professional and societal contexts. I can consistently examine and cultivate my own value system in order to take initiative as a responsible self in personal, professional and societal contexts." Faculty members observed that 1) valuing criteria, when stated in the first person, were more likely to elicit self-reflection from students and 2) the recent literature makes a strong case for integrating, rather than separating, the intellectual with the interpersonal, the more abstract kind of reasoning with concurrent emotional development.[14]

A common value embedded in many professional and technical careers is quality. We will return to quality later in the chapter.

NARRATIVE

Vocabularies, and the narratives created with them, contribute to the formation of powerful, compelling vocational mental frameworks when they articulate altruistic, moral, and ethical values that help organize and guide one's life, including their profession. By the same token, a compelling narrative is one that you can organize your life around.

For example, a great many people in the industrialized world organize their lives around narratives of economic utility and consumerism and live their lives governed by the resulting materialistic and consumerist mental frameworks. An allied and equally powerful modern-day narrative exists around technology—that is, the transformative power of technology for good or ill.

Although these frameworks, and their supporting narratives, possess great power over large numbers of people, one could certainly debate their assets with reams of evidence showing their liabilities in a litany of harmful social, cultural, and individual repercussions. Two influential narratives that are gaining strength in industrialized societies as a counterpoint to those mentioned are "sustainability" and the closely allied narrative of "simplicity," also known as the "slow" movement.

Two important narratives that drive the motivations of many professional and technical science students in the fields of biology, environmental science, horticulture, restoration ecology, and so on are "one with nature" and "Earth stewardship," stories of people working and living in harmony with nature as stewards of the Earth. The resulting mental frameworks have an extraordinary potential for good in the face of the many environmental and social predicaments we face. William Sullivan, in his book *Liberal Learning as a Quest for Purpose*, describes the importance of a powerful narrative for the individual and like-minded groups:

> Narratives "make" the person as much as the person (or group) forms narratives. The positive implication of this approach is that persons can grow toward more vibrant and coherent lives by learning to imagine new stories for themselves and their future, seeking connections with others engaged in a similar quest.[15]

Our students are at the stage in their lives when recognizing and reflecting upon their life's narratives and using a shared vocabulary and style of storytelling is of critical importance for finding their purpose, meaning, and vocation. Douglas Henry, in his essay "Vocation and Story," underscores how important the collegiate experience is to finding one's calling:

> Of all times and places of our lives, the collegiate years offer one of the most auspicious occasions to discern the narrative threads running through otherwise episodic and disconnected life experiences. College invites the rehearsal of one's story and the hearing of others'; such rehearsals begin in de rigueur accounts of hometown, year, major, and aspirations. By moving past superficial summaries, and by recognizing the qualities of good life stories, students are better prepared to hear a genuine calling.[16]

The formation of a new frame of reference is based on the gravity of the perceived truth of the frame's narrative(s). In the *End of Education*, Neil Postman provides a moving explanation: "The measure of a narrative's 'truth' or 'falsity' is in its consequences: does it provide people with a sense of personal identity, a sense of community life, a basis for moral conduct, explanations of that which cannot be known? Without a narrative, life has no meaning. Without meaning, learning has no purpose."[17]

Vaclav Havel famously observed that in America, we have a "crisis in narrative. We are looking for new scientific recipes, new ideologies, new control systems, new institutions."[18] At the time of this writing, it appears that even one of our most foundational narrative frameworks, one we might call the "sanctity of American democracy," or the "American experiment" narrative has lost its hold—its metaphysical raison d'être—on large numbers of citizens. Given this, we have an even more compelling mandate for new and vocationally oriented narratives in professional and technical education.

> Who creates the myths that bind a nation and give purpose and meaning to the idea of a public education? In America, it is the advertisers, the popular musicians and filmmakers . . . teachers are not on the list. It must be clear at the beginning

that schools have not and have never been organized to create forceful, inspiring narratives. They collect them, amplify them, distribute them, ennoble them. They sometimes refute them, mock them, or neglect them. This is why the narratives of economic utility, consumership, technology, and separatism are to be found in the schools now, exerting their force and commanding allegiance.[19]

As the quote on the previous page from Neil Postman points out, we're paddling upstream against a tide of social and cultural narratives that do not serve education well. We must use language and vocabulary carefully to craft new narratives and reframe a new perspective on education that includes a quest for purpose, meaning, and discerning vocation. As the philosopher Ludwig Wittgenstein reminds us, "language is not only the vehicle for thought, it is also the driver."[20] The linguist George Lakoff takes that thinking further: "the use of right language starts with ideas—with the right framing of the issues."[21] It's a framing that reflects the perspective sought.

Within the curriculum and at a classroom scale, a compelling narrative provides the fodder for analytical discourse and critical reflection contributing to the formation of a new frame of reference. In addition to promulgating a narrative(s) around the values associated with the professional practice or technical craft we teach, framing the program of study as a vocational exploration provides students with a narrative of a quest for purpose.

Faculty and instructors can contribute to and build narratives of professionalism that create a professional framework for discerning vocation. In this way, our intent is to create new frames of reference for our students' education and their subsequent life as a professional and practitioner. It invites students to understand themselves as protagonists in a collective drama with real import for their entire life.[22] Douglas Henry, in his essay "Vocation and Story," sums up the importance of narrative in education and finding a calling this way:

> Through its narratives—whether articulated or implied—education invites us to cherish some things and discount others. Education fits us for lives inhabiting particular framing narratives; our story-constituted selves take shape within these worlds. Educators concerned with helping students to explore their callings must therefore attend thoughtfully to the explicit and implicit narratives that they teach and model.[23]

To summarize, revising and amplifying our curriculum for vocation will require reframing our own educational perspectives and expectations as well as those of our students to make the new curriculum vocationally relevant and compelling. To do this we will need to craft new narratives that will provide the conceptual structure for our new frames of reference.

These narratives will be composed using carefully chosen, impactful language and vocabulary. Put simply and elegantly by Shirley Showalter,

"Applied across the curriculum, vocation consists of stories—educator stories, student stories, and stories about our disciplines. Out of these connected stories arise new narrative identities; these in turn can help us hear new and renewed callings."[24]

There are so many storytelling possibilities. For instance, what stories are most important to the vocation of the teacher and the student? We can all tell our students the story of when we first became engaged with our subject matter and it captured our attention and interest. We also have the vocational story about why we teach and what inspired us to become educators.

Regardless of the field of study, our students will have stories to tell us about their previous experiences with the subject matter, no matter how rudimentary. Most students discover some past connection to the subject of the class that informs their choice of study. Telling and revisiting these stories can evoke values, influences, and feelings that create incipient, if not stronger, notions of a calling and vocation.

Simple questions we can ask about our chosen profession will draw out interesting narratives. For instance, in how many ways and by what channels will our professional practice connect us to our community? Is it possible that our professional practice will, in some way, shape the community we serve?[25] Exploring the answers to these questions may produce lucrative narratives within which to frame our discipline as a vocation.

The "one with nature" and "stewardship of the Earth" narratives often resonate with a diverse array of professional and technical students. These narratives easily link scholarship, praxis, and the possibility of vocation in a powerful mental framework for a complete life. However, the initial connection is made to the professional or technical discipline and associated career paths and is then expanded to reveal larger vocational implications. The greater breadth and power of these frameworks and their narratives evolves over time and becomes more obvious as they play out through the curriculum.

The Earth stewardship and one-with-nature frameworks may be interpreted with broad, compelling narratives connected to several subframes having relevance and application in every segment of science and technology. Examples of those subframes are professional practice and craft, the metaphysics of quality, sustainability, and personal and professional fulfillment and well-being, to name a few. Closer examination probably will reveal few professional and technical programs of study where the Earth stewardship and one-with-nature frameworks and narratives are not applicable.

In further consideration of the previous two educational narratives, it is hard to imagine a set of academic narratives with greater need of emphasis in addressing our current and future predicaments as a species on this planet. Other examples of broad, far-reaching, compelling educational narratives that will contribute to the vocational reframing of professional and technical education are civic engagement and/or the American experiment, human well-being, service to humanity, the laws of diversity, and literacy as a key to human civilization, to name just a few.

Returning to the horticulture example, the one with nature and stewardship of the Earth narratives are relevant to every element of horticulture craft and practice, whether it be the technologies associated with plant cultivation, landscape design, or horticulture business practice. A particularly important sub-narrative mentioned earlier is sustainability and sustainable practice, which permeates several dimensions of horticulture practice. One may use the one with nature and stewardship of the Earth narrative frameworks to define and promote horticulture practice as a vocation in the following way.

- Horticulture students develop an intimate connection to nature that becomes their means for helping to sustainably steward the Earth for a meaningful and fulfilling professional and personal life.
- Horticulture graduates implement their practice and the associated crafts according to a metaphysics of quality that makes them a primary source of personal and professional fulfillment and well-being through community service and stewardship.

The previous narratives contribute to vocational frameworks with two important capacities contributing to their application and resilience as Michael Polanyi itemized: first, the power of our conceptual framework, based on reality, to assimilate new experiences; and second, the capacity to adapt this framework in the very act of applying it, so that it may increase its hold on reality.[26]

Regarding the horticulture program example, the Earth stewardship and one with nature narratives lend great meaning and purpose to the curriculum, thereby increasing its relevance, authority, and credibility in helping students visualize it as their vocation. The underlying outcome for horticulture students is that the students frame themselves in a professional/personal narrative as competent horticulture practitioners performing their craft in a sustainable manner to serve the needs of their communities.

LANGUAGE AND VOCABULARY

This brings us to language and vocabulary, the building blocks of narrative and framing. In the early stages of helping your students explore and identify their vocation, introduction of a vocabulary and language of vocation as part of an expanded curriculum can be most impactful. The language and vocabulary we choose for our framing narratives must be clearly defined and well received, and our students must own them. The relationship between language and framing is reciprocal and integral. Put another way by George Lakoff, "All words are defined relative to conceptual frames. When you hear a word, its frame (or collection of frames) is activated in your brain."[27]

A basic rule of thumb regarding language and the choice of vocabulary is to use the language associated with the thinking and concepts you wish to invoke. Another basic rule is that powerful framing language makes good use of metaphors and analogies.

To revise and amplify our curriculum to include teaching to inspire vocation, we must use the language of vocation to frame our students' professional and technical education. Put another way, from the service-learning guide *Looking In, Reaching Out*, "Explorations in and discovery of vocation is dependent upon vocabulary and words to describe concepts, practices, and to shape our thoughts, our associations, our values, and our orientation toward the discovery and support of vocation."[28] The power of a conceptual framework and its narratives grows and becomes more valuable as students use the vocabulary and key terminology more frequently.

For instance, important vocabulary in the example horticulture program includes craft, practice, quality (metaphysics of), stewardship, sustainability, spirituality, fulfillment, and well-being. As you might imagine, none of these words belongs to the lexicon of scientific or professional jargon common to horticulture, plant science, or their allied fields. However, they are important terms for bridging an understanding of the discipline with praxis and discerning vocation.

Throughout the units of study, laboratories, and field experiences, that vocabulary and elements of the framing narratives are used in conjunction with horticultural information to create mental images of professional practice as it relates to a life's vocation. For instance, this vocabulary may be used for making connections between successful plant propagation, sustainable practice, quality craftwork, community service, and professional/personal fulfillment. The vocabulary and narrative may be interspersed within your pedagogy, but most strongly emphasized within a moment of pause and reflection following instruction and practice on a particular technique or concept of study.

The language and vocabulary of vocation used in the horticulture program example is broad, dynamic, and flexible, making it very applicable to a range of other professional and technical curricula. The breadth of this language means that it stretches across questions of a students' potential work life, a major concern within the curriculum. But more than that, it also stretches into what sort of community involvements they may participate in and what their leisure and avocational lives might be like.

The vocabulary and language of vocation are dynamic in recognition of how students' professional life will evolve along with their personal life. We must remember that vocational exploration, analysis, and discernment is a process that continues throughout one's life. The flexibility of the language of vocation makes it possible for adoption by a variety of professional and technical programs.[29] Mindful of these important aspects of the language of vocation, consider carefully the underlying assumptions and concepts pertaining to your vision, goals, and strategies for expanding your curriculum and pedagogy to include explorations of purpose and vocation. These considerations will help you select and use the correct vocabulary to construct a helpful, compelling narrative in support of your vision.[30]

A vocational narrative often contains a highly diverse language of moral character, well-being, professional practice or craft, and community service. However, before pursuing those linguistic subjects, we need to reiterate the orthodox baggage with which the word "vocation" is freighted—usually a very narrow substitute for "gainful employment." This, of course, is why the term "vocational education" is still sometimes used to designate training for a particular trade. This presents a particular challenge for our vocational vocabulary and language to avoid creating an oversimplified narrative pigeonholed in job preparation and employment opportunities. Let's expand our vocational lexicon beginning with its moral implications.

Determining one's purpose requires judgments about what constitutes a worthy purpose and the necessary actions to pursue that purpose. Making judgments about a life that is worth living and how best to pursue such a life involves questions and issues of morality. Most of our students come to us with little experience deliberating moral questions and often don't possess the vocabulary for such in-depth explorations.

We can help our students develop a more extensive, more useful moral vocabulary that will provide them with the means to reflect on and evaluate their callings and potential vocations in a broader context than job and career. As David S. Cunningham points out, "Equipped with the language of virtue, our students will be able to ask a different set of questions about their potential vocations. [The] hope is that [students] will not only focus on what seems practical, but will also consider what goals and purposes can truly be called good—and how these might be rightly achieved."[31]

Discussing questions of morality—and its ally, spirituality—is a prickly matter. However, in this day and age, when high levels of white-collar crime and corruption most often revolve around matters of professional ethics, virtue, and morality, it seems clear that more attention needs to be paid to these subjects in professional and technical education. The exploration of ethics, morals, and virtues is certainly relevant to a professional and technical curriculum.

Every area of professional scholarship and technical practice has a code of ethics, although some are made more explicit than others. These codes exist within a moral framework that may form the basis of important lessons and conversations around what constitutes virtue and right livelihood.

Referring to the quote by David S. Cunningham, I appreciate his use of the word "virtue" as an all-encompassing, less threatening term for discussing questions of morality. A professional code of ethics provides a basis for moral conduct and a virtuous practice, craft, or service. A moral logic may be the basis for such a code articulated, for example, as participation in citizenship and a shared responsibility for the welfare of humanity and the environment.

Inevitably, discussions of professional codes of ethics, conduct, and virtues of character will lead to explorations of the same in the personal lives of students. Authenticity in professional ethics, conduct, and virtue can only be invoked if it is also reflected in our personal lives. Class discussions of professional ethics and virtues will orient and equip students to ask questions related to the professional and personal trajectories of their lives and about the potential for discovering a vocation connected to their areas of study. Cunningham provides some helpful questions to stimulate further discussion on this subject in Best Practices 6.1.

Best Practices 6.1: Self Query on Ethics and Virtues

- What are the excellences of character [virtues] that I hope my own life will exhibit?
- To what degree have I seen these character traits at work in other people, and what criteria do I use to evaluate whether a particular life is a "good" life?
- What will I need to do to be truly happy in life—not just in the sense of a passing emotion, but in the sense of living a truly fulfilled and fulfilling life?
- Does a particular vocational direction encourage me to develop excellences of character that will make me a better person?
- Conversely, does an apparent calling to which I feel particularly compelled have some (perhaps partially hidden) features that might obstruct my own moral development, or that might curtail my progress toward the good?
- What are my present character strengths, and how will they contribute to the vocational direction that I'm considering?
- What other character traits are necessary if I am to respond well to the calling that I am discerning, and how will I develop these?[32]

Questions and discussions of ethics, morals, and virtues naturally arise in connection with the narratives associated with established frameworks, such as the examples of sustainability and the metaphysics of quality mentioned earlier. Identify and take note of these possible discussion points in the curriculum as places to shape and reshape the narrative and reframe a vocational perspective.

Returning to our horticulture example, professional ethics and personal morals often factor into the metaphysics of quality and sustainability when it comes to implementing practice and craft. This blend of considerations and influences is part of the professional narrative and framework of practice and service. Included in this narrative is the understanding that if the budget, demands for service, the needs of the client, or a combination of all these factors prohibit a sustainable application, the practitioner may decline the project, contract, or service.

Students often raise the question of how to deal with circumstances where they are asked to do something that compromises their sustainability and/or quality ethic. The answer is that the necessary strength of resolve for supporting such professional and personal virtues develops by nurturing supporting ethical and moral frameworks. As instructors, we do this by sharing narratives, or stories, about how to invoke those frameworks to help students navigate such predicaments through client education, constructive compromise, or amicable separation.

The vocabulary of "practice," "craft," "sustainability," and "quality" and their narratives are brimming with meaning related to the virtues of character related to professional success, personal fulfillment, and discerning vocation. Coming back to the questions David S. Cunningham poses about virtues and vocation, the question may arise more than once in your classes about the kind of virtues necessary for a professional or technical practitioner to possess to develop a skilled and quality craft and a viable and sustainable practice. Such questions invariably touch on issues of character.

Students often feel called by the virtues of character associated with a particular vocation. As Mark Schwehn points out in his essay, "Good Teaching: Character Formation and Vocational Discernment," "Students look to educators as examples of how they should treat one another and one another's ideas in an effort to learn and live together in community. So, whether they realize it or not, faculty and staff are always about the business of character formation."[33]

CRAFT, PRACTICE, AND QUALITY

"Craft" and "practice," two important terms in the vocabulary of vocation, have already appeared several times in this text. Make it a point not to refer to the professional and technical practice and craft you teach as simply "employment," a "position," "work," or a "job." "Craft" is a term that has broad application to most of the areas of study and training within the domain of professional and technical education. Perhaps first and foremost, "to craft" means to make or do something skillfully, but it is more.

We should add three dimensions to the meaning of craft: intention, care (skill), and learning. When we set out to make or do something, we do so intentionally with a purpose in mind. Experienced, skilled craftsmen will reflect on and clarify their intention and purpose as they proceed toward completing their craft.

The intentionality of our craft translates into care for the process and the outcome, one we want to obtain to the best of our ability—part of the metaphysics of quality. With intention and care, we apply the most appropriate and focused skill to our craft. Finally, as purposeful, caring, and skillful craftsmen, we seek to improve our craft by learning as we practice through reflection, adjustment, and invention.

With that perspective, you can see why the multidimensional, deeply involved nature of craft is a powerful part of its allure and relevance to discerning and living a vocation. Our frames of reference, and the narratives we use to build and enforce those frames, define our profession and vocation as a practice involving a broad and sophisticated range of craft. Consider Sharon Parks's compelling explanation of those concepts:

> Every profession is an art and a practice. Becoming a professional requires knowledge of the field and the development of compassion and competence, grounded in a sense of deep purpose that can orient adaptive learning and adaptive leadership. It requires an initiation into practice (including always working on the edge of one's own knowing and learning from failure), which the art and practice of any true profession demands. If this promise of emerging adult lives is not met by this quality of commitment to excellence, professional education may be reduced to the acquisition of mere training and credentials.[34]

This quote articulates how apt the terms craft and practice are within narratives and frameworks for what your students become: scientists, artists, practitioners, and craftsmen—lifetime vocations.

A "metaphysics of quality" is a particularly important narrative and frame of practice for trade crafts, such as carpentry, and may constitute a "first principle" of that practice. The same may be said for many professional practices, certainly medicine. Metaphysics of quality (MOQ) is a theory of reality introduced in Robert Pirsig's philosophical novel *Zen and the Art of Motorcycle Maintenance* and most often used in reference to the Platonic conception of rationality that Pirsig sought to challenge by reconciling the spiritual (*Zen*), artistic (*art*), and scientific (*motorcycle maintenance*) realms within the unifying paradigm of the metaphysics of quality.[35]

However, as fascinating a subject as it is for a philosophy text, the focus here is on the simple element of MOQ dealing with attention to quality in practice, as opposed to the interpretation of reality embodied in the complete metaphysics of quality.

Those practicing a *craft*, whether it be horticulture, accounting, health care, or auto mechanics, live with an acute sense of technique and meaning giving them an immediacy that guides their work and dedication. "Craft," based on an entry in Wikipedia, comes from "Middle English craft ('strength, skill'), or Old English cræft, from Proto-West Germanic kraftu, from Proto-Germanic kraftuz ('strength, power'), or the cognate with German kraft ('strength, power, force, energy, employee')."[36]

In this country, we tend to stereotype our understanding of craft to mean skill and design associated with art, although following the German definition of kraft, it should also be about doing as well as making. Hence my inclusion of accounting in the above statement about those practicing craft. Attentiveness, patience, accuracy, precision, interpretation, and other qualities are important to practicing the craft of accounting.

Richard Sennett makes the case for the broad application of the word "craft":

> Craftsmanship names an enduring, basic human impulse, the desire to do a job well for its own sake. Craftsmanship cuts a far wider swath than skilled manual labor; it serves the computer programmer, the doctor, and the artist; parenting improves when it is practiced as a skilled craft, as does citizenship.[37]

Craft often involves the combination of abstract intellect with practical intelligence; a perfect example is farming, particularly bio-intensive and organic farming. A craft may be identified as any practice that involves a blend of skills and capabilities within the cognitive, kinesthetic, and affective domains—in other words, head, hands, and heart.

From a vocational standpoint, and contained within the metaphysics of quality, is the understanding that a good life is made through craftsmanship—that is, the craftsmanlike engagement with the actions, objects, and relationships of ordinary experience through caring about what you do, be it working in an office, on a motorcycle, the CEO of a large company, or as a shepherd. Practicing a craft, in the words of craftsman Peter Korn, "calls forth a symphony of human capacities that are intrinsically fulfilling"[38] to any craft professional. "Intrinsically fulfilling" is a critical element of vocation.

Our exploration of craft brings us back to an important component of craft: having a sense of "flow" in your work. The groundbreaking work of Csikszentmihalyi on the concept of flow was first described in chapter 5. Csikszentmihalyi observed a number of painters as part of a study carried out in the early 1970s. He noted how artists became completely engrossed in the process of making a painting, the work filling their thoughts twenty-four hours a day, yet he was surprised to find that

> the artists I was observing almost immediately lost interest in the canvas they had just painted. Typically, they turned the finished canvas around and stacked it against a wall. Nor were they particularly eager to show it off, or very hopeful about selling it. They could hardly wait to start on a new one.[39]

Whether we're talking about painters, accountants, designers, or a host of other practitioners involved in their craft, satisfaction and fulfillment most often come in the process, being in the flow of their craft.

Most people experience immersion in a transcendent flow of experience through the practice of a hobby or an avocation, such that when they emerge from the experience, they're startled to realize how much time has passed and how relaxed and revitalized they feel. A transcendent flow is also the hallmark of a practice, craft, and endeavor that has vocational significance. Experiencing flow is a great subject to share with your students in reflection, particularly after a successful experiential learning interval, such as a hands-on laboratory or project.

It's critically important to talk about and create narrative around shared experiences of flow to sensitize students to its possibility and importance to their professional and personal fulfillment and discerning vocation. The ceramicist, poet, and teacher M. C. Richards puts the practice of craft and flow into wonderful relief:

> The [craftsman] has an experience of meaning. He feels himself drawn in a kind of spiritual traffic; sensations of energy and excitement course through him like a new life; sensations of import are unmistakable; the value is the response that is taking place in him organically; it is his nature to respond more than ordinary men do. "Awe before the pure phenomenon." Goethe. Out of this spiritual traffic is born a [product] through the channel of breath, the *spiritus* of the poet. The experience flows like a charge into the organism. It spreads, its stirs, it breeds sound and picture, it warms and enlightens.[40]

Experiencing a sense of flow in our practice is wonderful and meaningful. However, even the most dedicated practitioners may only experience flow on occasion. It is all too easy to inflate the discussion and discovery of vocation and calling into an overarching and noble quest for a supreme epiphany of who we are and what we are to do. We must keep in mind that any of our students who shows a special skill in a craft or practice, be it bookkeeping, carpentry, or physician's assistant, is also engaged in universal values of creativity, expressiveness, and caring. These are the products of vocation that are as important in small things as they are in big ones. The sense of destiny in our vocation can give profound significance to the seemingly day-to-day insignificant things we do.

When dedicated practitioners in any field are fully engaged in what they are doing for its own sake, they are practicing a craft. Those of you teaching professional and technical subjects outside the orthodox arenas of craft work (e.g., woodworking, textile arts, ceramics) will have a greater challenge framing your subjects as practices involving craft. You will need to rely on compelling narratives to establish that framing. In so doing, you will be helping your students perceive their career path as a calling and a vocation by reframing their perspective on the nature of what they are learning and how the associated profession (practice) is defined.

Many people, in their personal search for meaning and purpose in their work, can find new definition and perspective in their profession as they gain experience. This kind of creative "job crafting" elicits a stronger sense of purpose, meaning, engagement, resilience, and thriving from their work. It may involve, for example, building stronger relationships with coworkers, or evolving some of the specific tasks associated with their work, changes that can help evoke the same psychological outcomes that accompany discerning your vocation.

Some might consider business as a difficult collegiate major with which to discern a vocation. It's not that business, and its many sub-specialties, are inherently difficult to find vocation in; it's about how they are framed in education and in practice. As Jay J. Janney and Della Stanley-Green point out in *Engaging with Vocation on Campus*,

> Business schools encourage students to develop more specialized knowledge, so employers are more likely to hire them upon graduation. What they do not ask of students is discernment of their sense of vocation: Instead, students choose their majors because of market demand, income, and prestige. We do not seek to diminish the value of those attributes, noting only they are less suited for contributing to deep satisfaction in a person's career.[41]

Not surprisingly, and as implied in the quote above, business schools emphasize an instrumental approach to success in business measured by market share, profit, and prestige. So, though business graduates may be successful by those metrics, they may still be left feeling empty. As business educators, we need to augment those requirements for business success with the noninstrumental elements that will help them to discover their vocation in this field of endeavor.

As with other, similar professional and technical majors focused on strictly instrumental approaches to success, business educators may craft vocational narratives using codes of professionalism and ethics to provide purpose and meaning to their discipline, thereby reframing for discerning vocation. As pointed out earlier in this chapter, these codes exist within a moral framework that may form the basis of important lessons and conversations around what constitutes a meaningful practice and vocation. Building narratives around these concepts, coupled with intervals of critical reflection, will help to form a framework for making meaning, finding purpose, and discerning vocation.

You may go on from that point to expand such a framework to include the technical and task-oriented elements of your major area of study, framed as professional "practices" and "craft," creating an entirely new perspective on their relevance and impact. Another domain in need of reframing or highlighting is the profession's social environment, the various and sundry array of relationships one may look forward to and cultivate.

Finally, cognitive elements of the profession may be framed to enrich the students' understanding of and appreciation for the purpose of their work.[42] In other words, create an attitude adjustment narrative for the discipline that provides students with new ways of thinking about the profession's nature, purpose, and impact, all of which have a positive influence on discerning vocation.

Those of you teaching in the traditional technical and trade skill disciplines, particularly those considered traditional "handcrafts," should find teaching to inspire vocation a much easier proposition. The idea of these professions as practice, craft, and a vocation are a common part of the narrative and the overall educational framework. Still, the tendency may be to focus only on the technical skills and their instrumental application, assuming that the affective and more metaphysical aspects of the craft are perceived, interpreted, and internalized by students as part of an implicit process.

The poet, philosopher, ceramicist, and educator M. C. Richards speaks for all craft makers and artists when she writes, "The handcrafts stand to perpetuate the living experience of contact with natural elements—something primal, immediate, personal, material, a dialogue between our dreams and the forces of nature." Identifying and focusing on this dynamic forms much of the basis for her work as a ceramics educator; it's a major part of her educational narrative and artistic framework for becoming a ceramicist. Many neophyte ceramic artists likely come to this understanding through their craft, but Richards makes a point of it in her teaching as a core cognitive and affective element of this practice.

Richards goes on to write compellingly about the impact of handcraft on the breadth of the practitioner's life, a concept that is applicable within all the domains of professional and technical education:

> the craftsman has the opportunity to extend, throughout all aspects of his life, the process and insights of his craft. Deeply experiencing the processes of his labor and his inspiration, he may deepen his perceptions of quality and relationship. Moral capacity may be thought of as the ability to be guided in one's behavior

by the standards of quality to which one gives inner allegiance. Centering in the moral sphere enables one to extend one's commitment to quality from one point through all other points.[43]

Consider further Richards's portrayal of the deep "perceptions of quality and relationship" that craftsmen have in their practice as a means of identifying affective elements you can use for crafting narratives within other professions.

The perception that craft brings deeper, more meaningful rewards to the practitioner goes back centuries. One can find in the writings of Alfred the Great, King of Wessex from 871 to 899, the use of the word "cræft" to describe a state of knowledge or wisdom combined with talent, skill, and merit associated with a physical skill. He also uses cræft as a kind of synonym for virtue, in the sense of spiritual skill or excellence.[44]

The "moral capacity" and "standards of quality" to which Richards refers as "extended process" and "insights" developed through the practice of handcraft touched on in Robert Pirsig's metaphysics of quality and, to reiterate a previous point, are applicable to all areas of study in professional and technical education.

The narratives associated with handcrafts and the crafts movement are useful for framing an educational approach to exploring purpose, meaning, and vocation, particularly as they empower the word "craft" and "practice" with a range of useful meanings for professional and technical education. These narratives, as pointed out above, began centuries ago but became pointedly refined at the beginning of the industrial age through the work of John Ruskin and William Morris, described in chapter 2. The philosopher and historian Thomas Carlyle expressed concern about the growing change of mind-set toward product and profit in the early days of the industrial revolution when he wrote, "Men are grown mechanical in head and heart, as well as hand."[45]

Carlyle was worried about the degrading influence on the understanding of and appreciation for craft as it relates to the quality of life. Ruskin and Morris recognized this concern and worked to push back against the dehumanizing impacts of industrialization with the birth of the Arts and Crafts Movement. Their belief was that local communities of craftsmen should make things through concentrated, heartfelt attention to materials to produce quality products for the community.

Maggie Jackson, in her insightful and instructive book *Distracted: The Erosion of Attention and the Coming Dark Age*, points out that Morris

> argued that happiness will elude us "if we hand over the whole responsibility of the detail of our daily lives to machines and their drivers." [Morris's] genius lay in the totality of his efforts and his ability to see clearly the steep costs of an age that values the material and the efficient above the immeasurable and the human.[46]

Morris was particularly sensitive to the importance of work as a mind and body experience that resulted in a state he called "repose amidst energy," another name for Csikszentmihalyi's concept of flow. Morris, Richards, and many other craftsmen understand that their work is an experience of meaning. Working with Morris's "state of repose amidst energy" places the craftsman into a kind of spiritual traffic where sensations of energy and excitement bring new life.

The crux of concern by the writers and activists referred to previously is that, against the rising tide of automation and increasing digital complexity, we are becoming further divorced from one of the principal characteristics that defines us as human beings: we are makers and crafters of things. Not only that, but we have created a society that looks down on tradespeople who use their hands in their vocation.

In Matthew Crawford's book *Shop Class as Soulcraft*, he makes a critical point about the requirements for and capabilities of tradespeople:

> Their relationship to objects enacts a more solid sort of command, based on real understanding. For this very reason, his work also chastens the easy fantasy of mastery that permeates modern culture. Such work requires that the craftsmen, tradesmen, and repairmen begin each project or job by getting outside of their own head and notice things . . . in fact, in areas of well-developed craft practices, technological developments typically preceded and gave rise to advances in scientific understanding, not vice versa. The surgeon's judgement is simultaneously technical and deliberative, and that mix is the source of its power. This could be said of any manual skill that is diagnostic.[47]

Creativity is an all-important ingredient in the cognitive capabilities of craftmen. Both Crawford and Pirsig make the point that a large part of that creativity must be directed at "problem finding" as well as the commonly thought of element of "problem solving." The challenge of recognizing the correct or offending problem is held out as a critical capability for craftsmen, and not just them, but for all careers and areas of study common to professional and technical education programs.

When it comes to the preservation and repair of machines, Crawford—a PhD in political philosophy and skilled motorcycle mechanic—states that "this challenge demands cognitive skills in a range of areas from mathematics to physics."[48] It also requires that the practitioners care personally about what they are doing, a measure of their understanding and grasp of purpose, meaning, and sense that they are living their vocation.

Robert Pirsig describes a comical but frustrating experience in *Zen and the Art of Motorcycle Maintenance* about dealing with ineffectual mechanics who did more damage to his motorcycle than good. The reason the mechanics were so ineffectual, counterproductive, and damaging is because they did their work with "nothing personal in it." They felt no loyalty, dedication, or calling in their work and, therefore, possessed no ethic of quality in their practice.

The level of care and attention to performance is well known to top-flight athletes. Reflecting on her perfect score at the 1976 Olympic Games, gymnast Nadia Comaneci said, "During my routine and even after it, I did not think it was all that perfect. I thought it was pretty good, but athletes don't think about history when making history. They think about what they're doing, and that's how it gets done."[49]

Comaneci's point is that one's attention is focused on standards intrinsic to the practice. Other than service to a client and/or the community, other externalities that may be acquired through one's practice and craft, typically money or recognition, are secondary if of concern at all.

An intrinsic part of the point being made about attention and care in our work relates, again, to a metaphysics of quality. When we are living out our vocation, we engage in our practice and craft (and other aspects of our lives) with an attention to quality that often boils down to being concerned about *what is best*. An expression of this concern in practice and craft is expressed in the use of the word "preservation" rather than "maintenance" or "upkeep." Preservation means to protect a thing or a group of things from different hazards such as destruction or deterioration—to preserve it in its primary, or *best*, condition.

A determination of what is best involves our full cognitive capabilities, beginning with the right hemisphere of our brain for a complete contextualization of what we perceive, the full picture of the project, work, or item. Then, it takes a detailed scrutiny using our left hemisphere to notice the underlying form(s) of the idea or work before us, which is returned to the right hemisphere for a summary view and assessment.

This fully cognitive approach is the only one that will provide a complete understanding of what constitutes "what is best" and how to proceed accordingly. Being fully cognitive requires great peace of mind, or a state of mindfulness, as explained in chapter 5 on contemplative practice. Instructions for any practice, craft, or process should begin with the recommendation: "requires great peace of mind."

Peter Korn summarizes an important element of Robert Pirsig's metaphysics of quality as well as his own take on the importance of craft in his observation that "a good life may be found through craftsman-like engagement with the actions, objects, and relationships of ordinary experience, through caring about what you do."[50] This perspective is certainly one we want to achieve in educational narratives and framing using the vocabulary of vocation in our curriculum. One more parting thought on framing from Peter Korn:

Every person on the planet navigates his life according to a singular, fluid, highly complex mental map [frame] that determines his goals, strategies, and tactics, his ideas of selfhood and truth.[51]

Textbox 6.1 Teaching Takeaways

- Intentional vocabulary, narrative, and framing are of critical importance to discoveries of meaning, purpose, and vocation.
- Any discussion of meaning, purpose, and vocation is inherently personal, and some would say, somewhat spiritual.
- Use a bridging vocabulary between the "language of scholarship" and the "language of spirituality" to bring out meaning, purpose, and vocation in your pedagogy.
- Frames of reference are the structures of assumptions through which we understand our experiences. Careful framing is important for melding explorations of purpose, meaning, and vocation together with professional and technical education.
- "Reframing is changing the way the students see the world. It is changing what counts as common sense. Because language activates frames, new language is required for new frames. Thinking differently requires speaking differently." (George Lakoff)
- The power of a conceptual framework and its narratives grows and becomes more valuable as students use the vocabulary and reference the narrative more frequently.
- A vocational narrative contains a highly diverse language of moral character, well-being, professional practice or craft, and community service.
- "To craft" means to make or do something skillfully.
- Craftsmanship cuts a far wider swath than skilled manual labor; it serves the computer programmer, the doctor, and the artist; parenting improves when it is practiced as a skilled craft, as does citizenship. (Richard Sennett)
- It is possible and necessary to reframe the nature of any profession as one of craft and special practice that can evoke a sense of calling and vocation.
- A good life may be found through craftsmanlike engagement with the actions, objects, and relationships of ordinary experience, through caring about what you do. (Peter Korn)
- Working in groups, ask students to identify elements of their profession or technical area of study that require a craftwork approach for success.

NOTES

1. Steven C. Hayes, Eric Fox, Elizabeth V. Gifford, and Kelly G. Wilson, "Derived Relational Responding as Learned Behavior," in *Relational Frame Theory: A Post-Skinnerian Account of Human Language and Cognition*, ed. Steven C. Hayes, Dermot Barnes-Holmes, and Bryan Roche (New York: Kluwer Academic/Plenum, 2001), 3.
2. Neil Postman, *The End of Education* (New York: Vintage, 1995), 7.
3. Elaine K. Ikeda, Marie G. Sandy, and David M. Donahue, "Navigating the Sea of Definitions," in *Looking In, Reaching Out*, ed. Barbara Jacoby and Pamela Mutascio (Boston: Campus Compact, 2010), 20.
4. A. W. Chickering, J. C. Dalton, and L. Stamm, *Encouraging Authenticity and Spirituality in Higher Education* (San Francisco: Jossey-Bass, 2006), 117.
5. Andrew Delbanco, *College: What It Was, Is, and Should Be* (Princeton, NJ: Princeton University Press, 2012), 99.
6. Michael Polanyi, *Personal Knowledge* (Chicago: University of Chicago Press, 1974), 143.
7. William Deresiewicz, *Excellent Sheep: The Miseducation of the American Elite and the Way to a Meaningful Life* (New York: Free Press, 2014), 183–84.
8. George Lakoff, *Don't Think of an Elephant* (White River Junction, VT: Chelsea Green, 2004), xv.
9. J. Mezirow, "Transformative Learning: Theory to Practice," in *New Directions for Adult and Continuing Education*, 74 (1997): 5.
10. Mezirow, "Transformative Learning," 5.
11. Lakoff, *Don't Think of an Elephant*, xv.
12. Sharon Daloz Parks, *Big Questions, Worthy Dreams: Mentoring Emerging Adults in Their Search for Meaning, Purpose, and Faith* (San Francisco: Jossey-Bass, 2011), 246.
13. Hayes, Fox, Gifford, and Wilson, "Derived Relational Responding," 34.
14. Chickering, Dalton, and Stamm, *Encouraging Authenticity*, 237–38.
15. William Sullivan, *Liberal Learning as a Quest for Purpose* (New York: Oxford University Press, 2016), 84.
16. Douglas Henry, "Vocation and Story," in *At This Time and In This Place*, ed. David S. Cunningham (New York: Oxford University Press, 2016), 169.
17. Postman, *The End of Education*, 7.
18. Postman, *The End of Education*, 23.
19. Postman, *The End of Education*, 59.
20. Postman, *The End of Education*, 83.
21. Lakoff, *Don't Think of an Elephant*, 23.
22. Sullivan, *Liberal Learning*, 122.
23. Henry, "Vocation and Story," 187.
24. Shirley Showalter, "Called to Tell Our Stories," in *Vocation across the Academy: A New Vocabulary for Higher Education*, ed. David S. Cunningham (New York: Oxford University Press, 2017), 68.

25. Jeff Brown, "Unplugging the GPS: Rethinking Professional Undergraduate Degree Programs," in *Vocation across the Academy: A New Vocabulary for Higher Education*, ed. David S. Cunningham (New York: Oxford University Press, 2017), 223.

26. Polanyi, *Personal Knowledge*, 317.

27. Lakoff, *Don't Think of an Elephant*, preface.

28. Ikeda, Sandy, and Donahue, "Navigating the Sea of Definitions," 17.

29. David S. Cunningham, "Introduction," in *At This Time and In This Place: Vocation in Higher Education*, ed. David S. Cunningham (New York: Oxford University Press, 2016), 10–12.

30. Ikeda, Sandy, and Donahue, "Navigating the Sea of Definitions," 20.

31. David S. Cunningham, "Vocation and Virtue," in *At This Time and In This Place: Vocation in Higher Education*, ed. David S. Cunningham (New York: Oxford University Press, 2016), 191.

32. Cunningham, "Vocation and Virtue," 190.

33. David Schwehn, "Good Teaching: Character Development and Vocation Discernment," in *Vocation across the Academy: A New Vocabulary for Higher Education*, ed. David S. Cunningham (New York: Oxford University Press, 2017), 294.

34. Parks, *Big Questions*, 250–51.

35. Anthony McWatt, "Robert Pirsig & His Metaphysics of Quality" in *Philosophy Now*, https://philosophynow.org/issues/122/Robert_Pirsig_and_His_Metaphysics_of_Quality.

36. "Craft" etymology from Wikipedia, https://en.wiktionary.org/wiki/craft.

37. Richard Sennett, *The Craftsman* (New Haven, CT: Yale University Press, 2009).

38. Peter Korn, *Why We Make Things and Why It Matters: The Education of a Craftsman* (Boston: David R. Godine, 2015).

39. Mihaly Csikszentmihalyi, *Beyond Boredom and Anxiety: Experiencing Flow in Work and Play* (San Francisco: Jossey-Bass, 1975), xiv.

40. M. C. Richards, *Centering in Pottery, Poetry, and the Person* (Middletown, CT: Wesleyan University Press, 1989), 93.

41. Jay J. Janney and Della Stanley-Green, "An Instrumental Approach to Teaching a Non-instrumental View to Vocation within Business Schools," in *Engaging with Vocation on Campus*, ed. Karen Lovett and Stephen Wilhoit (New York: Routledge, 2022), 166.

42. Bryan J. Dik and Ryan D. Duffy, *Make Your Job a Calling* (West Conshohocken, PA; Templeton Press, 2012), 135.

43. Richards, *Centering in Pottery, Poetry, and the Person*, 62.

44. Alex Langlands, *Cræft: An Inquiry into the Origins and True Meaning of Traditional Crafts* (New York: Norton, 2019), 17.

45. David Levy, "Head, Heart, and Hand: Cultivating the Contemplative in Higher Education," at the First Annual Association for Contemplative Mind in Higher Education Conference: The Contemplative Heart of Higher Education, April 24–26, 2009, Amherst College, Amherst, Massachusetts.

46. Maggie Jackson, *Distracted: The Erosion of Attention and the Coming Dark Age* (New York: Prometheus Books, 2009), 88–89.

47. Matthew Crawford, *Shop Class as Soulcraft* (New York: Penguin, 2009), 16, 22, 25.

48. Crawford, *Shop Class as Soulcraft*, 36.

49. Bill Penington, "Perfection Is Afterthought, Some Perfect Examples Say," *New York Times*, February 3, 2008, 1, 20.

50. Peter Korn, *Why We Make Things and Why It Matters* (Boston: David R. Godine, 2013), 13.

51. Korn, *Why We Make Things*, 109.

7

Experiential Learning Element

Experiential learning allows us to reimagine what it means to be human through shared contexts of meaning and living. It allows us to reimagine our world.

—Parker Palmer[1]

We need to be intentional about helping students connect the processes they learn for good, sophisticated work in the classroom or lab to the ways they think about and act in civic space.

—Craig Kaplowitz[2]

What could be more basic to professional and technical education than experiential learning? How else to fully learn a practice, skill, or trade? For this reason, many professional and technical programs and courses include a laboratory, shop, studio, or other appropriate venue for students to learn hands-on procedures, conduct experiments, and practice craft techniques.

For example, horticulture programs usually have three such venues: a laboratory classroom used for dissecting and experimenting with plants to better understand their taxonomy, anatomy, and physiology; a greenhouse for research and practice in propagating and growing plants; the college campus for learning and practicing plant preservation and conservation techniques as well as landscape design.

Providing laboratories and relevant work spaces for students requires larger infrastructure budgets. It also means that, to take advantage of these facilities, we continuously work on our own professional and technical competency in the relevant skills, practices, craft, and techniques to effectively teach those skills to our students.

Laboratory and shop time is not only the kinesthetic, or hands-on, part of the program but is also an affective, or heartfelt, part of the program. After instruction and practice of any procedure or craft, allocate time to a mindful moment about the physical and emotional impact of the skill or process. For instance, after instruction and practice on a particular pruning method in a horticulture course on the subject, students spend a few minutes to examine and think about what they have done. The instructor spends another few minutes asking them about what they have done and how they felt about it. If warranted, the instructor provides some commentary about how this new skill fits into the entire practice and contributes to feelings of competence and capability in horticulture practice, considerations, and thoughts that contribute to a vocational framing of this part of the students' education.

Laboratories and shops are often essential elements of professional and technical education programs, but they may not go far enough in helping our students find meaning and purpose in what they are learning. Other types of experiential learning that "enable students to apply their knowledge in real time, in real places, with real people, and with real consequences"[3]—such as internships, apprenticeships, community engagement programs, and community-engaged learning—can be powerful generators of purpose, meaning, and discerning vocation.

Regarding faculty preparedness to lead experiential learning programs, it's incumbent upon professional and technical faculty to have a high degree of competence in the skills, practices, and technologies associated with their discipline. Still, it is unreasonable to assume that faculty have *every* competence required in fields with rapidly changing technologies. Also, within any given discipline often it is possible to apply skills and practices correctly or effectively in more than one way.

Bringing in an outside expert is often necessary to expose students to a range of practice and technology. It can also be a useful form of external validation and a source of attention-getting instructional diversity. Be sure to take advantage of experienced students as guides for small-group practice.

In disciplines with rapidly changing technologies and practices, and/or multiple application methods, focus hands-on practice on the most commonly implemented or basic techniques as standard approaches. For production or other kinds of technologies implemented by teams or in groups, choreograph student practice in the most common way used in the profession. Be sure to make variabilities in practice known to your students and encourage them to personalize, modify, and improve their technique.

The likelihood of discovering vocation is high when students invest their own ideas and approaches into a practice. Avoid the use of laboratory and other experiential learning time for rote instruction on new practices, techniques, and craft. Experiential learning is rife with opportunities to explore broader, deeper connections to knowledge, skills, and explorations in discerning vocation within their professional and technical education. In addition, the student as teacher, either through prior knowledge or personal innovation, can create a strong personal and professional investment in the practice and/or craft.

Regarding specific types of experiential learning, apprenticeships associated with craft guilds have a centuries-old history and are still important to trade and handcraft today. The relevance, quality, and efficacy of apprenticeships are strongly dependent upon the standards imposed by the trade association and the professional practice of the craftsman in charge of the apprentice. Apprentices usually have completed their formal craft education by the time they enter their apprenticeship and may already have discovered their vocation in the process.

Internships are a common experiential learning option within many professional and technical education programs. Internships often terminate the formal training of professional and technical education programs and may provide an opportunity for regular employment with the internship provider.

The internship experience provides an opportunity for students to enhance skill sets learned in the classroom and practiced in the laboratory or other hands-on venues. They provide an opportunity to work with professionals in the field to help students determine whether one has gained an accurate representation of what such a career involves and to confirm their career interests and their calling.

Many programs offer internship opportunities for students nearing completion of their degrees when they can provide useful service to the internship provider. Faculty maintain a list of potential internship providers that, ideally, have venues that help students find and develop their practice and explore a calling.

To ensure student commitment and buy-in, some faculty expect students to arrange for their own internship with an appropriate provider based on a prearranged structure and set of general objectives. Internship providers with specific intern job descriptions usually have preference. Carefully structure internships to be relevant and meaningful to their purpose.

After meeting all the preliminaries, have interns and internship providers sign an agreement outlining internship objectives and expectations. Also, require the interns to meet with you periodically through the internship period—usually a single quarter or semester—to discuss their progress. These meetings are a good time to identify the cognitive, kinesthetic, and affective elements of their experience and how they relate to course objectives and the implications for professional practice. A final report on the internship—including images of their work—is prepared by the intern and signed by the internship provider along with their assessment of the intern's experience.

COMMUNITY-ENGAGED LEARNING

Perhaps the most impactful type of experiential learning currently practiced within many collegiate and university professional and technical programs is community-engaged learning. Here are two helpful definitions:

> the accomplishment of tasks that meet genuine human needs in combination with conscious educational growth.[4]

> Service-learning is a teaching and learning method that integrates critical reflection and meaningful service in the community with academic learning, personal growth, and civic responsibility.[5]

Andrew Delbanco in his book *College: What It Was, Is, And Should Be* identifies a specific valuable element of community-engaged learning:

> Perhaps the brightest spot in the contemporary landscape of American higher education is the resurgence of interest in engaging students in civic life beyond campus. "Community service" organizations have long been a feature of most colleges, but explicit connection of coursework with service work is relatively new, and growing.[6]

Literature on community-engaged learning is extensive, and the intention here is to provide you with a primer on the subject as an important experiential learning opportunity and framing element for discerning vocation. Two important references are *Looking In, Reaching Out: A Reflective Guide for Community Service-Learning Professionals* (2010) edited by Barbara Jacoby and Pamela Mutascio and *Service-Learning Course Design for Community Colleges* (2007) by Marina Baratian, Donna K. Duffy, Robert Franco, Amy Hendricks, Roger Henry, and Tanya Renner. Both of these texts are published by Campus Compact in Boston, a very resourceful membership coalition of colleges and universities.

Community-engaged learning is growing in collegiate education since Delbanco's assessment in 2012 and is quickly becoming a necessary part of collegiate community engagement and experiential learning. In a study by Alexander Astin and his colleagues, they examined thirty-five measures of student outcomes concerning civic responsibility, academic development, and life skill development and found that all their outcome measures were enhanced by community-engaged learning. Not only that, and despite the additional time required for community-engaged learning, students who engaged in volunteer service spent more time with studies and homework than did nonparticipants.[7]

It seems that, through community-engaged learning, students found their studies more relevant, stimulating, and purposeful. William Sullivan puts community-engaged learning in a compelling perspective: "As we have seen in a number of cases, these programs enabled their participants to make sense of their experience of a particular community of vocational quest not only as an individual exploration but as connected to a much broader human horizon."[8]

As opposed to internships that terminate degree programs, insert community-engaged learning projects in the curriculum where they best fit based on units of study, the relative competence of the students at that point in the program, and the needs of the community partner. Generally, students have reached some midpoint in their degree program and possess a foundation of knowledge about their field of study to meet the community-engaged learning requirement for reciprocity.

Embed community-engaged learning projects in a particular course or offer them as stand-alone credit like internships or independent studies. This decision often revolves around the scale of the community-engaged learning opportunity. Large and/or time-consuming projects work better as stand-alone opportunities, whereas smaller, less-complex projects are embedded in existing courses.

TYPES OF COMMUNITY-ENGAGED LEARNING PROGRAMS

We may distinguish between traditional community-engaged learning projects described here and what are emerging as "critical" community-engaged learning projects of particular relevance to select academic (sociology, political science, etc.) and professional programs (social worker, lawyer, journalist, etc.) with a focus on social justice.

From "Traditional vs. Critical Service-Learning: Engaging the Literature to Differentiate Two Models" by Tania D. Mitchell of Stanford University: "There is an emerging body of literature advocating a 'critical' approach to community service learning with an explicit social justice aim. A social change orientation, working to redistribute power, and developing authentic relationships are most often cited in the literature as points of departure from traditional service-learning."[9]

The foundations of "critical community-engaged learning" are the same as those for traditional community-engaged learning. To be more specific, this chapter and text focus on "discipline-specific" community-engaged learning where "students are expected to have a presence in the community throughout the semester and reflect on their experiences on a regular basis using course content as a basis for their analysis and understanding."[10]

Some scholars break down community-engaged learning into several different modes: direct community-engaged learning, indirect community-engaged learning, research-based community-engaged learning, and advocacy-based community-engaged learning. Following this scheme, direct service involves working directly with a client population on an interpersonal level to provide a service, such as tutoring students, working with the elderly, or coaching a youth activity. Indirect community-engaged learning involves fulfilling a community need in general, such as renovating a park, working on low-income housing projects, or fund-raising.

Research-based community-engaged learning involves working with a community partner to gather helpful data such as sampling water, energy use, or demographic information. Last, advocacy-based community-engaged learning involves students in advocating for or educating others on topics of concern for a community partner or the community-at-large, such as organizing and hosting a public forum, composing and distributing a newsletter, or conducting surveys.[11]

THE NATURE OF COMMUNITY-ENGAGED LEARNING PROGRAMS

Community-engaged learning follows a signature pedagogy that focuses on head (learning), hands (service), and heart (affective) pioneered by the Waldorf School. The head and hands modes are particular to the needs of a given professional or technical academic program, but the affective component is common to all through reflection and other contemplative practices.

Community-engaged learning is particularly relevant to the aims of this text because of its reliance on reflection and other contemplative practices as well as its critical role in helping students discern their vocation. It is also an effective way to bring our program scholarship and applications together to strengthen and transform them both while generating opportunities for our students to engage in meaningful work.[12]

Freire addressed this dynamic between scholarship and service in the following way: "When we explore the act of service in the context of theoretical and other forms of knowledge, coupled with reflection on our perspective and position in the world, we can enhance and transform the quality of the service and of the learning."[13] Many educators are beginning to recognize that the best way to foster intelligence in education is through the firsthand knowledge provided by internships, community-engaged learning, and job shadowing combined with contemplative practice. Community-engaged programs provide an opportunity for students to reflect critically on their experience, examine their sense of self in light of the experience (values, assets, bias, purpose, etc.), and plan new courses of action while trying out new skill and mind-sets. This is rich ground for bringing them closer to finding their calling.

Community-engaged learning projects are often situated within community contexts where issues of social justice and economic equity are of concern. Projects with social justice and economic equity elements will bring out and test the compassion of students. In such cases, compassion practice will help students develop a deeper appreciation for community and the common good, a significant part of discerning vocation by helping students find their place in the community. The outcomes of this work begin to show in a deepening sense of community among the students in the course and, as time goes on, begin to extend to a stronger sense of the community at large.[14]

Well-developed community-engaged learning courses can contribute to an enhanced student experience in the following ways:

- Experience firsthand the complexity and interrelatedness of society's social problems.
- Explore multiple perspectives.
- Combine critical thinking with experiential feeling.
- Relate theory to classroom studies with practice and real-life experience.
- Connect with their personal lives.
- Develop habits of the heart and mind (weave together the cognitive domains of the right and left hemispheres).
- Journal and reflect on experiences and then share them in class.
- Develop a sense of civic responsibility.
- Work as a member of a team to solve real-life problems.
- Develop leadership skills.
- Put into practice, under supervision, an understanding of the issues involved.[15]

It's important to recognize how community-engaged learning differs from other forms of experiential learning. The contemplative practice element is an important difference that we'll come back to later in this segment.

A special programmatic mix is inherent in the name, "community-engaged learning," especially when carried out with the most intentional, significant, and balanced attention to "community-engaged" and "learning." The entire experience should involve a clear and meaningful interplay between learning and community engagement for students. Anyone experienced in community-engaged learning will tell you that this dynamic relationship is much easier written and talked about than done.

Typically, college partners will put greater priority on the academic, or learning, portion of the project—something that easily fits in the curriculum and pedagogy—whereas partner organizations and communities will put greater priority on the service they are seeking to obtain. Making sure that the project functions with the right balance of learning and service components requires thorough planning and thoughtful curriculum integration between the collegiate and community partners. Community-engaged learning done right is a win-win proposition for all involved.

Given the opening descriptions, it should be clear that successful collaboration is a hallmark of successful community-engaged learning projects. Be sure to identify and include all the necessary stakeholders in the planning of a community-engaged learning project—the circle of stakeholders is likely to be larger than you think. Stakeholder ripples will go out to several players at the educational institution and within the service recipient community. You may not need to connect directly with all of them, but make sure all the necessary stakeholders are in the loop.

Put another way, community-engaged learning projects require a great deal of mutuality between the subject matter and the service as well as all the cooperators. The mutuality between your program and the community partner may also be expressed as reciprocity. A reciprocal partnership is based on an understanding and respect for the expertise, skills, wisdom, emotions, and capacities that both the academic and community partners contribute to the community-engaged learning project.

Consider all the community-engaged learning partners directly responsible for the success of the project, as Kathleen Rice puts it in *Looking In, Reaching Out*, as "teachers, learners, servers, served, agents of change, and agents that can be changed by the relationships. Intentionality is required to create authentically reciprocal partnerships."[16]

Cultivating our students' attention has been a persistent theme of this text. Loss of attentiveness—an insidious by-product of social and cultural media and other information technologies—is crippling the learning ability and capacity of our students. Experiential learning—community-engaged learning in particular—is an important antidote. Kleinhans describes a critically important outcome of student community engagement in her essay "Places of Responsibility" in the text *At This Time and In This Place: Vocation and Higher Education*:

Community or civic engagement is sustained, shared work for the common good; as such, it can be habit-forming and character-shaping. It is generative of virtues such as practical wisdom, attentiveness, and generosity; it encourages practices such as deep listening, gratitude, and empathy. Perhaps most importantly [with respect to vocation] community engagement exposes participants to diverse worlds of experience and possibility. . . . Of the virtues cultivated by community engagement, one of the most important in today's world is surely attentiveness.[17]

Kleinhans' point that students working in community engagement projects are in a position where they must attend to the working, social, economic, and cultural context of those they are serving is well taken—this is a requirement important to the integrity of their assignment. An integrity based on dedication to purpose and empathy for those they serve leads to a reevaluation of what is important and what really matters in our lives. This is the foundation for the discovery of real purpose in one's work and life.

Take care to ensure that community-engaged learning projects not only involve relevant professional or technical practice but also allow students to make real contributions to the community and, if possible, work directly with people in need. This will enrich their experience, as Kathryn Kleinhans describes, and increase their capacity to show concern for others. The opportunity to reflect on the elements of each experience, as well as the experience itself, is a critical component of community-engaged learning programs in cultivating professionalism, empathy, prudence, purpose, and discerning vocation.

Community-engaged learning can also be a powerful experience as it relates to William May's definition of authentic professional practice:

> The professional's covenant, in my judgment, opens out in three directions that help distinguish professionals from careerists: The professional professes something (a body of knowledge and experience); on behalf of someone (or some institution); and in the setting of colleagues.[18]

Community-engaged learning connects all of May's characteristics of a professional covenant through applications of professional practice and engagement with a citizen group or other organization responsible for meeting community needs.

Take a moment to reflect on the potential place of community-engaged learning in your pedagogy. It is very important that you keep your program goals—knowledge, skills, and discerning vocation—clearly in mind during your early deliberations on the kind of community-engaged earning projects you will arrange and organize. In your planning, keep in mind three particularly important facets of successful community-engaged learning projects:

(1) they operate on a reciprocal and mutually reinforcing dynamic between academics and service, as well as (2) mutual trust; and (3) process these dynamics and experiences through contemplative practice.

Another early community-engaged learning consideration is to represent relevant narratives and frameworks in your community-engaged learning projects. An example is the sustainability narrative described in the previous chapter. With this in mind, look for community-engaged learning partners whose practice and/or business model revolves around sustainability so that your students can experience how to put what they've learned within that narrative into practical application.

PLANNING AND ORGANIZING COMMUNITY-ENGAGED LEARNING PROJECTS

Below is a best practices summary of the community-engaged learning basics introduced in the previous paragraphs to help you organize your thinking about developing community-engaged learning projects.

Best Practices 7.1. Community-Engaged Learning Basics

- Integrate service with academics.
- Ensure that credit is for learning outcomes, not good deeds.
- Define academic outcomes to include all relevant outcomes, including community development and workforce development outcomes.
- If possible, give students latitude in choosing projects and project locations.
- Conduct reflection activities to deepen learning.
- Find concrete ways to involve the community in the teaching and learning process.

A couple of new items here need explanation. Regarding learning outcomes versus "good deeds," you may wish to acknowledge good deeds as an expected part of project participation along with other behavioral attributes, such as a positive attitude. These may be covered as a single behavioral project outcome or accounted for in some other way.

Integrated academics and service are a critical part of community-engaged learning, so you must develop project outcomes for both of these major elements. Be sure to vet those outcomes with the community participants involved in the teaching and learning portion of the service experience making sure they are relevant and may be clearly assessed.

When it comes to giving students latitude in selecting community-engaged learning projects, this may be difficult at the beginning when you likely have only one or two projects available. At this early stage, it may only be possible to give your students latitude for selecting among different roles within a single community-engaged learning project. As your repertoire of community-engaged learning projects grows, you will be able to offer your students greater latitude to choose a project.

Considering the last bullet in the list, the prospect of involving members of the community in teaching and learning, must be considered from the beginning when you are selecting community-engaged learning community partners. The potential and/or presence of community participants that can play an important role in teaching and learning is an important criterion for choosing community-engaged learning partners. You will then need to work closely with those members who will work directly with students in a mentoring, teaching, and learning role.

A first step in conceiving, organizing, and implementing a community-engaged learning project is to scan your college and university for community-engaged learning resources, in particular, other faculty members who may serve as community-engaged learning mentors. You may be fortunate to have at your disposal a cocurricular center and other faculty on campus familiar with community-engaged learning to connect with for advice and support.

Seek out part-time instructors in your program, or allied programs, with some familiarity and interest in community-engaged learning and a willingness to incorporate it into their courses. It's quite possible that you'll discover relevant community-engaged learning partners from other programs that will provide opportunities for you and your students.

Another area of concern are your institution's priorities. To the extent that you are meeting those, you should receive broader support from the administration for your community-engaged learning program. As previously mentioned, many colleges and universities have a community-engaged learning objective within a cocurricular program in student services, if not a community-engaged learning center. These can be particularly important internal community-engaged learning partners. Your community-engaged learning program should also meet a broader goal outlined in the college's strategic plan. The greater your alignment with institutional goals and plans, the more likely you will receive program support. Be sure to document all the above considerations in a community-engaged learning plan.

As you move forward in your planning and organizing, start out cautiously and focus on quality. Concentrate on an initial partnership(s) that embodies as many of your measures of success previously described as possible—better to establish one good project than several with shortcomings or flaws. As already mentioned, it is possible that other community-engaged learning programmers at your institution may be able to share a successful partnership with you that will meet your community-engaged learning goals.

Program sharing, internal collaborating, and finding mentors all fall under the heading of making the most of your place in the institution. However, don't be persuaded to share in one that, although successful in one subject area, may not be a good fit for your program. From the standpoint of internal standing, be sure to keep track of numbers. As you know, data is a very important institutional measure of success on several fronts.

Again, choose quality partnerships based on educational goals, outcomes, and the alignment of community needs, resources, and capabilities. Be sure to consider the community partner's overall strengths and assets as well as the authenticity of the individuals who represent the partnership. Other important partnership attributes are the strength and trust between you and one or more of the leading individuals from the community partner.

Be sure to document the dynamics of the partnership as the project moves forward. An additional attribute to consider when choosing a community partner and project is the importance of "meaningful work" for student participants. This may require a definition in a community-engaged learning agreement of what constitutes "meaningful work" relative to your learning outcomes.

Putting several recommendations and principals together from the previous paragraphs, this short list below from Marina Baratian et al. serves as a useful best practices checklist of basic community-engaged learning attributes.:

Best Practices 7.2: Community-Engaged Learning Attributes

- *Engagement*: Does the community-engaged learning component meet a public good? How do you know this? Has the community been consulted? How? How have the campus/community boundaries been negotiated, and how will they be crossed?
- *Reflection*: Is there a mechanism that encourages students to link their service experience to course content and to reflect upon why the service is important?
- *Reciprocity*: Is reciprocity evident in the service component? How? Reciprocity suggests that every person, organization, and entity involved in the community-engaged learning functions as both a teacher and a learner. Participants are perceived as colleagues, not as servers and clients.
- *Public dissemination*: Is service work presented to the public or made an opportunity for the community to enter into a public dialogue? How?[19]

The first item in the list, *engagement*, is a sensitive issue, especially when you're considering "boundaries." Boundaries deal with lines of communication in the project and chains of command. Make sure those are clear to students and community partners. Perhaps of greater importance, clearly identify institutional boundaries that are without flexibility: codes, policies, rules, liabilities, and protocols. List all these along with the necessary permissions, accountabilities, authorizations, and so forth. Consider all potential emergencies and identify and outline protocols for them. Finally, consider what mistakes would be catastrophic to a student, a program, your institution, or a partnership and how they can be avoided.

Regarding *reflection*, we will review some specific contemplative practices pertinent to community-engaged learning projects later in this chapter. *Reciprocity* should be listed as a specification or requirement of the project in the proposal and outline accompanied by specific reciprocity nodes, intersections, and/or services. Consider structuring contemplative intervals around the subject of reciprocity that involve a collective of everyone in the project. Make sure the project and its processes are made transparent in *public dissemination* through various means of communication: social media, public forums, and so on.

Pay careful attention to the relational nature of community-engaged learning projects in respect to the curriculum, project focus, and framing narratives for teaching to inspire vocation. It begins with the careful integration of the community-engaged learning project into the course curriculum. View community-engaged learning projects embedded in existing courses as an alternative and more effective way of accomplishing some of the same objectives as the standard curriculum. Therefore, you will need to support and make room for community-engaged learning by making trade-offs in reading, writing, and other standard requirements.

You will need to develop explicit learning objectives and then work with students and partners to design community-engaged learning activities accordingly. Include the basic elements of project management in the curriculum, especially for more comprehensive, stand-alone community-engaged learning projects. Students earn full credit for community-engaged learning by demonstrating what they've learned from their participation. Consider carefully how you will orient students on the first day of class to what may be an unorthodox learning experience involving collaboration and somewhat ambiguous teaching and learning roles for all the community-engaged learning participants.

Considering your community-engaged learning dedication, outcomes, pedagogies, and assignments, take under advisement and reflect on this recommendation from Jacoby and Mutascio:

By definition, service-learning is oriented toward professional praxis as part of mastering course material and civic learning as it relates to discovering vocation. Disciplines, [craft, and practice] . . . have public purposes; they connect in meaningful ways with societal issues and concerns. Faculty members need to be clear, in their own minds and with their students, that academic learning is connected to civic learning and that developing the knowledge, skills, dispositions, and behaviors of citizens and civic-minded professionals is an important objective of service-learning.[20]

The word "praxis" appeared in the previous chapter. This is an important professional and technical as well as vocational word to add to our vocabulary. From the *Cambridge Dictionary*: "the process of using a theory or something that you have learned in a practical way. 'She is interested in both the theory and praxis of criminology.'"[21] In this text, the word "practice" has been used when the word "praxis" may be more appropriate. However, in the parlance of everyday use (e.g., "the practice of medicine or law"), the word practice is acceptable. If we are sharing with our students how a theory or concept in a professional and technical discipline is used in standard practice, we may use the term praxis.

Also from Jacoby and Mutascio's quote, the segment "Disciplines . . . have public purposes; they connect in meaningful ways with societal issues and concerns," is a powerful one when it comes to the raison d'être of professional and technical education, community-engaged learning, and discerning vocation.

Through studies and interviews, the best practices list below of student expectations has been compiled.

Best Practices 7.3: Meeting Student Expectations

1. Clarify and acknowledge the unorthodox nature of the community-engaged learning experience and the shared risk in such a collaboration. Discuss the shared responsibility for the success of all partners.
2. Develop and emphasize a personal investment in the project's success.
3. Ensure and facilitate clear and frequent communication among all participants.
4. Accept and enhance a fluid process and work flow. Invoke and demonstrate a tact of monitor and adjust to mitigate conflicts, stalled progress, and project integration. Demonstrate process flexibility and loose deadlines.
5. Practice what you preach. Show enthusiasm, empathy, and passion.
6. Keep everyone's feet to the fire and challenge students to perform.

7. Showcase student achievements and demonstrated learning.[22]

Given all of that, it is imperative that faculty be authentic and purposeful in their commitment, enthusiasm, and support of everyone involved in a community-engaged learning project, particularly the students. Beyond that, given the complexity of some community-engaged learning projects, find time during the experience to replenish yourself. Set clear boundaries around your availability to students, staff, and project partners. Don't be afraid to delegate as part of this collaborative endeavor and, in doing so, give everyone space to find their way. This includes forgiving and learning from mistakes.

At this point in your deliberations and planning, you should have a set of notes and/or documents that serve as a prospectus on a community-engaged learning course or unit of an existing course.

In this next section we will examine community-engaged learning course specifics with a consideration of community-engaged learning projects, levels of service, community partner obligations, student expectations, and documentation. Choice of community-engaged learning projects will be based on community needs and the sites and/or projects available to service those needs. Some community organizations and institutions that may be helpful in identifying potential community-engaged learning sites are social service agencies (e.g., DSHS) and nonprofit organizations (e.g., the United Way), neighborhood organizations, chambers of commerce, school boards, hospitals and health-care facilities, professional organizations, and special-interest groups (e.g., Rotary Club).

It is important to identify how and who benefits from the service provided. Be sure to focus on services that provide a public, rather than private, benefit. Also, remember to focus on quality rather than quantity when choosing projects, making sure that they will meet the learning objectives for your course. Other considerations are safety and liability issues as well as special requirements that may be outside the capability of your students.

Calculate the level of service that will be required for your students to meet the learning objectives, the needs of the community, and to complete the project. Describing the roles available for the students as part of the project will help determine what each job requires and the level of service necessary. Job descriptions provided by the community partner are also very helpful for assessing student performance and defining expectations.

The community partner should provide supervision, feedback, and job evaluation for students. The partner assigns tasks directly related to community-engaged learning objectives that take place within a safe and appropriate working environment. The students are naturally obligated to perform their duties to the best of their ability within the required time frame while adhering to the rules and policies of the community partner.

Outline community-engaged learning requirements in a project agreement. Be sure to include an agreed upon and regularly scheduled project meeting involving yourself, your students, and representatives of the community partner in order to stay up to date on the progress of the project to rectify issues and problems.

Be prepared to document the project thoroughly to show its efficacy, a record of accomplishments and issues, and for student and partner recognition. Types of documentation may include student application forms, progress reports, hour reports or time sheets, community partner student evaluation forms and narratives, and post-project student learning assessments. When it comes to community partner student evaluations, provide them with an evaluation form that contains all the important criteria with room for explanations and other narrative.

Regarding student assessment, several other means are available for evaluating student learning, both during and at the end of a project. In addition to the suggested service-partner evaluation, you may use the various forms of student documentation resulting from your community-engaged learning reflective practices. The most obvious evaluation tool will be the finished product of the community-engaged learning project, including a specific description and self-evaluation by students individually along with a summary of what they learned.

Another common assessment element is a class presentation by a student or students describing their accomplishments and how they met the outcomes for the project and the course. A student essay or journal submission is a common evaluation tool that includes excerpts from their reflective practice journals.

Below is a helpful troubleshooting list from Marina Baratian et al. in *Service-Learning Course Design for Community Colleges* that should help you in planning (author comments are in brackets).

- Student does not contact the service provider and/or is absent after an initial visit [regular and timely attendance is an expectation and outcome].
- Logistical impediments (time commitments, travel, agency fit) result in an unsatisfactory placement [should be worked out in advance but may require student consultation].
- Orientation is too time-consuming, too minimal, or does not seem to apply to academic work [a requirement in the community-engaged learning contract or agreement of understanding].
- The student or the partner does not plan adequately [review preliminary planning with partners and students, make it part of the regularly scheduled project meetings].
- Lack of appreciation for each community-engaged learning role—that of the student, the agency supervisor, or the college facilitator—leads to

resentment [monitor through regularly scheduled project meetings and consider job rotations].
- Lack of understanding or recognition of others' perspective, cultural differences, or values causes misunderstandings [a teaching moment!] to be resolved through reflection.
- Overconcern about liability on the part of the community partner, program, or student interferes with the ability to get work done [may require job modification, special training, or special supervision; monitor and adjust!].
- The agency is overly concerned about students' maturity and ability to maintain confidentiality and professionalism [calls for a special consultation session, perhaps something akin to nondisclosure agreements].
- The agency needs/wants student workers but has no support structure in place [funding is a common issue and leveraging is a common solution].
- The agency sees students as a free labor pool and assigns them to tasks that are inappropriate, not meaningful, or outside their abilities [make sure appropriate job descriptions are in place and review in regular meetings].
- Students become "crunched" at certain times of the semester, and service falls off [plan for that and allow a relative down time].
- After a period of time in placement, the student becomes disenchanted and loses interest [could be a moment of reckoning regarding vocation, or lack thereof].
- Students suffer end-of-semester burnout, including concern about grades, time constraints, and uncertainty about how to end the relationship with the agency [this is certainly a reflection and other contemplative practice moment individually and in group].
- The agency does not provide evaluation and feedback on the service experience [make sure that requirement is in the community-engaged learning agreement].[23]

As you can see, many of these issues can be resolved through group reflective practice and regular community-engaged learning project meetings involving everyone associated with the project.

CONTEMPLATIVE PRACTICE IN COMMUNITY-ENGAGED LEARNING

This next section provides recommendations and details on reflective practices to accompany community-engaged learning projects and exercises to facilitate them. Contemplative practice is a crucial component of the community-engaged learning experience. At this juncture, you might want to refer to chapter 5 for a refresher on contemplative practices—particularly the segments on reflection—before we consider specific examples for community-engaged learning projects.

In your research on community-engaged learning projects, you are sure to encounter examples that lack a contemplative practice element. These are incomplete, less impactful examples. Without the contemplative practice element, students lose a tremendous learning opportunity, even if the project itself is successful. Reflection is vital and unique in its importance and impact as part of community-engaged learning. It is not just a student-centered activity, but involves everyone in the project: faculty, staff, project partners, advisers, and other stakeholders.

Perhaps the most common and useful reflective tools for community-engaged learning participants (and students in general) are journals or essays. When asking students to keep a journal record of their reflections, it is important for you to structure these assignments and provide prompts that will elicit thoughtful, nuanced contributions as opposed to a simple account of activity. Build that expectation into the assessment rubric and provide examples and/or questions for students to answer. For example: if you ask students to write five hundred words reflecting on their first week of community-engaged learning, provide guidance in the form of questions to answer and specific data to include. Questions should relate to community-engaged learning outcomes, class material, and service partner community or business objectives.

A less common but useful reflective tool is a continuous journal, a single journal that is passed among the participants as the community-engaged learning project proceeds. The journal begins with a musing by a student who then poses a question for the next person to answer. Students sign and date their entries, and you decide on guidelines for their submissions and how often students should submit journal entries. Journal contents may then be used as fodder for group reflections in discussion.

You can modify a continuous journal into what is known as a double-entry journal. These contain "chapters" that begin with a provocative question or observation about classroom material or project site activities for student comment. You will provide the first question or observation, and students may contribute to these provocations as the journal develops. Below the starting question, divide the page into two columns. The left column is for student answers to questions or comments; the right column is for their justification and support of their answers and comments. The journal may have as many of these sections as there are weeks in the community-engaged learning project. Encourage students to supply the introduction to each of the weekly sections.

Another type of useful journal that sparks reflective group discussion is the one-word journal. This begins when you pose a question that the students must answer in one word. The students record their one-word answer in their journals along with an explanation for why they choose that word. You may then decide to have some discussion time for students to share their answers and explanations or simply end the exercise with a new journal entry.

A useful provocative writing exercise for municipal community-engaged learning projects is a letter to the editor of the local newspaper. This may be a hypothetical exercise or an actual letter submitted for publication. The point is for students to take a position on an issue in a persuasive letter (essay) that contributes to public dialogue and links their service experiences to course content. Environmental conservation includes any number of pertinent current events issues—economic equity, social justice, and education, just to name a few—that will fill the bill. Here's an opportunity to employ the maxim "think globally, act locally" as it relates to the project.

A similar form of documentation is data gathering. In fact, these two assignments may be easily merged. The data gathering may be done as another way to describe the project, or supplement a description, as well as be part of a project research goal. The data may be numerical, descriptive, or narrative and demonstrate different types of linkages within the project and between the project and the coursework or similar projects elsewhere in the community. In any case, project data and documentation form the basis for meaningful reflection as part of the assignment and as subject matter for journals, essays, and discussion.

Ask students to bring in news articles, editorials, and so forth that touch on topics relevant to class and community-engaged learning outcomes for reflective discussion. Have a set of questions ready pertaining to an assigned news article to prompt student discussion. These could be about conflicts within the profession or current and controversial practices and/or applications and how these would impact the current community-engaged learning project, and any other relationships with course material and community-engaged learning outcomes, skills, and craft. This exercise could also be reworked as a news article montage, student photo collage, or any other graphic presentation on their community-engaged learning project presented in a poster session.

These reflective exercises are designed to help students obtain a clearer, more meaningful understanding of their knowledge and experience. Consider these comments from a community-engaged learning student: "service-learning enables students to apply their knowledge in real time, in real places, with real people, and with real consequences. Community-engaged learning takes you to the edge of what you know and who you are."[24] That should underscore the power of community-engaged learning as a contributor to the discovery of meaning and purpose for discerning vocation.

Reflective exercises will be a principal means of assessing whether the students are fulfilling their community-engaged learning outcomes and objectives. Be sure to provide a student evaluation form for the partner-supervisor to complete as another means of student assessment.

COMMUNITY-ENGAGED LEARNING SUPPORT

What about a supportive infrastructure from the standpoint of authentic partnerships and funding? Build successful, sustaining community-engaged learning partnerships on the strength of relationships, partnership evaluations, and institutional commitment.[25] See the best practices for community partnerships from Torrey, Sinton, and White below.

Best Practices 7.4. Sustainable Community Partnerships

1. clarity of mission or vision;
2. community demand and strength of programs, services, or activities;
3. organizational leadership;
4. suitable organizational structures;
5. strong human resources programs;
6. adequate financial resources (internal and external); and
7. a willingness to assess, improve, and change.[26]

The issue of money is no small consideration for collegiate programs. Prepare yourself to demonstrate relevance, supportive relationships, documented results, and access to a diversity of resources using this list as a guide. This is part of building a solid strategy for growing and sustaining your community-engaged learning program. Here's a basic recommendation: the four Rs for leveraging funding from "Leveraging Financial Support for Service-learning: Relevance, Relationships, Results, Resources," by Barbara Holland and Mark N. Langseth in *Looking In, Reaching Out: A Reflective Guide for Community Service-Learning Professionals*.

Best Practices 7.5. Leveraging Financial Support

1. *Relevance*: the importance of considering the relevance of community-engaged learning from the perspective of resource providers. Situate your program within a larger context—how is it relevant and important to the whole campus and community.
2. *Relationships*: Strategies to generate resources are successful only in the context of an authentic relationship that is based on the articulation of shared goals and interests—this process is an end in itself.
3. *Results*: Assessment and documentation of community-engaged learning impact and results is important evidence for leveraging resources. Both quantitative and qualitative data are useful.
4. *Identifying the most important resource providers*: The goal of your efforts is to weave adequate funding for your program into your institution's annual operating budget to create a sustained base of support. This will require a diversity of funding resources, both internal and external.[27]

Something else regarding fund-raising: your community-engaged learning program may become a valuable resource generator. Stop and think about it: a community-engaged learning program may attract new donors who heretofore were not interested in an existing institutional program or programs. Also, current donors may expand their giving in response to the new educational dimension that community-engaged learning provides. Finally, the goodwill that a successful community-engaged learning program generates can lead to several kinds of new support.

COMMUNITY-ENGAGED LEARNING PROGRAM ASSESSMENT

Now, let's assume that you have developed and implemented a community-engaged learning or other experiential learning program and you are moving forward. As much as you'd like to celebrate a new beginning and being engaged in practice rather than planning, there is one more requirement. As seasoned educators, you know that program assessment is fundamental to good practice.

No matter how wonderful you think the new program is, stakeholders will expect to see an assessment of how the program meets expectations and outcomes. From your point of view, an assessment is critical for bringing to the fore new information and knowledge that will help you adjust and fine-tune your program for even greater institutional and community support, and more importantly, student success.

Hatcher and Bringle recommend an assessment strategy based on five components:

1. *Reflection*: oriented toward the self-assessment of persons who are engaged in an experience.
2. *Program process evaluation*: produces information about how a class, course, or program was implemented.
3. *Program outcome evaluation*: produces information about what outcomes occurred as a result of a class, course, or program.
4. *Correlational studies*: produce information about what relationship exists between aspects of a class, course, or program.
5. *Research, including experimental studies*: produces information about why a specific outcome occurred.[28]

A program assessment strategy should also rely on critical reflection involving the program stakeholders: faculty, community partners, and any other crucial stakeholders, as well as those directly involved in the community-engaged learning project. Program evaluation is the most commonly considered portion of any assessment. This part of an assessment involves program accountability for student learning goals and outcomes. Toward that end, it involves process evaluation (program implementation) and outcome evaluation (student impact).

Correlational studies are meant to show the extent to which the program impacts students in the way intended. For instance, does the community-engaged learning experience provide students with a meaningful perspective on their professional and technical career goals and convey a sense of purpose, meaning, and vocation? The research component of an assessment program usually revolves around an explanation of the program results. Good assessments must "link the abstract and the concrete; be structured; occur regularly; provide feedback for learning; and explore and qualify values."[29]

As teachers, we must recognize the difference between surface learning and deep learning. Deep learning helps students clarify issues of identity, integrity, purpose, and meaning in ways that encourage authenticity, spiritual growth, and discerning vocation. Community-engaged learning is an effective experiential, deep learning mode, as are the other elements of teaching to inspire vocation outlined in this text.

A survey of community-engaged learning students at Wellesley College revealed that they often experienced moments of meaning, inspiration, connection, wonder and awe in the classroom—indicators of deep learning. These experiences weren't confined to courses in philosophy and theology, but across the curriculum from biology and mathematics to the entire curriculum of professional and technical subjects. The students told story after story about moments when they awakened to a deeper understanding of themselves, of others around them, and of the world.

The Wellesley students also told of transformational experiences. These moments were most common in collaborative work with other students (learning communities), through community-engaged learning opportunities, with well-chosen texts, contemplative practice, and mentoring faculty. In each case the students talked about these moments as transformational in their lives. These are the learning contexts and experiences that bring about the discovery of vocation.[30]

The richness of student experience at Wellesley College extends to the faculty who also experience transformation in their experience. Richard Harris, director of community-engaged learning at James Madison University, writes of the transformation common among community-engaged learning professionals:

> The diversity of our experiences helps us understand that the discomfort of perplexity is also the spark of transformation. Our experiences, both inside and beyond our educational institutions, inform our understanding that the most powerful learning environment is that which partners the community experience with classroom instruction. In turn, this knowledge leads to an awareness that in each experience there are many different ways of seeing and knowing. The true understanding of any experience happens only when these different perspectives are shared and understood by all.[31]

Textbox 7.1 Teaching Takeaways

- Community-engaged learning is a teaching and learning method that integrates critical reflection and meaningful service in the community with academic learning, personal growth, and civic responsibility. (Marina Baratian et al.)
- Community-engaged learning follows a signature pedagogy that is focused on head (learning), hands (service), and heart (affective) similar to the Waldorf School.
- Community-engaged learning projects function with the right balance of learning and service through planning and thoughtful curriculum integration.
- Successful collaboration is a hallmark of successful community-engaged learning projects.
- Care must be taken to ensure that community-engaged learning projects not only involve real professional or technical practice but also allow students to make real contributions whenever possible to the community.
- Reflection and contemplative practice are crucial to community-engaged learning and too often are overlooked.
- Revisit the checklists and Best Practices contained in this chapter.

NOTES

1. Parker Palmer, *The Heart of Higher Education* (San Francisco: Jossey-Bass, 2010), 112.

2. Craig Kaplowitz, "Helping with the 'How': A Role for Honors in Civic Education," *JNCHC* 18, no. 2 (2017): 17–23.

3. Barbara Jacoby and Pamela Mutascio, eds., *Looking In, Reaching Out: A Reflective Guide for Community Service-Learning Professionals* (Boston: Campus Compact, 2010), v.

4. Jacoby and Mutascio, *Looking In, Reaching Out*, 20.

5. Marina Baratian, Donna K. Duffy, Robert Franco, Amy Hendricks, Roger Henry, and Tanya Renner, *Service-Learning Course Design for Community Colleges* (Boston: Campus Compact, 2007), 7.

6. Andrew Delbanco, *What It Was, Is, and Should Be* (Princeton, NJ: Princeton University Press, 2012), ch. 5.

7. A. W. Chickering, J. C. Dalton, and L. Stamm, *Encouraging Authenticity and Spirituality in Higher Education* (San Francisco: Jossey-Bass, 2006), 129–30.

8. William Sullivan, *Liberal Learning as a Quest for Purpose* (Oxford, UK: Oxford University Press, 2016), 125.

9. Tania Mitchell, "Traditional vs. Critical Service-Learning: Engaging the Literature to Differentiate Two Models," in *Michigan Journal of Community Service Learning* (Spring 2008): 50.

10. Kerrissa Heffernan, *Service-Learning in Higher Education* (Boston: Campus Compact), 3.

11. Barbara Jacoby, *Service-Learning Essentials: Questions, Answers and Lessons Learned* (San Francisco: Jossey-Bass, 2015), 21.

12. Kathleen Rice, "Becoming a Reflective Community Service-Learning Professional," in *Looking In, Reaching Out: A Reflective Guide for Community Service-Learning Professionals*, ed. Barbara Jacoby and Pamela Mutascio (Boston: Campus Compact, 2010), 1.

13. Rice, "Becoming a Reflective Community Service-Learning Professional," 2.

14. Daniel P. Barbezat and Mirabai Bush, *Contemplative Practices in Higher Education* (San Francisco: Jossey-Bass, 2014).

15. Larry A. Braskamp, Lois Trautvetter, and Kelly Ward, *Putting Students First: How Colleges Develop Students Purposefully* (San Francisco: Jossey-Bass, 2005), 118.

16. Rice, "Becoming a Reflective Community Service-Learning Professional," 3.

17. Kathryn Kleinhans, "Places of Responsibility," in *At This Time and In This Place: Vocation and Higher Education*, ed. David S. Cunningham (Oxford, UK: Oxford University Press, 2015), 318.

18. Jeff Brown, "Unplugging the GPS," in *Vocation across the Academy: A New Vocabulary for Higher Education*, ed. David S. Cunningham (Oxford, UK: Oxford University Press, 2017), 221.

19. Baratian et al., *Service-Learning Course Design*, 7.

20. Patty H. Clayton and Billy O'Steen, "Working with Faculty: Designing Customized Developmental Strategies," in *Looking In, Reaching Out: A Reflective Guide for Community Service-Learning Professionals*, ed. Barbara Jacoby and Pamela Mutascio (Boston: Campus Compact, 2010), 106.

21. *Cambridge Dictionary* online, https://dictionary.cambridge.org/us/dictionary/english/praxis.

22. https://dictionary.cambridge.org/us/dictionary/english/praxis, 144.

23. Baratian et al., *Service-Learning Course Design*, 33–34.

24. Jacoby and Mutascio, *Looking In, Reaching Out*, v.

25. J. Torres, R. Stinton, and A. White, *Establishing and Sustaining an Office of Community Service* (Providence, RI: Campus Compact, 2000), 14.

26. Torres, Stinton, and White, *Establishing and Sustaining an Office of Community Service*, 14.

27. Barbara Holland and Mark N. Langseth, "Leveraging Financial Support for Service-Learning: Relevance, Relationships, Results, Resources," in *Looking In, Reaching Out: A Reflective Guide for Community Service-Learning Professionals*, ed. Barbara Jacoby and Pamela Mutascio (Boston: Campus Compact, 2010), 186.

28. Julie A. Hatcher and Robert G. Bringle, "Developing Your Assessment Plan: A Key Component of Reflective Practice," in *Looking In, Reaching Out: A Reflective Guide for Community Service-Learning Professionals*, ed. Barbara Jacoby and Pamela Mutascio (Boston: Campus Compact, 2010), 212–13.

29. Hatcher and Bringle, "Developing Your Assessment Plan," 215.

30. Chickering, Dalton, and Stamm, *Encouraging Authenticity*, 116.

31. Richard Harris, "Forward," in *Looking In, Reaching Out: A Reflective Guide for Community Service-Learning Professionals*, ed. Barbara Jacoby and Pamela Mutascio (Boston: Campus Compact, 2010), iii.

8

Teaching to Inspire Vocation

> Finding purpose, meaning, and vocation is an integral part of the deep process by which we become at home in the universe.[1]
>
> —Sharon Daloz Parks

This chapter brings together all the elements of a framework for teaching to inspire vocation in a series of recommendations and examples to help you revise and amplify a course, a curriculum, and your pedagogy to teach for vocation. Research shows that your students are waiting; they are eager; they are ready.

You may approach this change in several ways, from a gradual shift in your curriculum and pedagogy to a planned and complete overhaul. Those of you with students who started down a path toward discerning their vocation through their own reckoning and/or by virtue of several natural elements in the curriculum may opt for a gradual shift in your program. Other programs will require a more deliberate approach that calls for a strategic plan to effectively guide those changes. If so, a great deal of instructive literature on educational strategic planning is available.

The approach here to put in place the elements of a framework for teaching vocation follows a linear progression. We begin with changes in vocabulary and narrative; next introduce contemplative practices and cultivating mindfulness; and, finally, add community-engaged learning. These elements can be introduced within a single course or as a flow of revision to an entire program corresponding to the progression of a class of students from their first course to graduation. As your students' knowledge and capabilities grow, so will their sense of meaning, purpose, and vocation through the changes you make.

However, it may be more sensible for you to take up this process more broadly, combining two or more elements simultaneously. There is no one best approach: it depends a great deal on the organization of your courses and curriculum, the flow of your pedagogy, and your level of commitment to the process.

Revising a course and/or curriculum to inspire vocation will naturally involve your scholarship in teaching and learning. As you move forward with the practices described in this text, you should analyze and reflect on the resulting student work, academic performance, and outcomes, as Hutchings and Schulman describe:

> The scholarship of teaching and learning . . . requires a kind of "going meta" in which faculty frame and systematically investigate questions related to student learning—the conditions under which it occurs, what it looks like, how to deepen it, and so forth—and do so with an eye to not only improving their own classroom but to advancing practice beyond it.[2]

Teaching to inspire vocation is a "going meta" opportunity. Many of you may proceed with this work in a way that naturally includes reflections and analysis of your efforts and their impact on students. If you normally keep detailed notes and other documentation related to curriculum development, then you are well equipped to reflect on and analyze the work you have undertaken relative to its outcomes. If not, you would be well advised to document your strategy of course and/or curriculum revision. More on this process at the end of this chapter.

A simple first step in teaching to inspire vocation is to obtain basic information from the students in the first meeting of the course you have chosen to revise. Have your students write answers to the following questions:

1. Why did you enroll in (course)?
2. What motivated your interest in taking this course?
3. How does this decision fit into your educational and career goals?
4. How does this decision fit into your life goals?

The answers to these questions will be wide ranging. Some will be straightforward and show evidence of great forethought by your students on their education, career aspirations, and vocation. For many others, their answers will be vague and/or uncertain. Several students will be taking the course simply to fulfill a requirement. In any case, the answers will be revealing and instructive in moving forward.

This first class meeting will begin your students' exposure to important professional, technical, and vocational vocabulary, marking not only the beginning of their scholarship but their potential discovery of vocation. Be sure to keep these papers, or instruct the students to do the same, as you will ask them to answer the same questions again at the end of the term.

USING VOCABULARY

As introduced in chapter 6, vocabulary and narrative are basic and necessary for framing a course, the curriculum, and your pedagogy to help students discern their vocation. David S. Cunningham points out a particularly important benefit: "The language of vocation does have the potential to bring the various academic disciplines and applied fields into a deeper, richer, and more lasting dialogue with one another."[3] Cunningham has encapsulated in his compelling observation about the language of vocation an important aspect of teaching to inspire vocation in general: its relevance to the full breadth of collegiate education without regard to subject matter specialties and professional programming. The language of vocation is a common thread across the curriculum for helping all students discover their vocation.

The focus of our goal to teach to inspire vocation has mostly to do with the affective realm of instruction and, to a lesser extent, the cognitive and kinesthetic realms. Hence, most of our effort is to elicit and identify emotions and feelings about our academics and reflect on their meaning and purpose toward our discipline.

To reiterate the basic explanation first used in chapter 6, you are cultivating an orientation, perspective, and gestalt around your discipline using intentional vocabulary and narratives that frame it as a worthy vocation. In short, you want your students to perceive and envision making a life for themselves as a dedicated professional in their field of practice.

Several valuable sources of vocabulary for framing a discipline as a vocation come from the virtues and first principles of that discipline as well as the services it provides. In many cases, the virtues and first principles of a discipline overlap or are identical. Medical school faculty have only to turn to the Hippocratic Oath as a rich source of vocabulary, professional and vocational narrative, and framing. An overarching and familiar principle that emerges from that oath is "do no harm." The oath prescribes several virtues doctors must possess and bring to their practice to fulfill the oath, such as compassion, trustworthiness, discernment, and moral integrity. One powerful narrative that emerges from the oath is the physician as the moral fiduciary of the patient. There are certainly many more.

Another example in a completely different professional realm is accounting. However, like a doctor, an accountant also provides a service that is guided by a set of principles and virtues. Important principles for the instrumental, or technical, side of accounting include competence, patience, and precision. A virtuous accountant is honest, straightforward, and truthful; objective, skeptical, and independent; competent and diligent; discreet; and upright.[4] These requirements and personal/professional traits are an important part of a vocabulary for building professional narratives that convey meaning, purpose, and a framework for discerning vocation.

Returning to the horticulture program example used in previous chapters, the first course in the curriculum introduces basic elements of plant science that form the foundation of this practice. The students are exposed during this introductory course to important vocabulary related to horticulture as a vocation, such as "science," "art," "craft," and "practice," among others. By the time they reach the end of their first quarter, students are quite familiar with the use of these terms, the context of their meaning in horticulture practice, and a perspective on and feeling for horticulture as a vocation.

The terms "practice" and "practitioner" are important components of a vocabulary of vocation. They help to create and expand a narrative around career competence, special knowledge, and refined skill important to a vocational framework. Those terms also cultivate a vocational perspective on those professional traits. They are part of using a shared, professionally relevant, vocationally oriented language for building and communicating meaning-making narratives. Another element of that vocabulary is "craft," an important term that conveys special and skilled capabilities within a practice—making or doing something skillfully.

"Craft," "practice," and "practitioner" have cognitive as well as kinesthetic importance, although they most generally apply to artisanship with tools and technologies. Referring to our horticulture example, craft has broad application in reference to environmental manipulation, alterations in plant physiology and response, plant propagation, uses of plants as groups within the built environment through landscape design (art), and other aspects of practical horticulture. But the same may be said of the practice of law, medicine, architecture, business management, and others. The elements of practice associated with those careers are a type of craft when they are applied skillfully and bring about the desired outcomes.

The quality of our practice is embodied and expressed in our craft. Our vocational narrative and framework must also include the concept of "quality." Attention to quality is not only important for developing and implementing a successful practice; it is also an important virtue that conveys meaning and purpose. Regarding horticulture, quality is a characteristic that is widely considered and commonly discussed in connection with the practice of all horticulture technologies, for-profit business practices, not-for-profit services, and overall craft.

Quality is also a linchpin of a sustainability narrative and professional framework. The perception, identification, and metaphysics of quality can be the subject of much reflection and contemplative practice within the curriculum and pedagogy, forming a connection between narratives of scholarship, ethics, and spirituality.

Caring about quality in our professional practice becomes a reflection of our moral character, represented by an array of important virtues such as empathy, courage, fortitude, honesty, and loyalty in addition to those previously identified. This moral grounding is a critical part of making meaning and finding purpose and is strengthened by our references to quality and virtue in our curriculum, pedagogy, and dialogue with students. Melding scholastic and moral narratives in our vocabulary endows our education with a unique power to inspire and motivate.

At this point, our goal is to build a vocational narrative as we move forward in our curriculum using a highly diverse language of professional practice, craft, quality, and moral character that contributes to a sense of purpose and feelings of well-being among our students. Add to this mix "community" and "community service," a natural component within certain professions with community service obligations, such as social worker. However, business training curricula also need this vocabulary to create the necessary narrative and framework for a broader sense of purpose and vocation.

In connection with business education, consider that the first corporations were created in Europe as not-for-profit entities to build institutions, such as hospitals and universities, for the *public good*. The American business corporation evolved from a limited, tightly controlled franchise incorporated to complete *public improvement projects* such as constructing bridges, roads, and canals, and to provide certain services deemed essential to a fledgling economy, such as banking and insurance. The original foundation of the corporation as a business rests on community service.

A vocational vocabulary, narrative, and framework of practice and craft is often a natural part of technical education, particularly classic trades such as carpenter and woodworker, plumber, electrician, and metallurgist as well as artisan crafts such as ceramicist, glass blower, and more. These manual trades and artisan skills are wonderful examples of practices that weave together thinking and doing, producing a genuinely useful outcome and tying craftspeople to those who benefit from their efforts. The reward is a comforting sense of purpose, meaning, and vocation.

Matthew Crawford, a PhD leading a high-profile Washington, D.C., think tank, quit that prestigious position to open his own small motorcycle repair shop. The author of the book *Shop Class as Soulcraft*, he reports that the identification, analysis, and repair of motorcycle problems has been one of the most challenging and rewarding endeavors in his life—a perfect blend of thinking, doing, and direct customer service that he labels "soul craft." Many tradespeople certainly would agree with his assessment. We need to find those elements in other areas of professional and technical education and underscore them with appropriate vocabulary, narrative, and framing.

The concepts and terms previously discussed may also be put into a context to help your students recognize and focus on their strengths. Apply the terms practice, craft, and quality when talking with students about their knowledge and skills. Use them to emphasize where students show a comprehensive knowledge and an accomplished skill. Compliment students on their knowledge and skill in this "practice" or with that "craft" resulting in quality work that will provide a valuable "community service" or contribution to the "common good." This type of feedback generates a sense of purpose, meaning, and vocation.

You may also help students identify their strengths during reflective and other contemplative moments. Provide them with well-chosen questions for discussion or comment in class journals, such as what did you do well and why; what was the outcome; and what personal/professional strength did you demonstrate?

Choose intentional professional and vocational vocabulary that associates the products or services within your discipline with outcomes that matter; for instance, community service, community development, and the public good. "Community service" is an important term, concept, and outcome that is closely tied to the common good.

A classic story of different perspectives on work and work outcomes begins with three workers assigned to break rocks. When asked to describe what they are doing, one worker responded, "Making little rocks out of big ones." Another said, "Making a living." The third declared, "Building a cathedral!" Each comment is accurate, but you can certainly imagine the range of feelings among these three workers based on their interpretations of their work outcomes. The third worker certainly derives the most meaning from his work because he understands how work contributes to something larger than himself and benefits the whole community.

Career orientation, perspective, and a focus on outcomes that matter are reasons to choose your vocabulary carefully to construct career- and life-building narratives and frameworks that convey purpose, meaning, and a sense of vocation for our students. Within the realm of professional and technical education, any subject of study and portrayals of any associated career can connect to a broader purpose. The premise is that focusing on broader purpose imbues the work with greater meaning.

Your vocational vocabulary and narrative should contain a diverse language of moral character, well-being, professional practice or craft, and community service. You may go further with your students to include quality, stewardship, sustainability, spirituality, and fulfillment—any vocabulary related to a narrative and framing with joint relevance to the discipline and for discerning vocation.

Constructing educational narratives that meet our teaching to inspire vocation goals will be made more powerful through relevant and guiding themes. Some of the vocabulary of vocation detailed previously serves a dual purpose: to establish and support important educational themes—for instance, quality, sustainability, and community service.

In the horticulture program example, vocabulary contributed to two overarching narrative themes: the Earth stewardship and one with nature narratives that most students visualized in one way or another for themselves and readily accept. The goal is for the students to envision themselves in a professional/personal narrative as competent horticulture practitioners performing their craft in a sustainable manner to serve the needs of their communities.

Neil Postman identifies the building blocks for a compelling narrative:

> to direct one's mind to an idea and . . . a story—not any kind of story, but one that tells of origins and envisions a future, a story that constructs ideals, prescribes rules of conduct, provides a source of authority, and, above all, gives a sense of continuity and purpose. [A great narrative, or story,] . . . is one that has sufficient credibility, complexity, and symbolic power to enable one to organize one's life around it.[5]

Helping our students find meaning and purpose in their work and in their lives means that we are obligated to create or identify relevant and compelling narratives to frame and provide a vocational context for their education. In doing so, we help clarify the present, give point to their education, and give direction to their future.

In the largest sense, we need to answer the question of what kind of public do we want to create through public education? To find the right answer, we must look beyond issues of school management, the use of instructional technology, and methods of accountability—in other words, school "engineering" issues—to compelling and shared narratives that provide the inspiration for school and higher education.[6]

In that context, the principal narrative themes and frameworks used in the horticulture program example—"Earth stewardship" and "one-with-nature," and their subsidiary narratives "sustainability," "quality," and "community service"—are highly relevant, widely applicable, and compelling for several other professional and technical education programs. Narrative themes and frameworks come with a specific vocabulary that you will add to your growing lexicon for teaching to inspire vocation.

Consider for a moment important educational elements of the previous narratives. First, the story and history of human beings as stewards of the Earth, living in harmony as part of nature, brings forward all kinds of educational opportunities in a range of professional and technical subjects from agriculture and architecture to environmental engineering, medicine, social work, and urban planning, to name just a few. These are also narratives that can unite and bind people together making issues of inequality, racism, and class conflict irrelevant. The problems of environmental degradation and extinction beset us all, not just small segments of humanity.

Considering a narrative of sustainability, we get into a broad range of opportunities for professional and technical areas of education dealing with economic equity, environmental preservation, social justice, and spiritual fulfillment—sustainability in several realms and at many levels. Business schools are working to incorporate sustainable models and practices into their curricula, including multiple metrics for measuring sustainability such as the triple bottom line (TBL); environmental, social and governance (ESG) strategies, and the UN sustainable development goals (SDGs). These specific business narrative themes are comprised of important vocabulary that will link the acquisition of business knowledge and skill to meaning, purpose, and discerning vocation.

We need to remind ourselves that our purpose in helping our students discern their vocation is as much about achieving personal and spiritual fulfillment as it is professional success. Spiritual fulfillment may be found in professional and technical education having to do with a strong moral grounding. Alasdair MacIntyre writes in *After Virtue* "that the modern world suffers from a moral amnesia, a vague awareness of a deficiency of virtue that we can no longer describe."[7]

It used to be, in our country, that virtue was founded on and conceived as an integral part of community, contributing to the common good. However, it seems that such a tradition of virtues from the past has now, as MacIntyre states, "been suppressed and replaced by the moral vacuity of modern economics, individualism, and consumption."[8]

David Orr rightly points out in *Earth in Mind*, "The problem is that we ignore moral problems and/or give them the wrong kind of attention by creating a maze of rules and regulations. Without the intrinsic motivation provided by a clear moral understanding, the rules simply become a challenge to evade."[9]

Consider the collapse of the banking system in 2008 as an example of ineffective rules and regulations without a moral foundation. There is also a false equivalence in the common perspective that material wealth will ameliorate or mitigate for the absence of morality. Our vocabulary and narratives, in addition to being academically relevant, must also be morally sound and enriching. The moral imperatives relevant to your professional and technical curricula are best explored through contemplative practice.

Returning to the horticulture program example, the "Earth stewardship" and "one-with-nature" narratives were used as principal outcomes and points of purpose for the curriculum and pedagogy—particularly the implementation of horticulture technologies. The particulars were often framed within a subsidiary narrative, such as "sustainability." For instance, the manipulation of the environment to achieve a particular horticultural outcome is done against a measure of sustainability as part and parcel of effective "Earth stewardship" with an understanding of being at "one with nature."

Every time these connections are made, our knowledge and skills are framed in a larger, unifying context that imbues what is being learned with greater meaning and purpose. These narratives, and the frameworks of understanding they support, are also used to evaluate the appropriateness of various experiential and community-engaged learning opportunities for students.

Within the broadest context of the "Earth stewardship" and "one-with-nature" narratives, it is important that students come to understand that they are, to paraphrase Aldo Leopold, an integral part of an ecological system. If they will work within that system, they may experience ongoing prosperity. If not, well, we're beginning to see for ourselves what kind of outcome that generates.

The vocabulary we use, the narratives we build, and the frames of reference we create should be relevant to our discipline, our explorations of purpose, meaning, and vocation, and to solving the predicaments of humankind—these are relational goals. The challenge isn't that there are too few narratives for us to choose from, but in meeting the broad test of relevance.

There must be room in the broad narratives we build in the curriculum for our students' narratives. As pointed out previously in this text, we talk too little about our motives and feelings in relation to our occupations, experiences, and professions. We are educators and practitioners in our disciplines for reasons of deep resonance between our subject specialties, our vocational choices, and ourselves. We need to be more forthcoming and candid with our students to help them create and recognize a similar resonance by acknowledging and including personal narratives.

Best Practices 8.1: Vocabulary and Narrative

- You are cultivating an orientation, perspective, and gestalt around your discipline using an intentional vocabulary and narratives that frame it as a worthy vocation.
- Several valuable sources of vocabulary for framing a discipline as a vocation come from the virtues and first principles of that discipline as well as the services it provides.
- The terms "practice" and "practitioner" help create and expand a narrative around career competence, special knowledge, and refined skill important to a vocational framework.

- "Craft" has a cognitive as well as kinesthetic importance, and most commonly refers to artisanship with tools and technologies. The elements of professional/technical practice are a type of craft when they are applied skillfully and bring about the desired outcomes.
- The quality of our practice is embodied and expressed in our craft. Our vocational narrative and framework must also include the concept of "quality."
- Melding scholastic and moral narratives in our vocabulary endows our education with a unique power to inspire and motivate.
- Apply the terms practice, craft, and quality when talking with students about their knowledge and skills. Use them to emphasize where students show a comprehensive knowledge and an accomplished skill.
- Constructing educational narratives that meet our teaching to inspire vocation goals will be made more powerful through relevant and guiding themes.

USING CONTEMPLATIVE PRACTICE

At this point in your curriculum and pedagogy, you are using an intentional vocabulary to begin forming a purposeful and vocational narrative. To be most effective, you combine this approach with contemplative practice where the power of reflection may be focused on your narratives, elements of study, and experiential learning.

Coming back to the new group of students who have finished the initial questionnaire described at the beginning of this chapter, you explain that their answers form the first page of a journal they will be keeping as they progress through the course. Their last page, at the end of the course, will be a second set of answers to the original questions. Journals, as presented in chapter 5, are useful tools for contemplative practice.

Step back on a regular basis to pause and reflect with your students on their perspective and attitude about their education. This engages their right hemispheres in exploring a larger context of meaning for what they are learning and what it means for their careers and their lives. These moments of pause are also a good time for other types of contemplative practice and may be invoked at any point in a unit of study or during the term.

Self-selected groups of students, often the more mature and/or career-changing students, are more inclined to pause on their own to consider what they are learning. Take advantage of these moments. Take advantage of student questions to reflect on the current subject. As you take advantage of these reflective moments, your students' wonder and dedication to the subject matter will grow along with their self-image as practitioners. The more frequently they experience reflective and what are often referred to as "a-ha moments" in the classroom, the more meaningful their study and purposeful to their lives. These moments should be diagnostic experiences for students and teachers. As Bryan Dik and Ryan Duffy underscore in *Make Your Job a Calling*, "If your life goals and career goals support each other, you are experiencing the kind of congruence that fosters meaning."[10]

Arthur Jersild worried that the education system placed too high a premium on speed and not enough on reflection. "It is essential for conceptual thought that a person give himself time to size up a situation, check the immediate pulse to act, and take in what's there. Listening is part of it, but contemplation and reflection would go deeper."[11] For a refresher on the basics of contemplative practice, refer to chapter 5.

It is pertinent at this point to reiterate that using contemplative practices in your pedagogy is not an all-or-nothing proposition. If you are just beginning to add contemplative practice, consider beginning in an informal, occasional, and easy fashion—an overall approach that might be considered contemplative practice "light." Consider beginning with a perspective on contemplative practice to cultivate attention to an area of study.

Use a vocabulary dependent upon simile, analogy, and metaphor to characterize what you are doing as ordinary, orthodox, and natural. This involves words and phrases like "attention," "awareness," "alert," "open," "pause," "slowing down," and "keeping watch." Something else worthy of reiteration: your class contemplative practices are meant to explore your students' own beliefs, views, feelings, and responses so that a first-person, critical inquiry becomes an investigation of your academic study rather than an imposition of specific views.

Meaningful reflection includes recapturing an experience to learn from it and develop new understanding. Bringle and Hatcher, in their article "Reflection on Service-Learning: Making Meaning of Experience" in *Educational Horizons*, provide a list of best practices.

Best Practices 8.2. Meaningful Reflection

- link experience to learning
- occur regularly
- involve feedback to the learner to enhance learning
- help clarify values
- be oriented toward specific objectives
- be successful in terms of critical thinking
- include goals for future actions

- generate change in the student's life[12]

It would be ideal if all reflective and contemplative practice spoke to every one of these goals, but in a more practical sense we might consider this list a cumulative set of contemplative practice outcomes for our curriculum.

One of the most prevalent and pervasive antagonists to contemplative practice and focused attention are portable devices, particularly smart phones. If you haven't already done so, establish a policy about the presence and use of smart phones and other devices in your courses. Try to ensure that these devices are put away, preferably in a separate location from their owners, such as lockers or other safe places. But what about those in training for computer technology and associated careers in the tech industry? Some of their needs regarding contemplative practice will be addressed later in this section.

Begin most contemplative practice intervals with a provocation that connects to the unit of study just completed or an upcoming unit. These provocations can be in the form of a question, a pointed observation, an image, a sound bite, a video clip, or any combination. They provide the focus of contemplative practice derived from the unit of study.

As an example, in a medical school unit on taking patient histories, the professor may show a short video of neurologist Oliver Sacks's approach to this subject for instruction and reflection. The professor will then ask the students to reflect on Dr. Sacks's technique relative to classroom instruction. After a few minutes of reflection, the students may share their reflections in class, within groups, or as notations in a journal.

Keeping a simple journal of their reflections and thoughts about class subjects, as noted at the beginning of this chapter, is a common method of processing and documentation. You might first introduce journaling as a required course element and mechanism to help them learn and internalize what is being covered. What you want to convey to your students is that this is simply a natural part of accumulating and processing the information as opposed to some new, unorthodox method that they may resist. Introduce the idea of using contemplative practices gradually so as not to create any awkwardness or impediment to your students' comfort level.

You may feel guilty or impatient as you begin implementing contemplative practices considering that class time is precious. During those moments, keep in mind that contemplative practice is not a diversion or a distraction but a means to find deeper meaning in the material or experience. Another challenge: conducting contemplative practices is not always stress-free—the guilt of time pressure is an example.

No matter how careful your first efforts are, you're likely to encounter resistance to contemplative practice and/or superficiality in student participation. Under these circumstances, your charge is one of patience, reasonable passivity, and care in not pushing too hard. In some cases, individual student advising and tutoring may be required.

If you are in the habit of conducting group work and activities as part of your pedagogy, consider including group reflection as an additional part of those activities. Of course, taking time for a few additional questions or comments to focus attention and prompt some reflective comments from the entire class is a common practice. Again, don't expect too much or push too hard with these initial efforts to produce profound reflections or probing thoughts; it's about developing habits of mind, or mindfulness. This goes hand in hand with creating narratives that inspire a great deal more thoughtfulness about what is being learned and the impact of various contexts of application and practice for that information.

As you move forward with these practices, you are cultivating mindfulness in your students as both a practice—pause to think or reflect—and an outcome—they are more mindful and aware going forward. This is a major focus of contemplative practice in the classroom: assisting students to dive deeply into the intellectual core of your coursework, and then translating (self-authoring) that core into their own terms and personal-professional context.[13]

MINDFULNESS PRACTICE: BREATHING

The previous examples of contemplative practice include reflection and the development of mindfulness. A simple, very useful mindfulness practice described in chapter 5 is mindful breathing. One useful application of mindful breathing, and a good point at which to introduce the practice, is as a short calming and centering interval prior to exams.

Ordinarily, introducing mindful breathing requires orientation and instruction and may be fraught with discomfort and resistance in the form of superficial and/or inappropriate participation. However, this practice may be more readily accepted and appreciated as an "attitude adjustment" in preparation for a quiz or exam. Some students are often quiet and subdued just prior to an exam, exercising their own version of mindful preparation. Mindful breathing will assist them in a process they may be struggling to implement themselves.

Mindfulness practice is impactful and relevant for helping students see themselves within the vocational narratives we tell and the frames we construct. Further, it not only helps students become more aware of the current focus of study but also builds their capacity for holding multiple perspectives in mind while being open to something new. Mindfulness practice is valuable for professional and technical careers that are fraught with hectic schedules, time lines, and other demands. A mindful "slow down" or "pause" gives students valuable moments to reflect on their current professional (and personal) milieu and identify their safe places and lifelines.

In fields of practice involving design (e.g., landscape design, interior design, architecture), students tend to be harsh judges of their own work in ways that stifle creativity. This can be a serious impediment to successful practice and discerning vocation. Mindful breathing helps cultivate non-judgmental approaches to learning and practice, freeing students to exercise greater creativity as they proceed in their work.

In response to mindful breathing, an art student at Syracuse University reports that they no longer "found myself judging my work while I was creating. I had a hard time staying in the present moment and allowing myself to relax and enjoy the process. I worried about what others would think of my art." Mindfulness practice helped them ignore "the judgmental opinion of others and simply did art for myself—connected and accepting."[14]

Knowledge and computer technology professionals are now a large part of the modern-day business community. A key requirement in those fields is the possession of a keen ability to pay attention during episodes of multitasking. Multitasking, as you know, means moving back and forth between two or more tasks. Multitasking places high demands on left hemisphere search pathways, thus strengthening them while right hemisphere pathways for mindful attention are neglected and weakened.

Professionals with large multitasking responsibilities need to develop the capacity for a balanced state of cognition to help them effectively navigate between the near chaos of multitasking and mindful attention. At the University of Washington, David Levy uses mindful breathing and other contemplative practices to help students interact with technology in a more mindful way. After an interval of mindful breathing, he asks his students to spend time with a device engaged in a typical task such as texting, emailing, or internet browsing and respond to three prompts:

- Observe your own patterns of behavior, bringing attention to your body, your breath, your emotions.
- Decide which dimensions of your experience you want to cultivate or minimize (e.g., attention, fatigue, anxiety).
- Make conscious choices to cultivate some states and minimize others.[15]

More on contemplative practice for computer science and technology career students later in this chapter.

Jeremy Hunter, who teaches in the Peter F. Drucker and Masatoshi Ito Graduate School of Management at Claremont Graduate University, uses a simple but effective mindfulness practice with his students. After a short period of mindfulness breathing, Hunter's students are instructed to look at a very familiar person or thing as if for the first time, mindfully attending to every detail.[16] Students come away surprised at how much detail they notice for the first time and how much they ordinarily miss.

A similar training in mindful attention may be accomplished using hidden picture puzzles that can only be solved through mindful observation and attention. All these simple contemplative practices are designed to help students, pursuing what are often intense and anxiety-producing careers, to find ways to come to terms with those conditions. In doing so, they will better cope with their circumstances, be more effective, and find a comfortable niche and a calling within these careers.

The Center for Contemplative Mind in Society hosts retreats for Yale Law School students for the purpose of improving their practice through mindfulness training. As a result of these retreats, it became clear that law school education could be improved in the areas of listening, conflict resolution, separation, and connection, as well as creating new perspectives on the dynamic of "winning" and "losing."

At the University of Missouri Law School, Len Riskin worked with the students in his Understanding Conflict course on integrating mindfulness practices with readings and discussions to help them be more compassionate and patient, identify more closely with clients, and make better decisions. Following the course, one student wrote:

> I think the most important thing the practice gives us is deliberation. I find I am less likely to jump to conclusions, the way your law professors try to get you to do. It's harder to push my buttons than it was before I started this practice. I'm cooler-headed and likely to see any issue from more angles, which is the key to solving legal problems.[17]

Similar mindfulness training has proved helpful at the Roger Williams University Law School. In David Zlotnick's Trial Advocacy: Integrating Mindfulness Theory and Practice course, students are asked to conduct direct examination of a witness while blindfolded, which requires the students to listen more carefully to the witness instead of focusing solely on their trial notes.

Zlotnick's students also undertake mock trials where students are deliberately interrupted with repeated objections, and at the point where they show frustration and anger, a bell is rung to remind them to use anger management mindfulness practice to help them let go of their anger and clear their mind to focus on the facts of the case.[18] Zlotnick's intent through mindfulness practice is to help his students stay in the moment and become agile in monitoring and adjusting their approach to trial law as compassionate, connected lawyers.

MINDFULNESS PRACTICE: LISTENING

After familiarizing your students with basic mindfulness breathing and its benefits, move on to mindful listening. Unless you know a student has a hearing disability, you presume they all can hear. The real question is, do they all possess an acute ability to listen? Listening is absorbing words, processing them, understanding them, and finally, analyzing them.

Good listening is a distinctly right-hemisphere capability that requires a mindful state of cognition to be most effective. Deep listening is a way of hearing that requires mindful attention to what is being heard in the moment without trying to control or judge it. It means that we listen to precisely what is being heard without stereotyping or imposing assumptive filters.

Students' deep listening in the classroom, and later in their professional and personal lives, requires that they hear precisely what is being presented while being aware of their resulting thoughts and emotions—attentive listening. Such practice discourages preemptive planning and formulating of responses or interruptions. Deep listening practice improves retention and encourages insight. Barbezat and Bush, in *Contemplative Practices in Higher Education*, elaborate on the importance of deep listening:

> Through teaching listening, we are directly exploring ways in which the contemplative can have a profound influence in the academy: the role of not knowing and not judging in the process of learning, . . . the power of simply bearing witness, and the role of receptivity and openness in understanding.[19]

Mindful and deep listening is crucial to professions and community lives that can be intensely interpersonal, such as the practices of medicine, psychiatry, psychology, law, social work, and several others.

Deep listening begins with an ability to switch off one's internal chatter and simply listen out to become aware of ambient sounds. This simple, mindful listening may be an extension of a mindful breathing interval. After several minutes of mindful breathing, ask your students to become aware of ambient sounds. Begin this exercise with a focus on sounds close by and then extending out further to awaken student sensitivity to listening.

To further this gradual progression in mindful listening toward the practice of deep listening, introduce ambient music into mindfulness practice. The music component of mindful listening can be very calming and centering for students and professionals working under stressful conditions. After an interval of mindful breathing, introduce a piece of soft classical or ambient music and instruct your students to focus on its attributes: individual musical elements, tempo and flow, changes in volume and emphasis, and so forth.

Remind your students that as other thoughts emerge, notice them, and return your attention to the music.

A combination of mindful breathing and listening to music can be a wonderful prelude to the deep listening, concentration, and the attentiveness required for the introduction of new information. If you like to begin class sessions with a mindful moment, a prelude of soft or ambient music when students are filtering into class is good preparation. Next steps in mindful and deep listening practice can focus on instruction and instructional material and exercises for students to listen to each other in discussion.

Several good protocols and exercises are useful for person-to-person mindful and deep listening training. These are basically speaking and listening encounters that require listeners to carefully and as precisely as possible repeat what they have heard. This will require that you break the class up into speaking and listening pairs of students. The students should use either class material that you provide or a personal story that, in either case, will provide a short (approximately three minutes) narrative for the other student to listen to. The students may decide who will start as speaker and who will start as listener.

The exercise begins with the chosen speaker reading or telling their short story and the listener charged with listening attentively without interruption. When the speaker is finished, the listener will paraphrase the speaker's story with as much detail as he can recall. The speaker will correct the listener when necessary. When each is satisfied that the listener fully comprehends the story, they switch roles and repeat the process. At the end of the reciprocal storytelling, the students should be given time to discuss the challenges and pitfalls of mindful and deep listening as experienced with this exercise. When this exercise is built around course material, the impact on processing and understanding that material is often much more comprehensive.

Today's challenges in listening are not only based on superficial listening skills but also on a utilitarian approach to dialogue that revolves around simply getting a point across rather than hearing another's story. Refer back to Best Practices 5.5. Mindful Listening on page 91.

Consider extending your mindful and deep listening practice to audio recordings and videos in addition to your classroom presentations and group discussions.

MINDFULNESS PRACTICE: READING

Use the reading and writing requirements in the curriculum as opportunities for contemplative practice, as was first presented in chapter 5. The added element of contemplative practice dovetails nicely with required reading and writing. Mindful reading will help students slow down and attend more carefully to their reading assignments. In some professional programs, such as law school where a great deal of emphasis is placed on the reading and discussion of cases, contemplative reading combines the explicit literal meaning and deeper meaning brought out through personal reflection to convey the full meaning of the text to each student.

An example of a basic approach to contemplative reading comes from biologist David Haskell's Food and Hunger course at the University of the South described in chapter 5. His participatory reading aloud approach proceeds at a slow and contemplative pace that immerses students in portions of the text Haskell feels are of particular importance. In addition to contemplative, or mindful reading, Haskell also employs mindful breathing and journal writing to help the students reflect on their scholarship.

A mindful reading of Martin Luther King's "Letter from the Birmingham Jail" is a common practice within some law school curricula. The letter is read one sentence at a time, each by a different student; a moving and impactful exercise that allows each student to contemplate its meaning relative to social justice and legal precedent. This experience amplifies each student's understanding of the work of Martin Luther King, the broad meaning and impact of this piece of writing, and their juxtaposition to it as evolving legal experts.

Many different narrative themes that you introduce, such as the one-with-nature and stewardship of the Earth examples used in this text, may by their very nature bring out a contemplative frame of mind, making mindfulness reading and other contemplative practices much easier for students to engage and participate in. Mary O'Reilley, at the University of Saint Thomas in Minnesota, engages her students in reflective reading with these instructions:

- Center yourself in your mind and body, place and purpose.
- Read the passage reflectively several times.
- Consider the questions: What speaks most profoundly to me here? What does my inner teacher want me to hear?
- Write for five or ten minutes.[20]

She may also involve her students in shared reflective reading this way:

- Keep a few minutes of silence together.
- One person reads the text aloud. All listen.
- Each one speaks to something the reading sparks in them.
- If appropriate, general discussion.[21]

Such slow reading is the focus of concentration and contemplation. This type of mindful reading not only reveals a deeper connection with the material but may also help students make deeper connections with their classmates.

Some instructors will conduct what might be called a "word slam" with their contemplative reading. Building on the shared reading process described above, have students select a single word that has meaning to them for discussion or a journal entry. After such an experience on the subject of immigration, a student at Temple University wrote in the journal, "I became absorbed in the word 'sanctuary.' What is sanctuary? How do we welcome individuals seeking it? Must we bar people from receiving sanctuary? Everyone should engage in daily contemplative reading because it relaxes the mind and body and can help you consider ideas and concepts with a fresh perspective."[22]

Contemplative reading exercises may be used in online courses as a one-on-one connection between you and individual students. You may find this a necessity in that student participation in online courses can be superficial. To encourage mindful and attentive reading, you will need to supply some prompts and questions to help your students focus, contemplate, and reflect on the material.

If you feel that the online subject is compelling and/or provocative enough, you may post the information in a group chat and guide the experience to elicit mindful reading and commentary on the part of everyone. Students who might be reluctant to participate in such an exercise in class are often more likely to participate online when they have more time to contemplate and deliberate before responding.

MINDFULNESS PRACTICE: WRITING

A common companion to academic reading is some form of documentation and analysis of what has been read: an essay, theme, or journal entry. Journal writing achieves a new, more explicit form of understanding through the additional mindfulness that thoughtful writing requires. Writing is another means for collecting and sharing our thoughts, if only with ourselves.

Mindfulness and other contemplative practices cultivate a capacity for improved, more meaningful writing. However, contemplative writing emphasizes the process as much or more than the product. This is especially important to keep in mind for early efforts at this kind of writing. Students require a quiet space for such work where they can think carefully about their writing without disturbance.

Student journal writing isn't about creating a scholarly piece of writing or journalism; it's about self-exploration and expression. Each entry is a reflection on and a response connected to their scholarship. A typical instruction for each journal entry is to write briefly about your thoughts, interpretations, insights, academic and personal responses to scholarly information or experience in the first person.

Journal entries should be composed soon after an associated unit of study, classroom or laboratory experience, in-community-engaged learning interval, or another learning opportunity. These need not, and probably should not, be lengthy treatises. The directions for journal entries should reflect the intentions of the course and focus on the immediate experience of the student. The journals become part and parcel of the course requirements and student assessment.

A simple mindful writing exercise is to ask students to record in a journal their thoughts and interpretations of a discussion, group exercise, media presentation, or other class event. You can issue the same instructions regarding their thoughts and reactions following another kind of contemplative practice. They may use individual notebook paper for these entries and then compile them into a journal at the end of the quarter. Layla Phillips at Georgia State University provided the following set of directions for her students:

> Every time we do a contemplative exercise in class or have a contemplative homework assignment, briefly comment in this journal. It may be handwritten. Please use a campus blue book or other small pamphlet you can hand in at the end of the term. Each entry should be about a paragraph. You should record your feelings, thoughts, sensations, and any related experiences or insights. Do this as soon after the exercise as possible, as you will lose clarity if you wait.[23]

Inevitably you will have students who are uncomfortable writing in a journal. Be sure to clarify for them that these are not composition assignments that will be graded as such. You may find it acceptable for them to write a series of declarative statements, or isolated thoughts that, ordinarily, could be construed as non sequiturs in conversation or creative writing. The point is that each student write, in whatever style or manner, their perceptions, feelings, and interpretations of their educational experience. Assure them that the process will become easier as they gain experience with it. Also, assure students that their journals are strictly confidential and that only you will read them.

Whenever possible, provide your students with time to write a journal entry immediately following the experience you want them to reflect on. A useful precursor to composing journal entries is an interval of mindful breathing that will help the previous experience and/or information settle into place. It may be helpful to make the structure and style of the journal very loose, such that it may include clippings, drawings, and so forth in the manner of a scrapbook if that will stimulate reticent journal writers to be more involved and creative.

Ask for examples of journal entries part way through the course so that you can check their progress and then arrange to meet with any students who are obviously struggling with this assignment.

Contemplative writing in the form of journal entries or other types of writing with students in a more advanced stage of their education will have a sharper focus on their professional practice. For example, you might ask them to reflect on practices and craft covered in a lab, studio, or field work with commentary on their experience, growing competency, skillfulness, and applications. Your students will likely find such writing experiences to be particularly impactful in self-evaluation and, ultimately, their growing sense of purpose, meaning, and vocation.

MINDFULNESS PRACTICE: CONTEMPLATIVE MOVEMENT

Contemplative movement is widely practiced among many of the world's cultures, especially in Asia. Contemplative walking takes many forms, from a simple constitutional stroll—an old-fashioned term related to walking to maintain a healthy "constitution"—to more deliberate and formalized walking rituals. Walking labyrinths have come back into vogue following a tradition that goes back thousands of years. A labyrinth is a meandering path, often unicursal, with a singular path leading to a center—a symbolic form of pilgrimage on a path rising toward greater understanding and enlightenment.

Tai chi is a slow-motion, soft martial art that groups of people practice every morning in parks and green spaces across China. Yoga is another widely practiced contemplative movement that connects the body and the fluctuations of the mind to the rhythms of breathing, resulting in a contemplative and mindful state.

Mindful and contemplative movement may be very effective in relieving stress and clearing one's mind to open space for focused or "centered" thought. Vietnamese Zen master Thich Nhat Hanh recommended a very simple mindful walking practice that, coordinated with breathing, focused on walking and mindful, mantra-like phrases, such as "I am home," or "all is calm." Such simple contemplative walking may be practiced anywhere and at any time, a good way for your students to extend and deepen their mindfulness practice. Many students report that mindful walking following a class meeting has helped them process what they have learned.

MINDFULNESS PRACTICE: INFORMATION TECHNOLOGY

Information technology students—including computer science, software technology, and their associated disciplines—will benefit from contemplative practice as much or more than other students. However, special mindful challenges are associated with these curricula and the training needs of those students and any others where computer technologies are an important component.

Our digital devices, be they smart phones, computers, or other devices are useful but, as we all know, they can also be distracting, even addictive. Anyone who uses these devices—which is almost everyone in the developed world—and perhaps those in the tech industry most of all, need to apply a mindful approach to avoid succumbing to their potential for distractions.

Recall the description earlier in this chapter of a recommended approach from David Levy for dealing with the distractions of multitasking. What about contemplative practice for tech students to help them be more attentive and mindful of how they put the power of technology to work without losing their focus?

As David Levy points out in his book *Mindful Tech*, "Our devices have vastly extended our attentional choices, but the human attentional capacity remains the same. . . . we must figure out how to make wise choices, so we can use our digital tools to their best advantage, and to ours."[24] The idea of our students developing a "practice" and a "craft" is an important one, and the same terminology and its implications may be applied to digital knowledge and skill.

Contemplative practice, in particular mindfulness practice, can be used to assist computer science and technology students—as well as anyone using digital devices—to refine and focus their digital craft through practice, observation, and reflection.[25] We must empower our technology students to discipline themselves in their use of these tools.

All the preceding recommendations in this chapter also apply to computer science and technology programs. The difference is that tech professionals are faced with two specific problems regarding the demands of multitasking: first is the need to remain fully cognitive (bi-hemispheric) while shifting focus to maintain a high degree of mindful attention; and second, to resist the pull of multitasking energy that speeds up and degrades the level of attention possible.

This is where contemplative practice comes into play by activating the contextualizing, meaning-making, and calming pathways of the right hemisphere alongside the purely analytical functioning of the left hemisphere. With the help of contemplative practice, students can learn to manage multitasking demands to maintain mindful and higher-quality levels of shifting attention.

The following protocols from Levy for developing mindful attention when multitasking revolve around three attentional skills: focusing, noticing, and choosing.[26] This description assumes that you are the student. Whenever your attention is drawn to a particular task, how much attention do you pay to that task? This question is important because, at the same time, you are noticing other potential tasks vying for your attention. At this point you choose to continue with your current task or shift your attention to a different one. Breaking down multitasking in this way is meant to make you more conscious, or mindful, of your multitasking behavior so that you're not on autopilot in responding to every potential new task, or stimulus, that appears.

The process starts by asking students to observe their own multitasking behavior and routine, documenting what they observe, and analyzing the results to inform useful changes in their multitasking behavior. In addition, a basic mindfulness practice, such as mindful breathing, will also assist tech students in navigating multitasking with greater attention and calm, supplying them with greater patience and stamina for this activity.

Levy also recommends a more comprehensive exercise for students and professionals to help them learn how to observe and modify their approach to multitasking. A key ingredient is computer screen recording software to track and document multitasking. Several downloadable options are available at the time of this writing, and it is important that they perform the following functions:

- Save recordings for later viewing.
- Recordings include the sounds made by the computer during multitasking.
- Recordings also include ambient sounds in the vicinity of the computer.
- Recordings also include Web cam images.[27]

Students may use a remote video recorder or simply log their multitasking behaviors as they go, but neither of these methods is as effective as the feedback that a screen recording provides. Once a tracking method is in place, students should begin recording their multitasking intervals and then review them. They should take notes from their recordings documenting their habits, idiosyncrasies, and broader tendencies, particularly regarding switching tasks.

Task switching tendencies and triggers are important for students to take note of as well as the opposite reaction, refraining from switching tasks. Ask students to analyze their documented multitasking behaviors to formulate a strategy for more organized and effective multitasking. Finally, they should share their observations and discoveries with the class.

It may seem to some that these recommendations for assisting students with the demands of multitasking are overwrought and pedantic. However, it is likely that few, if any, technology students have examined their own multitasking behavior with any real degree of scrutiny. Through this exercise, even the most sensitive multitasking students often come to recognize that some of their switching tendencies are driven by procrastination and/or avoidance.

The principal goal of this mindful use of technology is to develop a practice of focused multitasking for professionals whose work demands it. Coming back to the larger point of this text, our effort to promote mindfulness for all students is to help ground them in their profession of choice, a condition that is ripe for inspiring vocation.

USING COMMUNITY-ENGAGED LEARNING

At this point in our process of curriculum and/or course revision, you should be using a vocabulary to build a narrative within your units of study in ways that imbue the scholarship and frame the profession with greater purpose and meaning. Our students' understanding of their education, their career perspective, and view of life should also be growing deeper and more meaningful through contemplative practice. Now is the time to add an element of community-engaged learning. The justifications, possibilities, and preliminaries for incorporating a community-engaged learning project in a course or curriculum are described in chapter 7.

Many of you probably have your students engaged in experiential learning in some form already, be it laboratories, shops, studios, or internships. Many professional and technical programs consider community-engaged learning experiences a special type of laboratory. This type of labeling and framing may make good sense for your program as well.

The next section will focus on examples of community-engaged learning practicums to assist readers new to this type of experiential learning in getting started. If you have community-engaged learning experience, you may find new information and ideas in these examples to improve your community-engaged learning practicums.

Before getting into the specifics of community-engaged learning practicums, consider one more perspective on the utility of experiential learning. It serves as a professional, personal, and vocational "prototyping" opportunity, which some of you may feel is implicit in experiential learning but is worth making more explicit before going ahead. When students are thinking about their future careers and lives, they must do a great deal of extrapolating with a limited amount of information resulting in a vague perception. One of the great advantages of experiential learning that takes place off campus in real career and working environments is the prototyping aspects of those experiences.

By prototyping, I mean an internal prototype that helps a student construct an idea and a mental image of what a particular career and lifestyle might be like *for them*. Prototyping, according to Burnett and Evans in *Designing Your Life*, is "asking good questions, outing our hidden biases and assumptions, iterating rapidly, and creating momentum for a path we'd like to try out."[28] The prototyping aspect of experiential learning—being engaged in a hands-on business or service in a career field of interest—is extremely valuable.

Before presenting community-engaged learning examples, consider this brief summary of the benefits of community-engaged learning as reported by students at Brevard Community College: "enriched learning, skill development, increased self-esteem, job contacts, enhanced critical thinking skills, increased civic literacy, and an appreciation of diversity both in the classroom and the service-learning site and community."[29]

Community-engaged learning practicums may be made part of a particular course or offered as a stand-alone course such as internships or independent studies. This decision revolves around the scale of the community-engaged learning opportunity and the appropriateness and flexibility of any single course. Large and/or time-consuming projects often work better as stand-alone credit offerings, whereas smaller and/or less-complex projects may be most successfully embedded in existing courses. The recommendations here will be geared primarily toward embedding a community-engaged learning practicum in an existing course.

Be advised that literature, examples, and supporting documents on stand-alone community-engaged learning courses may be found for multiple disciplines via online and other types of information searches. Also, the national coalition of colleges and universities known as Campus Compact (https://compact.org) is an invaluable resource on this subject. Among their many publications, the *Service-Learning Toolkit* and *Essential Resources for Campus-Based Service, Service-Learning, and Civic Engagement* are particularly useful.

PLANNING AND ORGANIZATION

The community-engaged learning component of a professional or technical course of study may be structured several ways. A major planning consideration depends upon whether you are working with multiple community-engaged learning providers or only one. In either case, you will need to allow the necessary time in the course (or curriculum) for student participation in community-engaged learning. If there are multiple community-engaged learning providers, this may benefit from a more student-driven organization because the community-engaged learning details connected with each provider will differ.

With a single community-engaged learning provider, you will likely work more directly with that provider to organize the experience. With single providers you may choose to be part of the community-engaged learning experience right along with your students to ensure curricular relevance. For multiple community-engaged learning providers, you may rotate between sites on a "drop-in" basis to observe, assist, and augment the experience with scholastic information and conduct contemplative practice.

The most important element in community-engaged learning practicums is a clear, mutualist relationship between the course objectives, units of study, and the community-engaged learning experience—an important point that will be reiterated several times. These ties may be created and expressed in several ways as you will see as we move forward with a community-engaged learning practicum description. First, you need a written community-engaged learning plan to describe the project, its objectives, and requirements, for example:

- Objective: Gain experience in (subject area) in a setting that affords the student an opportunity to gain practical experience with the current applications of the concepts taught in the course.[30]
- Complete a community-engaged learning contract that shapes the commitment between the student, faculty, and community-engaged learning partner.
- 20(–40) documented hours with an approved community-engaged learning partner (these are minimums; students may spend more time in community-engaged learning).
- Completed journal, essay, or other reflection tool.[31]

This objective covers the core of a community-engaged learning practicum, although some programs also seek to provide their students with a personal experience of community service, citizenship, leadership, and cultural diversity. Major topics to be covered may also be listed on the course plan, description, and in the parent course syllabus.

As mentioned, community-engaged learning experiences are often structured to be student-driven, particularly if students have several community-engaged learning partners to choose from. In this case, the class must agree on a particular theme, or set of themes, that will be addressed by the community-engaged learning experience. This may be preordained by the subject of the course, such as trial law, finish carpentry, or container nursery production. Still, even these subjects may be broken into specialty themes for emphasis in community-engaged learning. No matter the specific professional or technical theme, you may also impose a broad theme of study such as leadership, business communication, or strategic planning.

In any case, you should set aside the first 3–4 weeks of the parent course as time for the students to become part of the community-engaged learning apparatus, decision making, and planning. This means that students are often engaged in community-engaged learning before the actual practicum begins. Include in the community-engaged learning plan and description a set of competencies the students must demonstrate. You may define these with the input of the students as part of a "student-driven" enterprise or compose them yourself when you are working on the requirements and objectives. Consider these general competencies:

- The student will be at each community-engaged learning date.
- Formulate measurable community-engaged learning goals.
- Interpret and/or demonstrate the connections between your community-engaged learning experience and course concepts and principles.
- Complete the major community-engaged learning documentation forms.[32]

Make a preliminary determination on when and how much class time and practicum time will be devoted to debriefing and reflecting on the community-engaged learning practicum. Reflection may be initiated with mindful breathing or other contemplative practice and include group discussion. You will need to stimulate these reflections and discussions with appropriate questions and other prompts. Don't overlook the opportunity to bring in guest speakers who may add another dimension to the experience.

One other important element that must not be overlooked is scheduling team meetings that involve the students, faculty, and community-engaged learning partner personnel. These often take place at the community-engaged learning practicum site. They may be scheduled weekly, biweekly, or at another interval that the group feels is necessary. Err on the side of scheduling these frequently and then modify that schedule as the group deems necessary.

Construct a community-engaged learning calendar (with the S-L partner) to help keep everyone apprised of what is coming. Service-learning experiences, no matter the amount of careful planning and organization involved, will require a good deal of monitoring and adaptive management, especially if they are student-driven.

COMMUNITY-ENGAGED LEARNING CONTEMPLATIVE PRACTICE

The contemplative component of a community-engaged learning practicum is usually spread out within class time and at the community-engaged learning site. In-class contemplative practices, take advantage of having all the students together for group reflection and discussion, an important node when multiple community-engaged learning sites are involved. On-site contemplative practices often involve mindfulness moments to enhance attention and to process the experience.

Include time for reflection following important practices and procedures to generate a greater understanding of the purpose, meaning, and competency levels for those practices and to explore and underscore their vocational impact. On-site reflection "provides an opportunity for students to critically reflect on their experience, examine one's sense of self in light of the experience (values, assets, bias, purpose, etc.), and plan new courses of action along with trying out new skill and mindsets."[33]

Journaling, as you know, is not only a common form of contemplative documentation in class but also in community-engaged learning practicums. Another type of contemplative documentation that is less common but that can be every bit as effective is "photovoice," or photo journaling. Community-engaged learning students take and select photographs they feel best represent aspects of their service-learning practicum. They then reflect upon and explore the reasons, emotions, and experiences that have guided their chosen images.[34] Some of the benefits of this type of contemplative documentation are:

- It is a creative alternative to journal writing.
- Visual images can be a powerful communication tool.
- Photographs capture the lived experience of participants and give insight and deeper understanding about their world.
- Participants choose the most important images and compose a reflective caption.[35]

Consider providing regular or weekly prompts to stimulate entries anytime you require a community-engaged learning journal, be it written or photographic (with written captions). Two general areas of query regarding community-engaged learning prompts for journal writing and photography are the relationship between the community-engaged learning experience and the course curriculum; and the nature of the community-engaged learning experience as it relates to personal and professional capabilities, vision, and the discovery of vocation (e.g., "how did this week's experience tap into your particular capabilities?").

Providing regular, evocative prompts encourages students to reflect critically on the work they have performed during their community-engaged learning experience and to connect that work to the application and cultivation of their knowledge, skills, talents, and abilities. The prompts may be intentionally built upon each other throughout the community-engaged learning practicum and designed to continue the ongoing work of vocational exploration.[36] Here is a collection of suggested community-engaged learning contemplative questions to consider from the criminal justice program at the University of Dayton:

Preliminary reflection:

- What are your expectations for this experience?
- What do you hope to accomplish?
- What are your specific goals?

Reflection at the beginning of the experience:

- What are your initial reactions to your first few weeks of experience?
- What are you excited about?
- What are your concerns?

Reflection in the middle of the experience:

- How is your experience different than you expected?
- How has your perspective changed since the beginning?
- Are you accomplishing your goals?
- What are the surprises and disappointments?

Final reflection:

- Did you accomplish your goals?
- What did you learn about your host that surprised you?
- What did you learn about yourself?
- How has this experience shaped your career aspirations?
- How has this experience shaped your views of (subject area) and your role in this profession?
- How has this experience changed your perception of what you want to do?
- What would you do differently?
- Would you recommend this experience to another student?[37]

A useful and captivating contemplative or mindful seeing example comes from George Haskell's exceptional book *The Forest Unseen* and Thomas Murphy, anthropology department at Edmonds College: the "sit spot." Haskell marked out a one square meter observation quadrat within a section of Tennessee temperate deciduous forest and set about regular, documented meditations on this quadrat for an entire year. What he saw through patient observation and mindful seeing was diverse and revealing, leading to a series of profound essays on seasonal change in the forest, the intricate habits of forest creatures, and the overall relevance of his observations for all life on our planet.

Tom Murphy asks his students to do something similar as part of their human ecology community-engaged learning practicum series: spend contemplative time at a chosen "sit spot" and document what they see, hear, smell, taste, and feel. Below is his interpretation of the exercise:

> We would like you to select and revisit a "sit spot." Select a special location with some plants and animals in the vicinity but accessible enough that you can return on a regular basis. This place should be removed from everyday life (i.e., not your backyard) but accessible enough that you can visit it easily, at least once every other week. It might be in a conservation area, park, a garden, along a stream or a beach. You should be able to sit quietly and comfortably for at least 15 minutes each time you visit. The longer you sit the more you will observe.[38]

A "sit spot" may be located within the confines of the community-engaged learning practicum for a very pointed mindfulness experience.

Include in your community-engaged learning schedule a final contemplative "retreat," a time for mindful debriefing of the entire community-engaged learning experience. This is an extremely important element of the practicum to detail, focus, and affirm student memories and embodied knowledge from their community-engaged learning experience. Consider coming together somewhere other than the classroom to avoid the feeling of simply falling back into a previous mind-set.

Begin the retreat with a mindfulness exercise, such as mindful breathing, followed by a quiet reflection on the entire community-engaged learning experience. You may wish to include a few gentle prompts on segments of the community-engaged learning experience for the students to focus on. Next, arrange students into focus groups and use the final reflection questions above to stimulate contemplation and discussion.

STUDENT ASSESSMENT

As part of your community-engaged learning planning, determine how you will assess the students relative to practicum objectives and outcomes. Some of the requirements and competencies may include documentation, demonstrable skill, or tangible product from the students. If not, you will need to create a line of questions or some other means of collecting evidence of student progress that may include, but not be limited to, a final exam.

Two common important sources of assessment are student journals and community-engaged learning provider evaluations. Providers should submit a midterm progress report and a final report. You may also require a student self-assessment report in this mix. When students work in cohort groups, you may ask the cohorts to evaluate each other. Construct a rubric for you and the students to use based on the practicum requirements and competencies.

An obvious means of student assessment will be in the form of a tangible final project. For example, students participating in a restoration ecology community-engaged learning practicum may design and/or implement a small stream restoration as a final project. Habitat for Humanity will engage students in planning and building structures. Such projects will need their own assessment rubrics, and the community-engaged learning providers should be able to provide these. The project possibilities for community-engaged learning practicums are endless.

As a first-time community-engaged learning educator, you will need to remind yourself and your students of the evolving nature of this portion of the course. Flexibility will be a key ingredient with a requirement for close monitoring and adjustment. Be prepared to alter some deadlines and/or keep those deadlines fluid; some tasks are sure to take longer than expected. Be sure to identify the nonnegotiable deadlines for you and your students and make the necessary accommodations for them. A community-engaged learning practicum must be built into the course requirements in terms of your time commitment and that of your students, not simply added onto the course.

Recognize that the planning and execution of community-engaged learning experiences will take up a certain amount of class time and course credit. The significance of community-engaged learning to student experience and understanding more than makes up for the proportion of class time required. The same may be said for the impact of community-engaged learning on faculty creativity, spontaneity, and self-discovery. For more resources on planning and implementing community-engaged learning practicums, refer to the bibliography as well as the collegiate membership organization Campus Compact.

COMMUNITY-ENGAGED LEARNING PROJECT EXAMPLES

Examples of community-engaged learning projects that may be applied to a variety of education programs follow. Our first, from Edmonds College, was introduced earlier with the "sit spot" example. Here is a summary of the Cascade Citizens Wildlife Monitoring Project, developed by Thomas Murphy, anthropology department, Edmonds College:

> The Cascade Citizens Wildlife Monitoring Project (CCWMP) is a service-learning activity through which students ... draw upon traditional ecological knowledge and observation skills to help solve a modern problem [wildlife migration corridors]. . . . In the winter, students assist the I-90 Wildlife Bridges Coalition with documentation of wildlife presence and movements along the primary east-west route across the Cascade Mountains. During the spring, summer and fall students collaborate with Conservation Northwest and Wilderness Awareness School to set up remote cameras to document the presence of rare carnivores in the Cascades. The data collected by students is shared with government officials, environmental organizations and land managers to help guide the protection of wildlife corridors and the placement of freeway crossings.[39]

Although this community-engaged learning project is part of a stand-alone course in the human ecology series of the anthropology department, it would be relevant for several other professional and technical education programs such as restoration ecology, urban planning, forestry, wildlife management, transportation engineering, and possibly others.

This wildlife monitoring project is a five-credit (quarter system), stand-alone community-engaged learning course that meets for one eight-hour day each week and is offered multiple times each year with a variety of community-engaged learning practicums. Students may work on several community-engaged learning projects each quarter, all of them in partnership with local tribes, governments, and nonprofits, as well as business and industry. This wildlife monitoring community-engaged learning practicum, in partnership with CCWMP, occurs in the winter with a day of training and three full days of field work.

Murphy spent just over a year planning this project with the CCWMP, including his volunteer time with the group to become familiar with the procedures. He also enrolled in the Wilderness Awareness School's Intensive Wildlife Tracking Course to develop his tracking skills. These skills and techniques are passed along to his students. Students are expected to establish a "sit spot" and record their observations, sensory inputs, and thoughts as part of this practicum.

Murphy also leads contemplative encounters with his students throughout their community-engaged learning experiences. These experiences contribute to the community-engaged learning assessment along with the student's participation, field notes, and quizzes. A more complete description of this community-engaged learning project can be viewed and downloaded at https://serc.carleton.edu/bioregion/examples/59094.html.

A different example comes from a course in global environmental politics taught by Sonalini Sapra at Saint Martin's University: community-engaged learning in agriculture, food systems, and, more specifically, sustainable urban agriculture. Here is the project summary:

> In a Global Environmental Politics class, I devoted several weeks to the different issues concerning the nature of contemporary global food systems. As part of their study of these systems, students partnered with Parsons Family Farm, an urban organic farm in Olympia, Washington. They spent 15–20 hours during the semester helping them grow food, which we subsequently donated to community food banks. This community-based activity provided a useful window into alternative agro-ecological food systems and helped them examine the different ways local farms are addressing environmental issues and hunger in their community.[40]

Again, as in the previous example, I hope you can see a broad application for this community-engaged learning project in any of several professional and technical programs, such as applied agroecology, bio-intensive farming, urban agriculture, food systems management, food distribution, agriculture business, and public administration, to name a few.

Professor Sapra's community-engaged learning project outcomes are to:

- understand the key issues in global food politics today;
- analyze how political institutions govern commodity chains;
- explore the political and ethical implications of what we eat and drink every day;
- gain practical skills around farming and agroecology;
- critically read and analyze texts from multiple disciplines; and
- improve overall ability to clearly express ideas and opinions, both orally and in writing.

The overall objective of this community-engaged learning practicum is to help students become sensitized to issues of sustainability, food justice, hard work, and climate resilience in addition to traditional Benedictine values of stewardship, moderation, community, and social justice. Imagine the significance: a rich, impactful mix of vocabulary and potential narrative for conveying a sense of meaning, purpose, and vocation. This practicum required twenty hours of participation on the farm involving a range of crop growing, harvesting, and distribution tasks culminating in a food donation to the local community kitchen.

Professor Sabra accompanied the students on this project and engaged them in reflection and analysis with the following questions: "What issues/questions do these types of farms raise from an equity perspective? Is the Parsons Family Farm a good example of a 'food justice' initiative? Can we effectively use capitalist tools to address climate change? How can social justice initiatives at Catholic institutions foster inclusive communities?"[41] Assessment involved participation at the project site, submittal of a journal of reflections on the experience based on prompts from the instructor, and a final essay. A more complete account of the project may be found at https://serc.carleton.edu/bioregion/examples/184997.html.

Rob Turner teaches interdisciplinary arts and sciences at the University of Washington and makes a point of involving his students in community-engaged learning practicums. As a community service, sustainability, urban planning, and hydrogeology community-engaged learning experience, he developed a stormwater runoff mapping project for his students with the city of Bothell, Washington. Working in small groups, the students

> were tasked with mapping the flow of stormwater runoff on newly developed or altered properties in the City of Bothell. Each group did reconnaissance during rain events, tracing stormwater flow and identifying problems. Then, they made maps using a GPS, an aerial photograph, and City of Bothell stormwater infrastructure symbols. The students shared their results with the city in a presentation and a report that compiled each group's map and text observations.[42]

The big ideas that this project addresses are the environmental and sustainability issues around stormwater runoff and urban impervious surfaces; how students can learn to monitor, map, and communicate information useful for environmental management, urban planning, and other practical applications, as well as fostering connections and working within local communities. The specific learning outcomes for this project are:

- Critical and quantitative thinking—including improving your ability to evaluate what you read and see; identifying underlying patterns, connections, and discrepancies in hydrogeologic data; and generating graphics that successfully communicate complex quantitative information.
- Collaboration—including an improved facility in working with partners in an equitable and reliable research and problem-solving collaboration.

- Research—as manifested by improvement in collecting and organizing high-quality data.
- Ability to explain how different landscapes and infrastructure are likely to impact the flow and quality of stormwater runoff, particularly in the city of Bothell.

This is a five-week community-engaged learning practicum embedded within a hydroecology course. The project calls for students to work independently in pairs or larger groups depending upon the size of the area and the complexity of the stormwater runoff infrastructure. Class time is devoted to training students in the use of a GPS unit, mapping techniques, standard reporting protocols and terms, as well as learning how to investigate stormwater infrastructure issues with a member of city staff.

City staff also identified stormwater runoff trouble spots to help direct the attention of the students and used the resulting project data to update city maps and databases. Student assessment is achieved "via a draft map and report, a final map and report and contribution to a presentation made to the community partner.

"Each student assesses the contribution they and their partners made to their field work, maps, and reports." There is no mention of contemplative practice connected to this experience but, upon looking at the details, it is easy to see where these interludes may be inserted for additional benefit to the students. Community-engaged learning project details and supporting documents may be reviewed at https://serc.carleton.edu/bioregion/examples/68954.html.

Gina Vega of the management department at Salem State University has conducted several community-engaged learning practicums in business with a focus on business ethics. She explains her emphasis on business ethics this way: "We have been challenged to get the message across to our students more effectively than in the past that people in business must act honestly, responsibly, and with integrity."[43]

Vega's business ethics community-engaged learning practicums are meant to instill in her students a sense of the importance of ethical management behaviors, a focus on corporate citizenship, recognition of principled leadership, moral awareness, and participation in social change—a broad range of powerful narratives that convey meaning and purpose to help business management students discern their vocation.

To drive home these concepts and narratives about business management, Vega developed a community-engaged learning experience that put her students to work helping elderly members of the community connect to the larger world with training for email and internet connectivity.

Vega's business management students designed and implemented training programs with each student dedicating twenty-four hours of service for at least six individuals totaling 575 service hours for the term and training more than seventy people. In doing so, the students needed to exhibit a variety of leadership skills, use their business computing skills, and provide meaningful service to the community as an example of ethical leadership.

This community-engaged learning practicum was conducted at area senior centers, assisted living communities, or within SSU computer labs. The students were required to keep a journal of their service interactions with "clients" and reflections on their experience based on prompts from Professor Vega. The clients also contributed informal evaluations of their experience.

One of the journal prompts the students responded to in reflection is the question, "What does ethical leadership mean?" One student noted:

> We are acting as incremental leaders. We are doing something good on a very small scale by teaching senior citizens how to use email. . . . We are also making them feel like they are a part of something, which is something that they may not have felt in a long time.[44]

One interpretation you may draw from this student's comments is the notion of social responsibility and the impact of small actions that can have significant results. In addition, Vega also reached these conclusions about the impact of this community-engaged learning project:

> The business school places a heavy emphasis on computer technology, and students are sometimes unaware of how much they have actually learned. They surprised themselves when they realized the extent of their own computer skills and the joy they derived from sharing knowledge with others. They developed a great sense of communal responsibility for their elderly students, and they matured considerably in the course of the project. They also developed a growing respect for the challenges inherent in teaching ("teaching is harder than it looks"), although that was not one my goals.[45]

Since this community-engaged learning project was first offered, students have continued to participate in it on an individual basis through the University Service-Learning Center. The program became so popular with elderly residents that it has been extended to formal classes at local high schools.

Kiesha Warren-Gordon teaches criminal justice and criminology at Ball State University. She developed a human services in criminal justice sixteen-week community-engaged learning based course for upper-level criminal justice majors after spending a spring and summer working with the president and executive director of the Whitely Community Council in Muncie, Indiana. These two crucial partners became co-teachers for the community-engaged learning practicum and were involved in the development of the community-engaged learning component of the course. The three community-engaged learning outcomes are

1. understanding the organization and functions of public and private social services agencies;
2. understanding how criminal-justice professionals deliver social-service support; and
3. understanding the impact of social problems on individuals, families, and communities.[46]

The class met twice a week throughout the semester with the students spending the first eight weeks becoming familiar with the Whitely Community of Muncie, Indiana, and working with the two members of the Whitely Community Council who are co-teachers. During the second eight weeks, the students worked in four groups of five to address one of four problems that the community had identified.

The students, although ill-equipped to address these problems directly, identified useful strategies and connections for addressing them and implemented those to help resolve the problems. Students were assigned weekly reflection questions and documented their reflections as part of the community-engaged learning practicum and student assessment. Warren-Gordon noted:

> Assessing students' reflection assignments, many spoke of valuing such direct contact with the community partners. They also appreciated the community partners acting as co-teachers throughout the semester. Moreover, the students highlighted their own reconceptualizing of what crime is, the causes of crime, and how to prevent crime.[47]

At the end of the semester, Warren-Gordon met with the co-teachers to assess the outcomes of the project, their role in developing and managing the projects, and the performance of the students. The partner co-teachers praised the collaboration and integration of the project that allowed them to participate as co-teachers. The collaboration with community co-teachers fostered greater levels of overall trust within the community that allowed the students to develop close, one-on-one relationships with community members for a more successful community-engaged learning outcome.

Warren-Gordon summarizes one important outcome this way: community-engaged learning "provided students in this course the opportunity to have a transformative experience that would stay with them beyond the semester's end. The students were able to address their positionality and understand how it frames how they view what is a crime and who is a criminal."[48]

Here are more ideas for community-engaged learning projects by discipline:

Accounting and Finance

- Students can help local organizations maximize their financial processes, prepare taxes, perform audits, and so forth.
- Work with neighborhood leadership or advisory boards to put on workshops for residents of low-income areas on household finances and budgeting.
- Assist nonprofits with fund-raising efforts (grant writing, investments, budgeting).
- Develop a free tax-preparation and counseling service for low-income individuals (VITA program from the IRS).
- Assist in running and staffing a cooperative food store and credit union.

Agriculture

- Partner with ranchers and farmers to help solve their issues.
- Partner with local agriculture banks to put on classes for farmers and ranchers regarding budgeting/finances.
- Volunteer as judges at stock shows, 4-H events.
- Partner with county extension office to create new programs for the community (college student lead).

Architecture, Engineering, Environmental Science

- Design and create a playground for a community organization.
- Work with local communities to help reduce water/air pollution.
- Partner with local businesses (research labs) to volunteer/run tests.
- Environmental science and biology classes can work with an elementary school and its students on a pilot project to compost cafeteria meals.
- Partner with maintenance on a university campus to help with specific chemical/energy/environmental issues.
- Help third-world countries with sustainable energy, fresh water supplies, and housing.
- Serve as judges for a science fair, or partner with local schools to help with science projects (college/middle school science fair partners).

Business

- Students can create business and/or strategic plans for small organizations to aid in fund search, business growth, improved service capacity, and so forth.
- Work with neighborhood leadership/advisory boards to put on workshops for residents of low-income areas on household finances, budgeting.
- Students may develop a business plan or marketing strategy to help high-school students in art or shop classes sell their works. At the same time, mentoring is happening, and awareness of higher education business opportunities is being shared.
- Create and conduct workshops for homeowners in low-income areas to brush up on budgeting and personal finance skills.
- Students work with faculty to secure research grants, assist with writing proposals and identifying possible funding outlets.
- Students survey food and drugstores in and around the community to establish the relative prices and quality of essential items. They issue a monthly listing of this information, which helps prevent stores in low-income communities from raising their prices above those found in surrounding areas.
- Work with the Junior Achievement Program to give students an overview of the free enterprise system and basic principles of business and economics. Lessons range in difficulty, as students can be placed in elementary, middle, and high-school classrooms.
- Partnering with banks to help with personal accounting and money management. (creating workshops for the community or students on campus)
- Communications and broadcasting arts
- Students can assist local organizations in preparing media releases for programming and upcoming events.

Computer Science and Technology

- Show elementary school students how to create a website, a PowerPoint presentation, an animated video, and the like. Have students focus on their elementary school events, community service projects, or learning objectives to be shared with parents and perhaps the community.
- Design personalized software for local nonprofits to better manage volunteers, resources, finances, inventories, and so forth. For example, a volunteer center may need a program to match volunteer needs and class goals with community and agency needs.
- Assist a nonprofit agency in developing a website to inform both its clients and the public of its purpose and activities.

- Design a computer program to assist students in matching interests and skills to find appropriate volunteer placement sites within a community.
- Help a nonprofit organization or human services agency create and maintain a data base.
- Teach computer skills to senior citizens or those with disabilities (how to work a phone or computer).
- Design an educational game to be used in schools.
- Develop a computer system to track a local business's inventory.

Culinary Arts

- Create a program in which students teach families to create low-cost, healthy meals from canned food and boxed food items from the food bank.

Fashion Design

- Students can design and construct clothing for various local organizations, shelters, and so forth; costumes for local school theater departments; uniforms for children of DPS that have a need.

Public Health, Medical Services, Nursing

- Students can provide research and practical services to community organizations to learn about human growth and development, the influence of people's environment on their health, and so forth.
- Students work with community-based organizations and public health agencies to develop health education workshops and informational fairs.
- Develop a campus event in which students give free blood pressure tests, provide free and relevant information on the importance of healthy eating, facilitate blood donation, and so forth.

Journalism

- Students can write news pieces, obituaries, and calendar of event pieces for the local newspapers.

Marketing

- Students can create a marketing plan for a local bank to increase the number of college-age students who do business there.
- Assist local businesses in building their revenue.

- Partner with local business to create a new/improve marketing plan.
- Help a nonprofit organization create a public awareness campaign; design logos or prepare reports, brochures, or newsletters.
- Help children produce a program on a local cable channel.
- Write for a newspaper or newsletter that focuses on public issues that concern you.
- Help start a small-town community newspaper; help with a community newspaper produced by schoolchildren.
- Partner with local business to help with website.

Sports Management

- Partner with local rehab clinics to shadow and create new rehab ideas.
- Partner with schools to volunteer coaching and rehab.
- Partner with retirement homes to help with rehab.
- Serve as a coach or referee for a youth sports league.
- Teach aerobics classes.
- Help at local YMCAs or Boys/Girls Clubs with their activities.

The community-engaged learning academy is large and diverse with a plethora of resources to help educators in any field get started. Online searches using any number of keyword phrases structured around "community-engaged learning" will yield an abundance of useful results, including other examples of community-engaged learning projects. And don't forget Campus Compact as an invaluable resource with a highly informative website and many publications of interest. Finally, on the efficacy of community-engaged learning, this observation comes from Darby Ray:

> Connecting classroom learning to real-world situations and challenges has been shown, time and again, to increase students' investment in their learning, enhance their mastery of course concepts, build their awareness of themselves as public actors, and contribute to their psychological well-being.[49]

PROGRAM ASSESSMENT

The subject of teaching and learning scholarship was raised at the beginning of this chapter with a concern for how to assess your teaching to inspire vocation effectiveness. Many of you may have your own way of accomplishing this through a personalized approach to program reflection and analysis. If not, the advice that follows may help you review and assess your effort.

Begin by reviewing your vision for the work you have done to improve your course and/or curriculum. A good place to turn for this element are your course descriptions in the catalog, your syllabus, and anywhere else you have documented your purpose and vision.

Examine your vision for possible confusion or unnecessary complexity as well as gaps or omissions within either the subject matter content or the new material related to vocation. Consider as well how the addition of the new material and pedagogies related to and enhanced key course concepts. Were the vocabulary, narratives, themes, and frameworks well represented, and did they enhance the integrated learning that combines subject matter competency and the discovery of meaning, purpose, and vocation? Were you and the students overextended?

Another area to examine is course or curriculum design. Did the revised course and curriculum have continuity and connection? Were there conceptual or practical dead ends in the flow of the course or curriculum—dangling elements or practicums that seemed poorly connected to the rest of the course? Considering the course and curriculum as a whole, did segments or elements stand out? Were the various instructional modes within the course synergistic and cumulative in their effect, or were any isolated and ineffectual?

An assessment of connection and interaction is particularly important as it pertains to experiential learning, especially community-engaged learning. Look closely at the equivalency of different community-engaged learning and other experiential learning opportunities; did they all achieve an equivalent integrated learning opportunity between experience and scholarship?

These questions and analyses all point toward meeting course outcomes. One basic question: did the students demonstrate their understanding of the course concepts and practices as well as gain a sense of purpose, meaning, and vocation? In other words, could they demonstrate knowledge of the subject and skill in practice, and were they enthusiastic about their professional and personal prospects in this field? If not, were problems nested in the presentation, practice, and assessment of the subject matter and/or a misunderstanding or poor implementation of the vocational elements of the course in terms of vocabulary and narrative, contemplative practice, or experiential learning?

After all the hard work of planning and implementing a course and/or curriculum revision, along with the altered pedagogy to present the new material effectively, it can be very difficult to muster the additional time, energy, and *courage* to assess and analyze your work for improvement. Some of you may have the capacity to effectively assess your progress as it unfolds whereas others may need to take a more deliberate and concerted approach to assessment. In either case, consider it an inherent part of your vocation as an effective educator, and the results will be self-evident and transforming.

At this point in your teaching to inspire vocation project, you've implemented a range of practices that revise and enhance your course, curriculum, and pedagogy to help students discern their vocation. You have created a vocational framework in your pedagogy using language and narrative to make the professional or technical subject matter, practice, and life in this field of service more compelling and meaningful to your students. You should find yourself engaged in livelier, more meaningful conversations with students about your field of endeavor.

Another side to teaching vocation is often unrecognized: the fate of students who do not discover their vocation in your field of study. Some may find sufficient stimulus and competence in their scholarship and practice to continue toward graduation and a satisfactory career without the specific level of dedication and reward that comes with the discovery of vocation. Others may recognize that their vocation lies elsewhere, leading them to shift to another area of study altogether. And still others may drop out of college to take stock of their overall situation, hoping to identify a new educational path forward toward the discovery of their vocation. In any case, you have performed a valuable educational service in helping these students to see themselves and their educational, career, and life goals more clearly.

In teaching to inspire vocation, we build a unified framework for both *doing* and *being* in our professional or technical discipline that helps students discern their vocation. This means explorations of a broader range of actions beyond the instrumental requirements of our career fields to what we might *do* with our lives. In addition, it includes explorations of how we should *be*: our approach to life, evidenced by how we behave and conduct ourselves within our discipline, our personal lives, and our community.

Explorations of doing and being in life were principal elements of the curriculum in the antebellum colleges of the early nineteenth century. They accomplished this with a dynamic integration of intellectual and spiritual education that produced literacy, rationality, and wisdom. Teaching to inspire vocation is even more relevant today. Go back to the future and make what is old new again.

Textbox 8.1 Teaching Takeaways

- Begin your teaching vocation efforts with changes in vocabulary and narrative; move to contemplative practices and cultivating mindfulness, then into experiential learning.

- Vocabulary and narrative are good starting points for framing a course, the curriculum, and your pedagogy for helping students discern their vocation.
- With each new group of students, be sure to obtain basic information about their interest in your program and discipline with a questionnaire. Follow at the end of the term with the same questionnaire; note the differences.
- Teaching vocation involves providing an orientation and perspective on your discipline using intentional vocabulary for narratives that frame it as a worthy vocation.
- Three valuable sources of vocabulary for framing academics as a vocation come from the virtues and first principles that guide the discipline as well as the services it provides. Good examples are quality, craftsmanship, and practice.
- Moral grounding is a crucial part of making meaning and finding purpose, and it is strengthened by references to quality and virtue in your curriculum, pedagogy, and dialogue with students.
- Melding scholastic and spiritual narratives in our vocabulary endows our education with a unique power to inspire and motivate.
- Constructing educational narratives that meet our teaching vocation goals will be made more powerful through a relevant and guiding theme, such as sustainability, quality, community service, and so forth.
- A great narrative, or story, is one that has sufficient credibility, complexity, and symbolic power to enable one to organize one's life around it. (Neil Postman)
- We must make room in the broad narratives we build in the curriculum for students' personal narratives.
- Take time for reflection on a regular basis to examine student perspectives and attitudes about their education.
- If you are just beginning to add contemplative practice, consider beginning in an informal, occasional, and easy fashion—an overall approach that might be considered contemplative practice "light."
- Contemplative practice should link narratives and experience to learning, help clarify values, involve feedback to students to enhance learning, and occur regularly.
- Be patient in the face of student resistance or superficiality toward contemplative practice and avoid pushing too hard.

- A major focus of contemplative practice is to assist student understanding of the coursework and translate (self-author) it into their own terms and personal-professional context.
- Mindful breathing is the easiest, most widely used mindfulness practice.
- For professions dependent upon multitasking, mindful observation of multitasking patterns of behavior is an effective discipline.
- Consider using the full panoply of mindfulness practice involving breathing, reading, writing, seeing, listening, and movement.
- Community-engaged learning practicums serve as important vocational "prototyping" opportunities.
- Some community-engaged learning benefits reported by students: "enriched learning, skill development, increased self-esteem, job contacts, enhanced critical thinking skills, increased civic literacy, and an appreciation of diversity both in the classroom and the community-engaged learning site and community."
- Start with a community-engaged learning opportunity embedded in a course or as an additional course requirement similar to an internship.
- Important service-learning documents: community-engaged learning contract or agreement, student syllabus, and job descriptions. Include outcomes and a calendar in these documents.
- Whenever possible and relevant, engage community-engaged learning providers in the curriculum as adjunct instructors.
- It is imperative to include community-engaged learning on-site and/or classroom contemplative practices as part of the community-engaged learning practicum. Group reflection and individual journaling are common practices.
- Assess your teaching vocation efforts after implementing the important elements of a framework for teaching vocation: intentional vocabulary and narrative, contemplative practice, and community-engaged learning.

NOTES

1. Sharon Daloz Parks, *Big Questions, Worthy Dreams: Mentoring Emerging Adults in Their Search for Meaning, Purpose, and Faith* (San Francisco: Jossey-Bass, 2011), 44.

2. P. Hutchings and L. S. Shulman, "The Scholarship of Teaching: New Elaborations, New Developments," in *Change 31*, no. 5, 11–15.

3. David S. Cunningham, "Introduction: Language That Works," in *Vocation across the Academy: A New Vocabulary for Higher Education*, ed. David S. Cunningham (New York: Oxford University Press, 2017), 3.

4. C. J. Cowton, "Virtue Theory and Accounting," in *Handbook of Virtue Ethics in Business and Management*, ed. A. Sison (New York: Springer, 2016), 1129–40 Dordrecht. https://doi.org/10.1007/978-94-007-6729-4_74-1.

5. Neil Postman, *The End of Education: Redefining the Value of School* (New York: Vintage, 1996).

6. Postman, *The End of Education*.

7. Alisdair MacIntyre, *After Virtue* (South Bend, IN: University of Notre Dame Press, 2007), 2.

8. MacIntyre, *After Virtue*, 2.

9. David W. Orr, *Earth in Mind* (Washington, DC: Island Press, 2004).

10. Bryan J. Dik and Ryan D. Duffy, *Make Your Job a Calling* (Conshohocken, PA: Templeton Press, 2012), 67.

11. Maggie Jackson, *Distracted: The Erosion of Attention and the Coming Dark Age* (Amherst, NY: Prometheus Books, 2009), 93–94.

12. R. G. Bringle and J. A. Hatcher, "Reflection on Service-Learning: Making Meaning of Experience," in *Educational Horizons* (Summer 1999): 179–85.

13. Daniel P. Barbezat and Mirabai Bush, *Contemplative Practices in Higher Education* (San Francisco: Jossey-Bass, 2014), 99.

14. Barbezat and Bush, *Contemplative Practices*, 102.

15. David Levy, *Mindful Tech* (New Haven, CT: Yale University Press, 2016), 105.

16. Barbezat and Bush, *Contemplative Practices*, 103.

17. Barbezat and Bush, *Contemplative Practices*, 106.

18. Barbezat and Bush, *Contemplative Practices*, 107.

19. Barbezat and Bush, *Contemplative Practices*, 139.

20. Barbezat and Bush, *Contemplative Practices*, 118.

21. Barbezat and Bush, *Contemplative Practices*.

22. Barbezat and Bush, *Contemplative Practices*, 119.

23. Barbezat and Bush, *Contemplative Practices*, 126.

24. Levy, *Mindful Tech*, 3.

25. Levy, *Mindful Tech*, 6.

26. Levy, *Mindful Tech*, 88.

27. Levy, *Mindful Tech*, 93.

28. Bill Burnett and Dave Evans, *Designing Your Life* (New York: Knopf, 2016), 112.

29. Brevard Community College, Center for Service-Learning. *Student Volunteer/Service-Learning Questionnaire Results* (unpublished, Fall 2005–Spring 2006).

30. *Student Volunteer/Service-Learning Questionnaire Results*, 58.

31. Marina Baratian et al., *Service-Learning Course Design for Community Colleges* (Providence, RI: Campus Compact, 2007), 50.

32. Baratian et al., *Service-Learning Course Design*, 59.

33. Kelly Bohrer et al., "A Transdisciplinary Journey of Vocational Reflection through Immersion Programs," in *Engaging with Vocation on Campus*, ed. Karen Lovett and Stephen Wilhoit (New York: Routledge, 2022), 18.

34. Bohrer et al., "A Transdisciplinary Journey," 19.

35. Howard League for Penal Reform, "Factsheet: What Is Photovoice Methodology and Why Is It Important?," 2016, https://howardleague.org/wp-content/uploads/2016/04/Photovoice-factsheet.pdf.

36. Bohrer et al., "A Transdisciplinary Journey," 20.

37. Martha H. Hurley and Stacey Siekman Hall, "Helping Students Who Enter College with a Desire to Serve Discern Vocation: A Criminal Justice Example," in *Engaging with Vocation on Campus*, ed. Karen Lovett and Stephen Wilhoit (New York: Routledge, 2022), 53.

38. Thomas Murphy, "Cascade Citizens Wildlife Monitoring Project," in *Curriculum for the Bioregion Activity Collection*, https://serc.carleton.edu/bioregion/examples/59094.html.

39. Murphy, "Cascade Citizens Wildlife Monitoring Project."

40. Sonalini Sapra, "Growing Food and Justice in Catholic Universities: Urban Farming and Community-University Partnerships," in *Curriculum for the Bioregion Activity Collection*, https://serc.carleton.edu/bioregion/examples/184997.html.

41. Sapra, "Growing Food and Justice in Catholic Universities."

42. Rob Turner, "Mapping Stormwater Runoff Infrastructure for the City of Bothell," in *Curriculum for the Bioregion Activity Collection*, https://serc.carleton.edu/bioregion/examples/68954.html.

43. Gina Vega, "Teaching Business Ethics through Service-Learning Metaprojects," *Journal of Management Education 31*, no. 5 (October 2007): 648.

44. Vega, "Teaching Business Ethics," 659.

45. Vega, "Teaching Business Ethics," 665.

46. K. Warren-Gordon, "A Critical Approach to Service-Learning Criminal Justice and Criminology Courses," *Collaborations: A Journal of Community-Based Research and Practice 4*, no. 1 (2021): 3.

47. Warren-Gordon, "A Critical Approach," 3.

48. Warren-Gordon, "A Critical Approach," 4.

49. Darby Ray, "Essay 13: Self, World, and the Space Between," in *At This Time and In This Place: Vocation and Higher Education*, ed. David S. Cunningham (New York: Oxford University Press, 2016), 307.

9

Conclusion

> My work is loving the world . . . which is mostly standing still and learning to be astonished.
>
> —Mary Oliver, "Loving the World"

It seems fitting to end this exploration on teaching to inspire vocation where we began, with Mary Oliver. Our students come to us with questions about life, learning, and their place in the world. They are eager to find meaning and purpose. The "loving" vision that Oliver suggested is often eclipsed in professional and technical education by an instrumental focus on job training. This focus is incomplete and unsatisfactory as well as antithetical to personal and professional well-being. As such, it fails to prepare students to function holistically in the twenty-first century.

Forward-looking professional and technical education must provide relevant knowledge, skills, and context for a changing world, grounded in meaning and purpose. As illustrated in the preceding chapters, an authentic vocational framework can be created that includes intentional vocabulary, compelling narrative, self-reflection, and community interaction. In the words of philosopher and educator William Sullivan, "The vocational narrative, when embodied in a community of learning gathered around its goals, can promote both Socratic engagement with self-reflection and self-development and an ethic of responsibility toward the larger world."[1] In this light, our students evolve from being passive recipients of their education to active protagonists in the pursuit of learning with lifelong significance.[2]

Discovering vocation is of particular relevance to emerging adults deciding how they will live their lives and by what means. More to the point, students in professional and technical programs are intent on finding a place for themselves within a specific career path. Therefore, they are *primed* for such explorations of vocation. We also know that a person's undergraduate years have significant impact on their future.

Some believe that vocation is of such a personal nature that it cannot be taught. This text is meant to show that vocation can be successfully taught—albeit indirectly—by building an intentional vocational framework in the curriculum. As you implement this approach, your pedagogy will naturally evolve to carry these attributes forward with less effort and with growing competency.

Taking to heart the advice of David S. Cunningham, I'm reminded of an important teaching maxim, "monitor and adjust." Dr. Cunningham invokes the theme of "provisionality" to emphasize the need for prudence in teaching to inspire vocation. Specifically, that "it is wise to avoid the temptation to press for definitive conclusions or to describe the state of a person's life and learning with too much confidence."[3] Discerning a vocation(s) is an evolving process, one that will exist for different people at different stages of clarity, requiring flexibility in our approach to teaching.

When I began the research for this text, I was pleased to find substantial literature related to vocation in higher education, some of which you'll find in the bibliography. I encourage you to make use of the Network for Vocation in Undergraduate Education (NetVUE) within the Council for Independent Colleges professional membership organization. NetVUE is a nationwide network of private, four-year colleges and universities formed to enrich the intellectual and theological exploration of vocation among undergraduate students.[4]

Know that you are not alone in your pursuit of a more meaningful and significant education for your students. Be confident and committed in your teaching to help your students live their lives more sincerely, being who they are called to be, and doing what they are called to do. This is a great privilege, given that so many people in the world lead lives predetermined by external forces beyond their control. Remind them that their vocations and callings will evolve, reshaping their lives in a multitude of interesting ways. Go forward in the knowledge that you are helping your students find a more meaningful and significant life within the broad context of what you have to give.

NOTES

1. William M. Sullivan, *Liberal Learning as a Quest for Purpose* (New York: Oxford University Press, 2016), 189.

2. Sullivan, *Liberal Learning as a Quest for Purpose*, 193.

3. David S. Cunningham, "Epilogue: At Various Times and in Sundry Places: Pedagogies of Vocation/Vocation as Pedagogy," in *At This Time and In This Place: Vocation and Higher Education*, ed. David S. Cunningham (New York: Oxford University Press, 2016), 328.

4. Council of Independent Colleges, Network for Vocation in Undergraduate Education, https://www.cic.edu/programs/netvue.

Bibliography

Adamson, Glenn. *Thinking through Craft*. London, UK: Berg, 2007.
Annas, Julia. *Intelligent Virtue*. Oxford, UK: Oxford University Press, 2011.
Aristotle. *Aristotle's Politics*. Oxford: Clarendon Press, 1905.
Astin, A. W., and L. Sax. "How Undergraduates are Effected by Service Participation," *Journal of College Student Development*, 39.
Astin, Alexander W., Helen S. Astin, and Jennifer A. Lindholm. *Cultivating the Spirit: How College Can Enhance Students' Inner Lives*. San Francisco: Jossey-Bass, 2010.
Awbrey, S. M. *Integrative Learning and Action: A Call to Wholeness*. New York: Peter Lang, 2006.
Baratian, Marina, Donna K. Duffy, Robert Franco, Amy Hendricks, Roger Henry, and Tanya Renner. *Service-Learning Course Design for Community Colleges*. Boston: Campus Compact, 2007.
Barbezat, Daniel, and Mirabai Bush. *Contemplative Practices in Higher Education*. San Francisco: Jossey-Bass, 2014.
Baumard, N., A. Hyafil, and P. Boyer. "What Changed during the Axial Age: Cognitive Styles or Reward Systems." *Communicative & Integrative Biology 8*, no. 5 (September–October 2015): e1046657.
Begley, Sharon. *Train Your Mind, Change Your Brain*. New York: Ballantine, 2007.
Bennett, William J., and David Wilezol. *Is College Worth It?* Nashville, TN: Thomas Nelson, 2013.
Berry, Wendell. *Home Economics*. San Francisco: North Point Press, 1987.
Bohrer, Kelly, Maria Ollier Burkett, Castel Sweet, Mary Niebler, and Matthew A. Witenstein. "A Transdisciplinary Journey of Vocational Reflection through Immersion Programs." In *Engaging with Vocation on Campus*, ed. Karen Lovett and Stephen Wilhoit, 15–29. New York: Routledge, 2022.
Bok, Derek. *Our Underachieving Colleges*. Princeton, NJ: Princeton University Press, 2006.
Brady, Mark. *Right Listening*. Jordan Station, Ontario, Canada: Paideia Press, 2009.
Braskamp, Larry A., Lois Trautvetter, and Kelly Ward. *Putting Students First: How Colleges Develop Students Purposefully*. San Francisco: Jossey-Bass, 2005.
Brevard Community College, Center for Service-Learning. *Student Volunteer/Service-Learning Questionnaire Results*. Unpublished, Fall 2005–Spring 2006.

Bringle, R. G., and J. A. Hatcher. "Reflection on Service-Learning: Making Meaning of Experience." *Educational Horizons*, Summer 1999, 179–85.

Brisson, L. "Presuppposes et consequences d'une interpretation esoteriste de Platon," *Les Etudes Philosophiques*, 4, Octobre-Décembre 1993, 475–95.

Brown, Jeff. "Unplugging the GPS." In *Vocation across the Academy: A New Vocabulary for Higher Education*, ed. David S. Cunningham, 204–24. Oxford, UK: Oxford University Press, 2017.

Burnett, Bill, and Dave Evans. *Designing Your Life*. New York: Knopf, 2016.

Bush, Mirabai. "Uncovering the Heart of Higher Education: The Contemplative Practice Fellowship Program." In *The Heart of Higher Education*, ed. Parker J. Palmer and Arthur Zajonc, 161–65. San Francisco: Jossey-Bass, 2010.

Butin, D. *Service-Learning in Higher Education: Critical Issues and Directions*. New York: Palgrave Macmillan, 2005.

Cage, John, and Joan Retallack. *Musicage: Cage Muses on Words *Art* Music*. Middletown, CT: Wesleyan University Press, 2011.

Cambridge Dictionary online, https://dictionary.cambridge.org/us/dictionary/english/praxis.

Campbell, William D. "Vocation as Grace." In *Callings!*, ed. James Y. Holloway and William D. Campbell, 279–80. New York: Paulist Press, 1974.

Carnegie quoted in Frank Donohue. *The Last Professors: The Corporate University and the Fate of the Humanities*, 4. New York: Fordham University Press, 2008.

Carr, Nicholas. *The Shallows: What the Internet Is Doing to Our Brains*. New York: Norton, 2011.

Chickering, A. W., J. C. Dalton, and L. Stamm. *Encouraging Authenticity and Spirituality in Higher Education*. San Francisco: Jossey-Bass, 2006.

Clayton, Patty H., and M. G. Moses. *Integrating Service-Learning: A Resource Guide*. Boston: Jumpstart, 2006.

Clayton, Patty H., and Billy O'Steen. "Working with Faculty: Designing Customized Developmental Strategies." In *Looking In, Reaching Out: A Reflective Guide for Community Service-Learning Professionals*, ed. Barbara Jacoby and Pamela Mutascio, 95–136. Boston: Campus Compact, 2010.

Clydesdale, Tim. *The Purposeful Graduate*. Chicago and London: University of Chicago Press, 2015.

Colby, A., T. Ehrlich, E. Beaumont, and J. Stephens. *Educating Citizens: Preparing America's Undergraduates for Lives of Moral and Civic Responsibility*. San Francisco: Jossey-Bass, 2003.

Coleman, Liz. "A Call to Reinvent Liberal Arts Education." TED, https://www.ted.com/talks/liz_coleman_a_call_to_reinvent_liberal_arts_education?language=en.

Conyers, A. J. *The Listening Heart: Vocation and the Crisis of Modern Culture*. Waco, TX: Baylor University Press, 2009.

Crawford, Matthew. *Shop Class as Soulcraft*. New York: Penguin, 2009.

Crews, R. J. *Higher Education Service-Learning Sourcebook*. Westport, CT: Oryx Press, 2002.

Csikszentmihalyi, Mihaly. *Beyond Boredom and Anxiety: Experiencing*. San Francisco: Jossey-Bass, 2000.

———. *Flow: The Psychology of Optimal Experience.* New York: Harper Perennial, 1991.
Cunningham, David S. "Introduction: Language That Works." In *Vocation across the Academy: A New Vocabulary for Higher Education,* ed. David S. Cunningham, 3–12. New York: Oxford University Press, 2017.
———. "Vocation and Virtue." In *At This Time and In This Place: Vocation in Higher Education,* ed, David S. Cunningham, 189–91. New York: Oxford University Press, 2016.
Damon, William. *The Path to Purpose: How Young People Find Their Calling in Life.* New York: Free Press, 2009.
de Lille, Alain. *Anticlaudianus: The Good and Perfect Man,* trans. James J. Sheridan. Toronto: Pontifical Institute of Medieval Studies, 1973.
Delbanco, Andrew. *College: What It Was, Is, and Should Be.* Princeton, NJ: Princeton University Press, 2012.
Deresiewicz, William. *Excellent Sheep: The Miseducation of the American Elite and the Way to a Meaningful Life.* New York: Free Press, 2015.
Dewey, J. *How We Think.* Boston: Heath, 1933.
Dik, Bryan J., and Ryan D. Duffy. *Make Your Job a Calling.* Conshohocken, PA: Templeton Press, 2012.
Dillard, Annie. *Pilgrim at Tinker Creek.* New York: Harper Perennial, 2013.
Dormer, Peter, ed. *The Culture of Craft.* Manchester, UK: Manchester University Press, 1997.
Dreher, Diane. *Your Personal Renaissance: 12 Steps to Finding Your Life's True Calling.* Philadelphia: DeCapo, 2008.
Dustin, C. A., and J. E. Zeigler. *Practicing Mortality: Art, Philosophy, and Contemplative Seeing.* London, UK: Palgrave Macmillan, 2007.
Ebertz, Roger. "What Is Vocation." University of Dubuque, dbq.edu, http://www.dbq.edu/CampusLife/OfficeofStudentLife/VocationalServices/WhatisVocation/.
Eck, Diane. *Encountering God: A Spiritual Journey from Bozeman to Banaras.* Boston: Beacon Press, 1993.
Eyler, J. D. Giles, and A. Schmiede. *A Practitioner's Guide to Reflection in Service-Learning.* Nashville, TN: Vanderbilt University, 1996.
Falk, John H., Joe E. Heimlich, and Susan Foutz. *Free-Choice Learning and the Environment.* Lanham, MD: AltaMira, 2009.
Fortin, Jack. *The Centered Life.* Minneapolis, MN: Augsberg Fortress, 2006.
Frankl, Victor. *Man's Search for Meaning.* Boston: Beacon Press, 2006.
Fredericks, Jennifer, Phyllis Blumenfeld, and Alison Paris. "School Engagement: Potential of the Concept, State of the Evidence." *Review of Educational Research* 74, no. 1 (2004): 59–109.
Freire, Paulo. *Pedagogy of the Oppressed.* London: Penguin, 1972.
Furco, A. *Service Learning: A Balanced Approach to Experiential Learning.* Washington, DC: Corporation for National Service, 1996.
Garber, Steven. *Visions of Vocation.* Downers Grove, IL: InterVarsity Press, 2014.
Gardner, Howard. *Frames of Mind: The Theory of Multiple Intelligences.* New York: Basic Books, 2004.

Gardner, Howard, Mihaly Csikszentmihalyi, and William Damon. *Good Work: When Excellence and Ethics Meet*. New York: Basic Books, 2001.

Goleman, D. *Emotional Intelligence*. New York: Bantam, 2006.

Gordon, Howard R. D. *The History and Growth of Career and Technical Education in America*. Long Grove, IL: Waveland Press, 2008.

Hadot, Pierre. *What Is Ancient Philosophy?*, trans. Michael Chase. Cambridge, MA: Harvard University Press, 2002.

Hanson, Rick, and Richard Mendius. *Buddha's Brain: The Practical Neuroscience of Love, Happiness and Wisdom*. Oakland, CA: New Harbinger, 2009.

Harris, Richard. "Forward." In *Looking In, Reaching Out: A Reflective Guide for Community Service Learning Professionals*, ed. Barbara Jacoby and Pamela Mutascio, iii–iv. Boston: Campus Compact, 2010.

Hatcher, Julie A., and Robert G. Bringle. "Developing Your Assessment Plan: A Key Component of Reflective Practice." In *Looking In, Reaching Out: A Reflective Guide for Community Service-Learning Professionals*, ed. Barbara Jacoby and Pamela Mutascio, 212–13. Boston: Campus Compact, 2011.

Hayes, Steven C., Eric Fox, Elizabeth V. Gifford, and Kelly G. Wilson. "Derived Relational Responding as Learned Behavior." In *Relational Frame Theory: A Post-Skinnerian Account of Human Language and Cognition*, ed. Steven C. Hayes, Dermot Barnes-Holmes, and Bryan Roche, 21–49. New York: Kluwer Academic/Plenum Publishers, 2001.

Heffernan, Kerrissa. *Service-Learning in Higher Education*. Boston: Campus Compact, 2001.

Henry, Douglas. "Vocation and Story." In *At This Time and In This Place*, ed. David S. Cunningham, 169. New York: Oxford University Press, 2016.

Holland, Barbara, and Mark N. Langseth. "Leveraging Financial Support for Service-Learning: Relevance, Relationships, Results, Resources." In *Looking In, Reaching Out: A Reflective Guide for Community Service-Learning Professionals*, ed. Barbara Jacoby and Pamela Mutascio, 185–210. Boston: Campus Compact, 2010.

Howard League for Penal Reform. "Factsheet: What Is Photovoice Methodology and Why Is It Important?," 2016. https://howardleague.org/wp-content/uploads/2016/04/Photovoice-factsheet.pdf.

Howard, J. *Service-Learning Course Design Workbook*. Ann Arbor: Edward Ginsberg Center for Community Service and Learning, University of Michigan, 2001.

Huber, Mary, and Pat Hutchings. *Integrative Learning: Mapping the Terrain*. Washington, DC: AAC&U, 2004.

Hurley, Martha H., and Stacey Siekman Hall. "Helping Students Who Enter College with a Desire to Serve Discern Vocation: A Criminal Justice Example." In *Engaging with Vocation on Campus*, ed. Karen Lovett and Stephen Wilhoit, 51–65. New York: Routledge, 2022.

Hutchings, P., and L. S. Shulman. "The Scholarship of Teaching: New Elaborations, New Developments." In *Change: The Magazine of Higher Learning* 31, no. 5: 11–15.

Ikeda, Elaine K., Marie G. Sandy, and David M. Donahue. "Navigating the Sea of Definitions." In *Looking In, Reaching Out*, ed. Barbara Jacoby and Pamela Mutascio, 17–37. Boston: Campus Compact, 2010.
Jackson, Maggie. *Distracted: The Erosion of Attention and the Coming Dark Age*. Amherst, NY: Prometheus Books, 2009.
Jacoby, Barbara. *Service-Learning Essentials: Questions, Answers and Lessons Learned*. San Francisco: Jossey-Bass, 2015.
Jacoby, Barbara, and Pamela Mutascio, eds. *Looking In, Reaching Out: A Reflective Guide for Community Service-Learning Professionals*. Boston: Campus Compact, 2010.
Janney, Jay J., and Della Stanley-Green. "An Instrumental Approach to Teaching a Non-Instrumental View to Vocation within Business Schools." In *Engaging with Vocation on Campus*, ed. Karen Lovett and Stephen Wilhoit, 166–77. New York: Routledge, 2022.
Jaspers, K. *The Origin and Goal of History*. New York: Routledge, 2010.
Kaplowitz, Craig. "Helping with the 'How': A Role for Honors in Civic Education." *JNCHC* 18, no. 2 (2017): 17–23.
Keeling, Richard P., and Richard H. Hersh. *We're Losing Our Minds: Re-Thinking American Higher Education*. New York: Palgrave Macmillan, 2011.
Kegan, Robert. *In Over Our Heads*. Boston: Harvard University Press, 1998.
Kleinhans, Kathryn. "Places of Responsibility." In *At This Time and In This Place: Vocation and Higher Education*, ed. David S. Cunningham, 99–121. Oxford, UK: Oxford University Press, 2015.
Kolb, D. *Experiential Learning: Experience as the Source of Learning and Development*. Englewood Cliffs, NJ: Prentice Hall, 1984.
Korn, Peter. *Why We Make Things and Why It Matters: The Education of a Craftsman*. Boston: David R. Godine, 2015.
Kroll, K., ed. *Contemplative Teaching and Learning*. San Francisco: Jossey-Bass, 2010.
Kronman, Anthony. *Education's End: Why Our Colleges and Universities Have Given Up on the Meaning of Life*. New Haven, CT, and London: Yale University Press, 2007.
Lakoff, George. *Don't Think of An Elephant*. White River Junction, VT: Chelsea Green, 2004.
Langer, Ellen J. *Mindfulness*. Boston: De Capo, 2014.
———. *The Power of Mindful Learning*. Reading, MA: Addison-Wesley, 1997.
Langlands, Alex. *Cræft: An Inquiry into the Origins and True Meaning of Traditional Crafts*. New York: Norton, 2019.
LaReau, Renee M. *Getting a Life: How to Find Your True Vocation*. Maryknoll, NY: Orbis Books, 2003.
Levine, Arthur, and Diane R. Dean. *Generation on a Tightrope: A Portrait of Today's College Students*. San Francisco: Jossey-Bass, 2013.
Levine, Donald N. *Powers of the Mind: The Reinvention of Liberal Learning in America*. Chicago: University of Chicago Press, 2006.
Levinson, Daniel J. *The Seasons of Man's Life*. New York: Ballantine, 1978.

Levy, David M. "Head, Heart, and Hand: Cultivating the Contemplative in Higher Education." First Annual Association for Contemplative Mind in Higher Education Conference: The Contemplative Heart of Higher Education, April 24–26, 2009, Amherst College, Amherst, Massachusetts. https://vimeo.com/5187656.
———. *Mindful Tech.* New Haven, CT: Yale University Press, 2016.
———. "No Time to Think: Reflections on Information Technology and Contemplative Scholarship." *Ethics & Information Technology* 9, no. 4 (2007): 237–49.
Light, Richard J. *Making the Most of College: Students Speak Their Minds.* Cambridge, MA: Harvard University Press, 2001.
Listening Center, http://www.sacredlistening.com/tlc_about.htm.
Lynch, John P. *Aristotle's School: A Study of a Greek Educational Institution.* Berkeley: University of California Press, 1972.
MacIntyre, Alisdair. *After Virtue.* South Bend, IN: University of Notre Dame Press, 2007.
Mackness, Jenny. *The Master and His Emissary Wiki,* https://jennymackness.wordpress.com/2020/07/03/the-master-and-his-emissary-notes/.
Mahan, Brian J. *Forgetting Ourselves on Purpose.* San Francisco: Jossey-Bass, 2002.
McCabe, Herbert, O. P. *The Good Life: Ethics and the Pursuit of Happiness.* New York: Continuum, 2005.
McGilchrist, Iain. *The Master and His Emissary.* New Haven, CT: Yale University Press, 2009.
McWatt, Anthony. "Robert Pirsig & His Metaphysics of Quality." *Philosophy Now,* https://philosophynow.org/issues/122/Robert_Pirsig_and_His_Metaphysics_of_Quality.
Merriam Webster Dictionary online, https://www.merriam-webster.com/dictionary/praxis.
Merton, Thomas. *Learning To Love.* London, UK: HarperCollins, 1999.
Mezirow, J. "Transformative Learning: Theory to Practice." In *New Directions for Adult and Continuing Education 74* (1997): 5–12.
Mitchell, Stephen. *Parables and Portraits.* New York: Harper, 1990.
Mitchell, Tania. "Traditional vs. Critical Service-Learning: Engaging the Literature to Differentiate Two Models." In *Michigan Journal of Community Service Learning* (Spring 2008): 50.
Moore, Thomas. *A Life at Work.* Easton, PA: Harmony Press, 2009.
Murphy, Thomas. "Cascade Citizens Wildlife Monitoring Project." In *Curriculum for the Bioregion Activity Collection,* https://serc.carleton.edu/bioregion/examples/59094.html.
Neafsey, John. *A Sacred Voice Is Calling.* Maryknoll, NY: Orbis Books, 2011.
Oliver, Mary. "A Summer Day." In *House of Light.* Boston: Beacon Press, 1990.
Oppland, Mike. "8 Traits of Flow According to Mihaly Csikszentmihalyi." In PositivePsychology.com, https://positivepsychology.com/mihaly-csikszentmihalyi-father-of-flow/#flow-types-characteristics.
O'Reilley, M. R. *Radical Presence: Teaching as Contemplative Practice.* Portsmouth, NH: Heinemann, 1998.

Orr, David W. *Earth in Mind: On Education, Environment, and the Human Prospect.* Washington, DC: Island Press, 2004.

Palmer, Parker. *The Courage to Teach: Exploring the Inner Landscape of a Teacher's Life.* San Francisco: Jossey-Bass, 1998.

———. *A Hidden Wholeness: The Journey Toward an Undivided Life.* San Francisco: Jossey-Bass, 2004.

———. *Let Your Life Speak: Listening for the Voice of Vocation.* San Francisco: Jossey-Bass, 2000.

Palmer, Parker, and Arthur Zajonc. *The Heart of Higher Education.* San Francisco: Jossey-Bass, 2010.

Parks, Sharon Daloz. *Big Questions, Worthy Dreams: Mentoring Emerging Adults in Their Search for Meaning, Purpose, and Faith.* San Francisco: Jossey-Bass, 2011.

Pennington, Bill. "Perfection Is Afterthought, Perfect Examples Say." *New York Times*, February 3, 2008.

Persky, H., M. Daane, and Y. Jin. *The Nation's Report Card: Writing 2002.* Washington DC: U.S. Department of Education, Institute of Educational Sciences, 2003.

Petrash, Jack. *Understanding Waldorf Education.* Lewisville, NC: Gryphon House, 2002.

Pigza, Jennifer M. "Developing Your Ability to Foster Student Learning and Development through Reflection." In *Looking In, Reaching Out: A Reflective Guide for Community Service-Learning Professionals*, ed. Barbara Jacoby and Pamela Mutascio, 73–95. Boston: Campus Compact, 2010.

Piper, John. *Don't Waste Your Life.* Wheaton, IL: Crossway Books, 2003.

Pirsig, Robert M. *Zen and the Art of Motorcycle Maintenance.* Cambridge, UK: Cambridge University Press, 1974.

Polanyi, Michael. *Personal Knowledge.* Chicago: University of Chicago Press, 1974.

Postman, Neil. *The End of Education: Redefining the Value of School.* New York: Vintage, 1995.

Problem Solving for Tomorrow's World. Paris: Organization for Economic Cooperation and Development, 2004.

Pye, David. *The Nature and Art of Workmanship.* Cambridge, UK: Cambridge University Press, 1968.

Ray, Darby Kathleen. "Essay 13: Self, World, and the Space Between: Community Engagement as Vocational Discernment." In *At This Time and In This Place: Vocation in Higher Education*, ed. David S. Cunningham, 301–20. New York: Oxford University Press, 2016.

Rechtschaffen, Daniel. *The Mindful Education Workbook.* New York: Norton, 2016.

Reed, J., and C. Koliba. *Facilitating Reflection: A Manual for Leaders and Educators.* Burlington: University of Vermont, 2003. https://www.uvm.edu/~dewey/reflect.pdf.

Rhoads, R. A., and J. Howard. *Academic Service Learning: A Pedagogy of Action and Reflection.* San Francisco: Jossey-Bass, 1998.

Rice, Kathleen. "Becoming a Reflective Community Service-Learning Professional." In *Looking In, Reaching Out: A Reflective Guide for Community Service-Learning*

Professionals, ed. Barbara Jacoby and Pamela Mutascio, 1–16. Boston: Campus Compact, 2010.

Richards, M. C. *Centering in Pottery, Poetry, and the Person*. Middletown, CT: Wesleyan University Press, 1989.

Robinson, Ken. "Do Schools Kill Creativity." TED, https://www.ted.com/talks/sir_ken_robinson_do_schools_kill_creativity?language=en.

———. *The Element: How Finding Your Passion Changes Everything*. New York: Penguin, 2009.

Rosenthal, Michael. *Nicholas Miraculous: The Amazing Career of the Redoubtable Dr. Nicholas Murray Butler*. New York: Farrar, Straus & Giroux, 2006.

Sapra, Sonalini. "Growing Food and Justice in Catholic Universities: Urban Farming and Community-University Partnerships." In *Curriculum for the Bioregion Activity Collection*, https://serc.carleton.edu/bioregion/examples/184997.html.

Sayers, Dorothy L. *Letters to a Diminished Church: Passionate Arguments for the Relevance of Christian Doctrine*. Nashville, TN: W. Publishing Group, 2004.

Schell, Hannah. "Commitment and Community: The Virtue of Loyalty and Vocational Discernment." In *At This Time and In This Place: Vocation and Higher Education*, ed. David S. Cunningham, 235–54. New York: Oxford University Press, 2016.

Schoem, David. "Essay 24: Honoring the Humanity of Our Students." In *Well-Being in Higher Education*, ed. Donald Harward, 217–27. Washington, DC: Bringing Theory to Practice, 2016.

Schuurman, Douglas J. *Vocation: Discerning Our Callings in Life*. Grand Rapids, MI: William B. Eerdmans, 2004.

Schwartz, Barry, and Kenneth Sharpe. *Practical Wisdom: The Right Way to Do the Right Thing*. New York: Riverhead Books, 2010.

Schwehn, Kaethe, and L. DeAne Lagerquist, eds. *Claiming Our Callings: Toward a New Understanding of Vocation in the Liberal Arts*. New York: Oxford University Press, 2014.

Schwehn, Mark R. "Good Teaching: Character Development and Vocation Discernment." In *Vocation across the Academy: A New Vocabulary for Higher Education*, ed. David S. Cunningham, 294–315. New York: Oxford University Press, 2017.

Schwehn, Mark R., and Dorothy C. Bass. *Leading Lives That Matter: What We Should Do and Who We Should Be*. Grand Rapids, MI: William B. Eerdmans, 2006.

Seligman, Martin. *A Visionary New Understanding of Happiness and Well-Being*. New York: Free Press, 2011.

Seligman, Martin, and Angela Duckworth. "Self-Discipline Outdoes IQ in Predicting Academic Performance of Adolescents." *Psychological Science* 16, no. 12 (2005): 939–44.

Sennett, Richard. *The Corrosion of Character: The Personal Consequences of Work in the New Capitalism*. New York: Norton, 1996.

———. *The Craftsman*. New Haven, CT: Yale University Press, 2009.

———. *Flesh and Stone: The Body and the City in Western Civilization*. New York: Norton, 1993.

Showalter, Shirley Hershey. "Called to Tell Our Stories: The Narrative Structure of Vocation." In *Vocation across the Academy: A New Vocabulary for Higher Education*, ed. David S. Cunningham, 67–86. New York: Oxford University Press, 2017.

Siegel, D. J. *The Mindful Brain: Reflection and Attunement in the Cultivation of Well-Being*. New York: Norton, 2007.

Simmer-Brown, J. "Training the Heart Responsibly: Ethical Considerations in Contemplative Teaching." In *Meditation and the Classroom: Contemplative Pedagogy and Religious Studies*, ed. J. Simmer-Brown and F. Grace, 107–20. Albany, NY: SUNY Press, 2011.

Stafford, William. *Stories That Could Be True*. New York: Harper & Row, 1977.

Stansberry Beard, Karen, and Wayne K. Hoy. "The Nature, Meaning, and Measure of Teacher Flow in Elementary Schools: A Test of Rival Hypotheses." *Educational Administration Quarterly* 46, no. 3 (2010): 426–58.

Stoecker, R., and E. A. Tryon. *The Unheard Voices: Community Organizations and Service-Learning*. Philadelphia: Temple University Press, 2009.

Sullivan, William. *Liberal Learning as a Quest for Purpose*. New York: Oxford University Press, 2016.

Teasdale, Wayne. *Mystic Heart: Discovering a Universal Spirituality in the World's Religions*. Novato, CA: New World Library, 1999.

Torres, J., R. Stinton, and A. White. *Establishing and Sustaining an Office of Community Service*. Providence, RI: Campus Compact, 2000.

Turner, Rob. "Mapping Stormwater Runoff Infrastructure for the City of Bothell." In *Curriculum for the Bioregion Activity Collection*, https://serc.carleton.edu/bioregion/examples/68954.html.

Varela, Francisco J., Evan Thompson, and Eleanor Rosch. *The Embodied Mind*. Cambridge, MA: MIT Press, 1992.

Vega, Gina. "Teaching Business Ethics Through Service-Learning Metaprojects." In *Journal of Management Education* 31, no. 5 (October 2007): 647–78.

Wallace, B. Alan. *The Taboo of Subjectivity: Toward a New Science of Consciousness*. New York: Oxford University Press, 2000.

Warren-Gordon, K. "A Critical Approach to Service-Learning Criminal Justice and Criminology Courses." In *Collaborations: A Journal of Community-Based Research and Practice* 4, no. 1 (2021): 3.

Wells, Cynthia. "Finding the Center as Things Fly Apart." In *At This Time and In This Place: Vocation and Higher Education*, ed. David S. Cunningham, 47–72. New York: Oxford University Press, 2016.

Whitehead, Alfred North. *The Aims of Education*. New York: Free Press, 1967.

Zajonc, Arthur. *Meditation as Contemplative Inquiry*. Great Barrington, MA: Lindisfarne Press, 2009.

Zakaria, Fareed. *In Defense of a Liberal Education*. New York: Norton, 2015.

Zlotkowski, E., ed. *Concepts and Models for Service-Learning in the Disciplines Series*. Sterling, VA: Stylus Publishing, 2006.

About the Author

Timothy C. Hohn is a retired faculty member and chair of the horticulture department at Edmonds College, where he taught horticulture for twenty-two years. Previously, he was curator at the University of Washington Botanical Gardens, which includes the Washington Park Arboretum, and was the first curator of plants for Wildlife Conservation International at the Bronx Zoo. He received a master's degree in public garden management from the University of Delaware's Longwood Program in 1986 and is the author of *Curatorial Practices for Botanical Gardens*, also by Rowman & Littlefield.

www.ingramcontent.com/pod-product-compliance
Lightning Source LLC
Chambersburg PA
CBHW032023230426
43671CB00005B/187